Assessment in Infancy

Assessment in Infancy

ORDINAL SCALES OF PSYCHOLOGICAL DEVELOPMENT

Ina Č. Užgiris AND *J. McV. Hunt*

UNIVERSITY OF ILLINOIS PRESS

URBANA : CHICAGO : LONDON

Library of Congress Cataloging in Publication Data

Užgiris, Ina Č.
    Assessment in infancy.

    Bibliography: p.
    Includes index.
        1. Infant psychology. 2. Personality assessment.
I. Hunt, Joseph McVicker, 1906–   joint author.
II. Title. [DNLM: 1. Child development. 2. Child
psychology. 3. Psychological tests—In infancy and
childhood. WS105 U99a]
    BF723.I6U9 1975   155.4'22   74-31461
    ISBN 0-252-00465-5

Contents

PART III : ARRANGING THE ELICITING
SITUATIONS AND RECORDING THE CRITICAL
ACTIONS FOR THE VARIOUS STEPS IN EACH
OF THE SCALES

List of Tables

vii

Introduction

This book describes a novel approach to the assessment of psychological development in infancy. Piaget's (1936, 1937, 1945) observations of the development of his own three children combined with other evidence of hierarchical organization in the development of intelligence and motivation (see Hunt, 1961) inspired us to take this approach. The approach is novel in that the apparent order in the behavioral manifestations of the progressive levels of organization of central processes forms the framework for the assessment sequences.

We have devised scales pertaining to six branches of psychological development. The description of each scale is in three sections: (1) an abstract conception of each level of organization tapped in the sequence, (2) a series of situations designed to elicit behaviors critical as evidence for each conceptualized level of organization, and (3) an ordering of critical actions. The behavioral landmarks of progressive organization implicit in the critical actions in the eliciting situations appear on theoretical grounds and from the evidence now available to have an invariant order which makes these scales ordinal in character. The ordinality of the scales permits new ways of assessing the level of development in individual infants, new ways of comparing the levels of cognitive organization achieved by different infants, and a way of determining the influence of various constellations of environmental circumstances on early development. The work reported here was originally undertaken with a view toward devising ordinal scales with which to uncover, in longitudinal studies, differing rates of development associated with various child-rearing practices.

Strictly speaking, this book is a report of progress. The work originally planned is still incomplete. It is incomplete in the sense that we have not yet undertaken the longitudinal studies in which we had hoped to use the scales to investigate the effects of various kinds of child-rearing and through which we had hoped to determine more definitely the ordinality which appears, from the cross-sectional evidence in hand, to characterize these six scales. It is also incomplete in that we have made no attempt to standardize the scales by obtaining distributions of the ages at which representative samples of the infants of America achieve the various steps on the scales indicative of progressive levels of cognitive organization. Although such standardization is possible, at no time did we have any intention of doing it, because the various levels of organization tapped by the scales have psychological significance in their own right and stand by themselves. They have, indeed, what Robert Gagné has termed intrinsic validity. Thus, with ordinal scales, assessment of development need not be based on the individual's comparative status in a statistical distribution.

This report consists of three parts. The first summarizes the theoretical background and reinterpretations of the development of intelligence and motivation which have given direction to our effort to construct ordinal scales of psychological development in infancy. The second part describes the investigation. From the beginning, guided by the hypothesis of definite order in cognitive development, our effort was aimed toward devising ordinal scales for assessing the levels of competence commonly shown during the first two years of life. The third part of the report consists of a set of directions for choosing the materials to be used in the eliciting situations, for arranging these situations, and for observing and recording the critical actions for each of the six scales. Those wishing to use these scales can readily supplement these directions by viewing the sound films which we have prepared, one for each of the six scales. These demonstration films appear under the generic title "Ordinal Scales of Infant Psychological Development." They were produced by the Motion Picture Service of the University of Illinois at Urbana-Champaign, where they are available for purchase through the Film Department of the Division of Broadcasting. They are also available for rental through Visual Aids Service at the University.

The development of these ordinal scales and the production of the demonstration films were supported by the United States Public Health Service through Grants No. MH–08468, No. MH–11321, No. K6–18567. We acknowledge this support with gratitude.

Investigators incur debts in every scientific enterprise they undertake. Many of these debts must go without explicit acknowledgment. We wish, however, to acknowledge the help of those who participated in this work. At various stages in the development of what have become the six scales Donald Heil, Melissa Galloway Kaplan, and Tam Wei all participated in the examining of infants. At these various stages in producing the interim reports and the mimeographed versions of earlier forms of the assessment sequences we had the secretarial help of Sharon Ferguson and Merle Thorne. We are indebted to Bonnie B. Stone, Merle Thorne, Janice E. Langlois, and Vonice Wohlstein for transcribing the dictation and making the revisions which have resulted in the manuscript of this monograph; they have done a noble job. We are additionally indebted to Bonnie B. Stone for a splendid job of typing the final manuscript and making the author index. Above all, we wish to acknowledge with appreciation the participation of the parents and their infants who served as the subjects of this investigation.

INA Č. UŽGIRIS

J. McV. HUNT

Part I

Theoretical Background and Reinterpretations

CHAPTER 1

The Concept of Development

The differing assumptions implicit in various perspectives on change in the course of ontogenesis have recently been receiving increasing attention. It has been shown that the prevailing conceptions of onto-genetic development relate to different philosophical positions with respect to the nature of reality, the nature of man, the metaphoric model for the functioning of man, and even to the truth-criteria deemed significant. An examination of these premises is without question extremely important both for the sake of clarity in theoretical discussions and for consistency of approach to empirical work. However, since several good discussions of the various views on development are readily available (Kaplan, 1967a; Kessen, 1966; Langer, 1969; Reese and Overton, 1970), only an outline review of the relevant considerations will be undertaken here.

Inasmuch as any discussion of development implies a recognition of certain continuities between diverse organizational states of the object of study and of the pervasiveness of change within which certain configurations are taken to be states, the discussion has to address questions pertaining to the characterization of the various organizational states, the nature of change between states, the principles for ordering the diverse states, and the processes which account for change from one state to another. We maintain that positions with respect to these four issues are not completely interdependent and thus allow for a number of views on development, seemingly related, and yet discrepant from each other in important ways.

An example from biology may help to make these four issues concrete. In order to discuss egg-larva-pupa-imago as states of anatomical structure in the development of an insect of the order Lepidoptera, one must first of all recognize these states as related in some meaningful manner, in this case, by their occurrence in the life-cycle of the butterfly or moth. The issues then must be formulated as: (1) a description of each of the states to permit their unequivocal identification (either as idealized abstractions or as exemplified in reality), so that, for example, the larval state can be identified during the course of several molts or with respect to other members of the Lepidoptera order; (2) an indication of the nature of change occurring in the transformation from egg to larva to pupa (epigenesis, epimorphosis, etc.); (3) an ordering of the various states according to some principle, in this case, their sequential occurrence in the life-span of the organism; and (4) an indication of the processes accounting for the transformations from egg to larva to pupa or pupa to moth. In the discussion which follows, these four issues will be considered with respect to human psychological development.

Probably the sharpest distinction may be drawn between development conceived of as the accretion of behavior patterns and skills during ontogenesis or the life-span in a qualitatively unchanging organism, in which case some would even object to the use of the term development, and development conceived of as the transformation of interrelated competencies to progressively higher levels in accord with some specifiable criteria. With development conceived of as accretious, any descriptive distinctions between separate states tend to be minimized. The apparent existence of states which differ in organization is considered to be a reflection of the crudity of analysis and of a lack of knowledge of the intervening gradations between the successive states which appear to differ in their organization. At most, differing states may be defined in terms of central tendencies in normal distributions and employed on practical rather than on theoretical grounds. With development conceived in terms of transformations of competencies, however, distinctions among states tend to be emphasized. They are delineated as stages of development, and attempts are made to identify the network of competencies which gives the organi-

zational structure or form of each state. A different way of phrasing
the polarity is to say that, in the first instance, changes in particulars
are taken to underlie all varieties of observed change, while in the
second, reorganizations of the whole are assumed to be expressed
through changes in particulars. The first, accretional, view of development is reflected in such notions as that of postnatal physical growth
and in a strict S-R approach to behavioral development; the second,
transformational, view is embodied in structural theories of development, most notably Piaget's (1968).

The issue concerned with the nature of change between states is
clearly related to conceptualization of the states themselves. The
position that diverse states are only labels of convenience is more compatible with the view that changes in the course of development are
small, gradual, and inherently unrelated to each other; change is
considered to be quantitative and no a priori assumptions are made
about the relationship of a given achievement to the one that follows.
In contrast, the view emphasizing diverse states or stages in development sees change in terms of specifiable alterations in the level of
organization, implying both qualitative transformations and an inherent relatedness between achievements of one level and those of the
next. Even when substantial change between delineated states is assumed, however, one may conceptualize the nature of transformations
in several ways, such as juxtaposition, substitution, superordination, and integration into an ordered system. That is, the characteristics of the new state may be viewed as being added onto those of the
previous one without any interdependence being established between
them. While it is difficult to envision a case of true juxtaposition which
would not result in conflict and tension for a living being, it nevertheless remains a conceivable possibility. Change between states may
occur as substitution, in that characteristics of the new state would
replace those of the previous one completely. The fate of the replaced
characteristics remains a question, for if they are assumed to reappear
under specified conditions, the notion of superordination might be
more applicable. Finally, change between states may be viewed as involving the integration of new achievements with previous ones along
lines of subordination–superordination and a reorganization of the
whole network of competencies in the organism. While at a general
level of discussion, the question of the nature of change between states

is a matter of theoretical perspective, it gains empirical interest as more restricted strands of the developmental progression are examined and the nature of the relationship between specific achievements at adjacent levels of development is studied. Since not all change need be considered developmental, it might be of particular interest to specify the types of relationship among achievements which are all characteristic of one state, which characterize a transition between successive states or stages, and which belong jointly to two adjacent stages (for a discussion see Flavell, 1972).

Furthermore, it is important to distinguish the nature of the change between states and the processes which are thought to bring about such change. Characterization of change in terms of qualitative transformations need not imply that the processes bringing about change are intrinsic to the organism and unresponsive to environmental circumstances; even an intrinsic process may depend on certain external conditions for occurrence. On the other hand, characterization of change as incremental and additive does not necessarily imply a direct mirroring of external conditions; an internal mechanism might be programmed equally well to bring about incremental change. The processes which may account for change will be taken up as the last issue.

The ordering of states or a conception of developmental sequence may be derived from various bases. The most common basis would seem to be sequential occurrence within the life-span of the organism, or within that portion of the life-span leading up to maturity. The division of the life-span into units of chronological age provides a measuring scale along which the recognized states may be anchored. A precise time-scale has both advantages and disadvantages: it may be a precise yardstick for comparative purposes, but it may turn into a prime system for conceptualizing development itself. It is but a short step from anchoring diverse states at different points on the age-scale to characterizing the diverse states in terms of co-occurrence of various achievements at the same point in chronology, without considering any other interrelationships between them. Thus, while most people of this earth may recognize a period of infancy, of childhood, and of maturity in the psychological development of the individual, only in the context of concern with and precise measurement of chronological age common to Western man do we find the notion of mental age, defined as a set of achievements for each unit of chronological age.

It may be worthwhile to emphasize that the chronological age scale provides but a precise guideline for a sequence derived from an observed progression toward maturity, however understood. Thus, an ordering of states without being specifically tied to chronological age may still rest on such sequential occurrence in the life-spans of at least some individuals. In fact, states may be characterized in terms of constellations of specific competencies, irrespective of the ages at which these constellations are observed, and yet be ordered, with an implicit reference to a normative life-span. Within this broad category, the constellations of competencies to be ordered may be derived empirically from normative groups and, thus, shade into a chronological sequencing of states, or, on the other side, they may be derived from an implicative relationship between achievements of adjacent states and shade into the ordering of states on logical grounds. For example, the sequence of infant motor development, which is often said to be based on the principle of maturation (Shirley, 1931), is, in fact, empirically derived from the typical order of occurrence in the life-spans of sample individuals. It should be noted that any empirically derived ordering is always subject to modification, since the states need not be linked by a relationship of necessity.

A different basis for ordering various states is found in reliance on some principle or a set of criteria which enable specification of order on logical rather than empirical grounds. The best example of such developmental ordering may be Werner's orthogenetic principle, particularly as recently explicated by Kaplan (1966, 1967b). The ordering is made independent not only of association with chronological age, but also of sequential occurrence in a lifetime, in evolution, or in history. Only a logically derived ordering may be expected to have complete immutability. While the specification of criteria for developmental ordering is crucial for a general method of analysis which might be called developmental, the study of the variety of actual developmental sequences which may be followed in different circumstances with respect to more delimited achievements during ontogensis is of considerable import for understanding human development. In sum, the ordering of states may be derived from association with chronological age, empirical observation of sequence, or logical implication.

Assumptions regarding the characterization of diverse states, the nature of change between states, and the developmental ordering of states still leave open the issue of the processes which account for the characteristics of states and the transformations in an actual organism from one state to the next. The question of processes has not received a great deal of systematic attention, except at a general level in the context of the nature-nurture controversy. This is unfortunate, since interesting observations are likely to come from more detailed analyses of the relationships between the type of transformation in competence and the process involved in the transformation. In the present discussion, only the general processes will be mentioned, without touching on the more specific mechanisms which have been suggested for mediating change (e.g., conditioning, generalization, accommodation, discrepancy reduction), in order to emphasize that the issue of processes bringing about change is not intrinsically linked to the issue of the nature of change between diverse states.

First, at one extreme is the conceptual position that developmental change may be accounted for by invoking maturation or organismic preprogramming. While a series of gradations of this position may be easily recognized, the unifying contention is that whatever the manner of change in development, the source of the change is an intrinsic organismic process. It may be conceded that external conditions might block, or impede, or even facilitate this process; however, the effect of external conditions is always thought to be a modulation of the internal preprogramming (see Gesell, 1954). In other words, the rate of progress along a developmental sequence may be subject to modification by environmental circumstances, but the characteristics of states and the manner of change from one state to the next are thought to be the product of an inherent regulatory process. A potentially important distinction within this conceptual position may lie between the view that external circumstances essentially have a threshold effect on the expression of the internal regulatory process and the view that their effect may be graded in agreement with some mathematical function.

Second, at the other extreme, is the conceptual position that developmental change may be accounted for exclusively by environmental inputs. It may be that such a view is more compatible with a gradual, incremental conceptualization of change, yet it is possible to see even qualitative change as the outcome of a strict sequential programming of the environment which is being directly mirrored by transformations in the organism. This would imply that not only the rate of progress along a developmental sequence but the nature of the sequence itself is a reflection of arrangements in external circumstances. While this view suggests that the order of achievements should be mutable by circumstances, it does not rule out all constraints on sequence arising from implicative relationships between competencies. It also has implications with respect to remediation of lacking competencies which differ from those derivable from the first view.

Finally, the process accounting for developmental change may be conceived of as an interaction of an organism possessing a certain configuration of competencies with a given set of environmental conditions. The ordering of transformations is thought to reside neither within the organism nor within environmental conditions separately, but in the back-and-forth transactions between them. An interactionist view is often expressed in order to indicate a middle-ground position in regard to the nature-nurture controversy. In regard to the question of processes accounting for developmental change, however, it is far from a compromise position. It posits a regulatory process in the "fit" of circumstances to the organism's level of organization with both organism and circumstances contributing to the regulation. Thus, it admits a variation in the rate of developmental progress depending on availability of environmental opportunities, but it also leaves open the possibility of alternate orders in the achievement of competencies arising from the plasticity of the organism in adapting to variations in opportunities. While in order to specify some alternative configurations of competencies which could be transformed to the next higher level of organization one would have to consider the flexibility of the organism, the possible variation in circumstances, and the extent of implicative relationships between competencies, it may be, nevertheless, important to recognize the possibility of such alternative outcomes of the interaction process. Conceptually, it suggests a way of viewing diversity in developmental progress other than as deviation from one normative sequence.

These four issues pertaining to developmental change sketched in the preceding paragraphs do not exhaust the relevant considerations for a conception of development. They have been discussed in order to furnish a setting for our position on assessment of developmental progress in infancy. Since the questions of consistent order in developmental achievements and the possible basis for observed order were particularly important for the present study, they will be taken up again in subsequent chapters.

CHAPTER 2

Ordinal Scales versus Traditional Scales

The conception of the organization and the development of intelligence and motivation which prompted our attempt to construct ordinal scales of psychological development seems to differ substantially from the traditional conceptions which underlie the existing tests of infant development. The most marked divergence pertains to the view of the nature of change with development. The traditional tests rest on an assumption of incremental progress, without much consideration of the interrelationships between achievements at one level and those at the next. In contrast, ordinal scales imply a hierarchical relationship between achievements at different levels, so that in principle the achievements of the higher level do not incidentally follow, but are intrinsically derived from those at the preceding level and encompass them within the higher level. Closely linked to this divergence is the difference in conception of the organization of achievements at any one level. In traditional tests of intelligence, achievements are grouped together on the basis of their co-occurrence at a particular chronological age in the population sampled for standardization; no inherent relationships between achievements are assumed. Ordinal scales, on the other hand, by separating the issue of sequence from association with chronological age, suggest more inherent grounds for the co-occurrence of achievements; the regular co-occurrence of a set of achievements becomes a finding worthy of study. Furthermore, while the basis for sequencing achievements both in traditional and ordinal scales may come from empirical observations of sequence in the ontogenesis of the individuals studied, in the case of ordinal scales, the mutability of an empirically derived sequence is recognized, and it is expected that the inherent relationships between achievements producing the sequence can be eventually explicated. Finally, even the "theory of data," to use Coombs's (1964) term, and the conception of measurement underlying ordinal scales differ from those for mental or developmental ages and intelligence or developmental quotients.

EXISTING TESTS AND THEIR ASSUMPTIONS

Existing tests of psychological development in infancy have been modeled, for the most part, on tests of intelligence for older children. These tests reflect the traditional assumptions made regarding the development of intelligence. First, those constructing the tests have traditionally assumed that psychological development in infancy reflects essentially a unitary process not unlike Spearman's (1904) "general intelligence." Some recognition of the untenableness of this assumption is indicated in the most recent revision of the Bayley Scales of Infant Development by their division into a Mental Scale and a Motor Scale (Bayley, 1969) as well as by attempts to construct sub-scales from various items of these scales (Kohen-Raz, 1967). Second, they have assumed that individual differences in intelligence may be measured in terms of differential rates of achievement as revealed by Stern's (1914) suggestion for the intelligence quotient (IQ). Thus, we have had the developmental quotient (DQ) in place of the IQ for measuring differential rates of progress in infancy. From these assumptions arose the expectation that development in infancy would be continuous with later intellectual development, that DQs based on early testings would predict IQs based on later testings and, hopefully, the ultimate level of intelligence and competence.

In constructing tests for infants, the lesson from the comparative success of the tests devised by Binet and those devised by Galton was largely forgotten. Perhaps it would be more correct to say that the lesson was neglected, because it was no easy matter to find tasks suitable for infants which require such complex processes as Binet had found to be more significant for prediction across situations at any given age during childhood than the simple actions that Galton had utilized in his anthropometric tests. Those who constructed tests for infants, for example Bayley (1933), Bühler and Hetzer (1927), Cattell (1947), and Gesell and Armatruda (1941), have used, for the most part, simple readily observable motor actions as items for their tests. The appearance of these various motor actions was found to be roughly correlated with age. It is important to note that these various actions were conceived to speak essentially for themselves; they were not selected to signify, even implicitly, progress in the level of organization of central neural processes or of thought-processes.

The computation of the developmental age (DA) for any individual infant involves two assumptions. The first is related to what Coombs (1964) has called a compensatory model of the theory of data. The DA consists of the sum of items successfully performed by the infant regardless of the nature of the items. Thus, in this summation, success on any given item can substitute or compensate for any other. Second, the summation procedure implies an additive view of developmental progress. The successful performance on each item is given equal weight, thus overlooking the possibility of interaction between performances on separate items. Since the test items have no special significance in themselves, the summation of credits for any individual gets meaning chiefly from comparison with the summations for other individuals. Thus, the measurement of development becomes a matter of the rank or status of the individual's performance among the performances of those constituting the standardization group.

THE ASSUMPTIONS AND THE EVIDENCE

Such assumptions concerning psychological development in infancy and such bases for the selection of test items have had several consequences. The assumption of predetermined rates of development led to the expectation that DQs and IQs would be constant, thereby permitting confidence that DQs derived from tests given during the first two years would predict later IQs. When evidence of gross variations in the DQ came repeatedly (Bayley, 1940; see also Hunt, 1961, pp. 19ff.), however, it did not immediately impune the assumption of predetermined rates of development. Rather it was taken to impune the reliability and validity of the infant tests. When Bayley (1940) found split-half reliabilities well above .9 and also found high test-retest reliability coefficients with short times between testings, defective reliability was ruled out. The defect was thereby limited to the validity of the infant tests, and specifically to their longitudinal validity. When DQs based on tests given during the first or second year failed to predict IQs derived from tests given ten or eighteen years later (see Jones, 1954, p. 642), it was the validity of the infant tests which was questioned rather than the assumption of predetermined rates of development. As Hunt (1961) has pointed out, it is important to distinguish such longitudinal validity, based upon the fallible assumption of predetermined rates of behavioral development, from contemporary validity, evidenced by substantial correlations between performance on the tests and performance by the infants or children tested in other situations. Moreover, because the DA was based on a compensatory model of scaling and because the various test items were selected without consideration of their implications as evidence for development of central processes, DAs and DQs yielded little information about the nature of development within individual infants as well as little information about the kinds of circumstances which will foster infant development. Even if such scores could serve only as the grossest indicators of the effects of circumstances encountered, they were expected to serve no such purpose, because it was assumed that the course and rate of development were predetermined.

More recently, evidence indicating lack of constancy in DQs and IQs of individual children led to the recognition that the linear relationship between increments in DA or MA and increments in chronological age assumed by those who devised the tests may not in fact hold, and that developmental progress of individuals may conform more closely to what may be described as a spiral function, rather than to a linear function. However, the notion of predetermined rates of development was maintained by assuming that the individual patterns of progress were predetermined and that the sharp variations sometimes observed represented the operation of some compensatory mechanism in response to temporary deflections from the predetermined pattern. While preserving the idea of set rates of development, this notion prompted the abandonment of chronological age as the ideal scale for anchoring developmental achievements. DA or MA came to be viewed as preferred indicators of status, without sufficient recognition, however, that these scores gain meaning only in comparison to the standardization group and, thus, are quite arbitrary.

ORDINAL SCALES AND THEIR ASSUMPTIONS

The ordinal scales proposed here derive from assumptions about development, from a model for scaling, and from a basis for selecting items all of which contrast sharply with those just described for traditional tests of psychological development in infancy. Where the traditional tests have presumed a predetermined rate of development, we have devised these ordinal scales in order to have better tools with which to investigate the effects of infants' encounters with various kinds of circumstances on the rate of their development. Where traditional tests have presumed competence and intelligence to be based, for the most part, upon a unitary ability, we have presumed that competence is based on a hierarchical organization of a number of abilities and motive systems with several relatively independent branches (see Hunt, 1961, Ch. 5). We have also presumed that this hierarchical organization of abilities and motives consists of coordinations and differentiations among the several sensorimotor organizations already present at birth, and that progress toward the symbolic representations and regulations comprising competence and intelligence undergoes an epigenetic development analogous to the embryonic development of organ structures from the single cell constituting the fertilized ovum. On the basis of Piaget's (1936, 1937) observations of the psychological development in his own three children, we have adopted the working assumption that the course of development within each of the several branches would follow a consistent order. We have focused more on delineating the sequence of development in each branch than on explicating the interrelationships among achievements in the various branches. Thus, we have made the issue of order rather than of stages central to our study.

Because all psychological investigators must depend upon observable items of behavior elicited in specifiable situations, we, like the authors of the traditional tests, have selected behavioral items for our critical actions. On the other hand, where the existing tests have typically accepted each item essentially for itself, we have selected our behavioral items for their value, in conjunction with the eliciting situations, as landmarks of implied levels of achievement and organization along the several branches of development. Thus, though it would be possible, for measurement purposes, to apply the notions of DA or DQ to the set of infant performances obtained with these scales, we can also describe an infant in terms of the level of organization achieved in each of the six branches. Most steps on these scales have immediate conceptual significance, or "intrinsic validity" in Gagné's words (personal communication), which, at least it is hoped, can be used to plan meaningful arrangements of circumstances that will promote development. We can also compare the development-fostering capacity of diverse child-rearing regimes in terms of the distributions of ages at which infants achieve given landmarks of development on these scales, insofar as they are indeed ordinal in character.

THE INSPIRATION FROM PIAGET

The observations of Piaget (1936, 1937) have provided us with both information and inspiration. They have supplied the most explicit picture available of the ongoing organism-environment interaction in the human infant. Coupled with the theorizing of Donald Hebb (1949) and various lines of empirical evidence (see Hunt, 1961), they have given us confidence that it is sensible to conceive of psychological development as an elaboration of cognitive structures which also have motivational and emotional significance. In addition, Piaget's observations have suggested to us how simple, easily observed actions can imply these cognitive structures, how changes of reaction to a given situation can imply a change in these structures, and how assumed changes in the organization of cognitive structures can be checked through systematic variations in the eliciting situations. Thus, an infant's following an object with his eyes and head implies a coordination of eye-movements with head-movements and an interest in the object as perceived at that moment. When an infant's reaction to an object disappearing from view changes from one of turning his gaze immediately from the point of disappearance to one of holding his gaze at the point of disappearance till the object returns, the change implies an increasing stability of those central processes through which the infant apprehends the object and which mediate what Piaget calls "object permanence."

We strongly suspect from various lines of evidence that these representational central processes develop in the course of repeated and progressively changing perceptual encounters with events, objects, persons, and places. This is especially true for those branches of cognitive development concerned with what Piaget (1937) has called the "construction of reality." These branches of development are tapped in the scales for visual following and the permanence of objects, for the construction of operational causality, and for the construction of object relations in space. Moreover, the response of imitation can be made to indicate the level of an infant's cognitive grasp as well as his motor competence, depending upon the behavioral pattern used as the model to be imitated. The other two scales, that concerned with the development of means for achieving desired environmental events and that concerned with the development of those sensorimotor organizations (henceforth called schemes) for relating to objects, both focus somewhat more directly on the attainment of certain motor competencies in addition to progress toward representational central processes.

Piaget's descriptions of sensorimotor stages have provided us with confidence that one may expect an order within the epigenetic course of each branch of development which may prove to be invariant across individuals. Although we were led by our preliminary findings to set aside, for the moment, Piaget's designation of six stages in sensorimotor development and to utilize for scaling the more numerous observable landmarks of development, it was his description of development in stages, with the changes in structure which make it epigenetic, that led us to consider seriously the hypothesis that it may be feasible to construct ordinal scales of cognitive development in infancy (see Hunt, 1961, p. 229).

IMPLICATIONS OF ORDINALITY
FOR DEVELOPMENTAL ASSESSMENT

The evidence to be reported in Part II of this monograph supports the existence of a definite, sequential order in the branches of psy-

chological development assessed by our six scales. The same issue
has been addressed in a more limited way by several investigators.
Décarie (1965), using Piaget's six stages to designate levels of development, verified the sequence of achievements pertaining to the construction of the object, while Corman and Escalona (1969), in
addition to object permanence, verified the sequences for prehension
and spatial relationships as well. On the other hand, using a modified
administration procedure Miller, Cohen, and Hill (1970) found support for the ordinal character of the major steps, but obtained minimal
scalability for curtailed ranges of items for object construction. Even
so, additional investigations will be needed to determine how regularly
these orders occur in individual infants retested repeatedly especially
when living under differing conditions.

Nevertheless, the evidence of sequential order in these six scales
suggests a novel approach to the assessment of psychological development. One may compare the development of two infants in terms of
their levels of achievement on each of the several scales, and these
comparisons may be, as we shall see in Chapter 3, relatively independent of the ages of the infants. Since the several scales differ qualitatively, and various kinds of evidence indicate that the rate of
development in these several branches may be relatively independent,
the information from such a comparison cannot help but be substantially greater than that obtained from a mental age or an IQ. As we
learn to use such instruments, the information from such an assessment
should help predict the kinds of circumstances best adapted to foster
development in an infant whose achievement is determined to be at
any given level on a particular scale.

One may also compare the degree to which one infant is advanced
or retarded with respect to others on each of the various scales in
terms of how his age compares with the ages of others at his level of
development. Such comparisons would demand age norms. The age
norms for such scales would take the form of a distribution of ages at
which a representative sample of children achieve each of the landmarks of development on each of the scales. Obtaining such norms
would be a tremendous task requiring periodic updating. It is a task
which has not been started and one which we shall not undertake.
Nevertheless, one may use these scales, as they now stand, to assess
the development-fostering quality of differing child-rearing regimes

simply by comparing the mean age of the infants at successive levels of development who are living under the differing regimes of child-rearing. Or, in longitudinal studies with repeated examinations of infants, one can compare the mean ages at which those living under differing regimes achieve specified behavioral landmarks. Moreover, one can also use these scales, as they are, to assess the degree to which development along any given branch is a function of encounters with particular kinds of circumstances by comparing the average time needed by infants in these differing kinds of circumstances to move from one step to another on an appropriate scale.

CHAPTER 3

Developmental Sequence and Chronological Age

The two main issues with respect to order in development pertain to: (1) conceptions regarding the basis for universally invariant sequences of achievements, and (2) conceptions concerning the rate of individual progress along developmental sequences. The first issue is not often raised and, when raised, is usually rapidly answered by invoking some inherent organismic process. This issue will be discussed more fully in Chapter 4. The second issue is most frequently answered in a normative fashion, creating the impression that chronological age is not only correlated with, but is also a causal determinant of individual progress. Several lines of evidence, however, strongly suggest the need to disengage the notion of developmental sequence from its tie to chronological age.

PIAGET'S STAGES AND AGES

Although Piaget (1936) attributes psychological development to an ongoing organism-environment interaction epitomized in his constructs of accommodation, assimilation, and equilibration, he has not been concerned with demonstrating the impact of differing circumstances or individual variability on developmental progress. By reporting an age at which children usually reach each stage in development, he has tended to foster the idea of an association between

20

chronological age and the level of development, even though the children whose protocols he cites for illustration usually span a considerable age range.

In regard to the sensorimotor period, Piaget has not been very explicit about the hypothesized organization of cognitive structures at each of the six stages nor about the transformations leading up to each higher stage; he has been much more explicit about this with respect to concrete operational structures and the transition from preoperational to operational thought. One wonders whether Piaget would now even wish to apply the concept of stage as recently elaborated (e.g., Pinard and Laurendeau, 1969) to each of the six levels of sensorimotor development. Nevertheless, the sequence of behavioral landmarks he has described in sensorimotor development clearly implies change in the organization of competencies, not only in their number, but change which culminates in a fairly well-defined structure at the highest of the sensorimotor levels. In contrast to his theoretical formulations, however, his empirical evidence for the sequential ordering of stages comes from observations of their regular occurrence in each of several subjects at successively higher ages in ontogenesis. Thus, the *empirical evidence* presented by Piaget for the sequential nature of his stages of development may seem as much tied to chronological age as the items in the various tests of mental age or the norms of Arnold Gesell and his collaborators (see Gesell et al., 1940).

Within the sensorimotor period, the primary circular reactions in which ready-made schemes become coordinated to form motor habits began to appear in Piaget's children during the second month of life. The secondary circular reactions comprising coordinations of motor habits and perceptions into intentional acts made their appearance during the fifth month. The coordination of secondary circular reactions evidenced in the separation of means from ends and in the active search for vanished objects made their appearance in the ninth month. The tertiary circular reactions manifested in the discovery of new means through active groping, interest in novelty, and search for objects following a series of displacements began to appear at about the end of the first year. The sensorimotor period terminates with the internalization of these sensorimotor schemes as implied by the invention of new means through mental combination, by search for objects even when some of their displacements have to be inferred, and by imitation of models no longer present, which all began to appear in Piaget's children at roughly eighteen months of age.

Similarly, beyond the sensorimotor period, the appearance of achievements marking each stage in development was observed at a particular age. Elaboration of the symbolic function and the development of intuitions during the preconceptual phase were repeatedly observed to terminate in the appearance of concrete operations at about the age of seven or eight years. The concrete operational structure is marked by conservation of quantity, length, and number; by the ability to manipulate reversible nestings of hierarchies of classes and relations; and by the inference pattern of transitivity for length, quantity, etc. Finally, the period of concrete operations, during which observation directs thought, was observed by Piaget and his collaborators (see Inhelder and Piaget, 1955) to terminate in the development of formal operational thought at approximately twelve years of age. The formal operational structure is marked behaviorally by ability to conserve volume, ability to decode properly propositions involving classes and transitive relationships, and by thought which reflects the hypothetico-deductive method (wherein thought directs observation), the proportionality schema, the sixteen binary propositional operations of bivalent logic, and the INRC group of Boole (1854) while attempting to solve various kinds of problems. Thus, the behavioral landmarks of psychological development were anchored not in terms of characteristic opportunities for and modes of organism-environment interaction, but largely in terms of the modal chronological age for their appearance.

EVIDENCE CALLING FOR SEPARATION

In addition to theoretical reasons for separating the sequence of development from linkage with chronological age, there are several lines of empirical evidence which indicate a lack of precise correspondence between the achievement of various landmarks of development and chronological age.

One line of evidence resides in the high variability of DQs and IQs in very young children (see Anderson, 1939; Bayley, 1940; Furfey and Muehlenbein, 1932; Goodenough and Maurer, 1942; Honzik, Mac-

Farlane, and Allen, 1948; Jones, 1954). While Anderson (1939), Goodenough (1939), and others attributed this variability in IQ to lack of validity of the infant tests, Goodenough and Maurer (1942) interpreted it to be the consequence of inherited patterns of growth, because they were unable to discern variations in the circumstances of children to which they felt they could attribute the observed variations in IQ. Murphy (1944), however, did report variations in circumstances associated with both changes of personality and of DQ or IQ and Sontag, Baker, and Nelson (1958) specifically examined personality and familial concomitants of marked IQ changes for the samples of families utilized in the investigations of the Fels Research Institute.

A second line of evidence resides in the various studies of the effects of orphanage-rearing and nursery-school experience on IQ. Orphanage-rearing has been commonly associated with the development of apathy and retardation (see Provence and Lipton, 1962; Skeels and Dye, 1939; Spitz, 1945, 1946a, 1946b; and for a survey, Hunt, 1961, pp. 27ff.). The apathy and retardation probably occur because orphanages typically provide little in the way of variations in ongoing or repeated receptor inputs and little in the way of responsive feedback to the infant's self-initiated actions. The adaptation and habituation resulting from unvaried inputs would be expected to result in apathy. Living apathetically without response from the environment would be expected to result in retardation.

Although the investigations of the effects of enrichment through nursery school experience by Skeels, Updegraff, Wellman, and Williams (1938) could be and were criticized on methodological grounds, their results were highly suggestive and deserved to be taken more seriously. Moreover, Skeels and Dye (1939) reported that the apathy and retardation associated with orphanage-rearing during the second and third year of life could readily be reversed by transferring the orphanage-reared children to the care of women in an institution for the mentally retarded. Where the children had been left largely alone in the orphanage, it was noted that in the institution for the mentally retarded, the women and girls on the ward became very much attached to the children and would play with them during most of their waking hours.

This study was prompted by a "clinical surprise." Two residents of a state orphanage, one aged 13 months with a Kuhlmann IQ of 46 and the other aged 16 months with an IQ of 35 were committed to a state institution for the mentally retarded. Some six months after this transfer, a psychologist visiting the wards noted with surprise that these two children had shown remarkable development. They were tested again with the Kuhlmann scale. The younger one had achieved an IQ of 77, and the older one an IQ of 87: improvements of 31 and 52 points respectively. At the end of a year on the ward, the IQ of the younger was 100, and that of the older one was 88. As a consequence of this incident, eleven additional infants ranging in age from 7 to 30 months, with IQ ranging from 36 to 89 and a mean IQ of 64.3, were deliberately transferred from the orphanage to wards for women in the state institution for the mentally retarded. After being on these wards for periods ranging from six months for the 7-month old infant to 52 months for the 30-month old youngster, the children were retested. Each showed a gain in IQ. The minimal gain was 7 points, the maximal gain was 58 points. All but four showed gains of over 20 points.

Contrariwise, 12 other infants ranging in age from 12 to 22 months and in IQ from 50 to 103, with a mean IQ of 87, were left in the orphanage. When these 12 children were retested after periods varying between 21 and 43 months, all but one showed a decrease in IQ. One of the children showed a decrease of only 8 points, but the remaining 10 showed decreases that ranged between 18 and 45 points, with five exceeding 35 points. At the time, these findings met with ridicule, which long deprived them of the highly suggestive import they should have had. The tremendous social consequences of these changes in tested ability associated with the transfer from the orphanage to the wards for mentally retarded girls has been brought out in a follow-up study of the adult status of these two sets of children with contrasting experiences (Skeels, 1966).

A third line of evidence suggesting the importance of separating developmental sequences from chronological age derives from investigations of neuroanatomical maturation inspired by the neuropsychological theorizing of Hebb (1949) and the neurobiochemical theorizing of Hydén (1943, 1950, 1960). In the earliest of those studies inspired by Hebb's theorizing, Riesen (1958) got evidence that rearing infant chimpanzees in darkness for periods ranging from 7 to 18 months of age delayed the appearance of a number of visuomotor functions, including the blink response to an object rapidly approaching the face, visual fixation and pursuit of objects, visual recognition of even such highly familiar objects as the feeding bottle, and fear of strange objects and persons. In the case of those chimpanzees kept in total darkness for as long as 16 or 18 months, these effects proved to be irreversible. Moreover, the functional defect was shown to have a basis in anatomical maturation. This was first manifest as a pallor of the optic disc. In histological examination following autopsy, however, this pallor proved to be based on a paucity of both nerve cells and Mueller fibers in the retinal ganglia (Rasch et al., 1961).

The earlier work on the effects of stimulation on the biochemical characteristics of the cells in the nuclei for various receptors by Hydén and his collaborators coupled with lack of evidence concerning possible effects of such stimulation early in life prompted Brattgård (1952) to rear rabbits in the dark. A histochemical analysis of the retinae of these dark-reared rabbits and those of their light-reared litter mates revealed a deficiency in RNA production in the retinal ganglion cells of those dark-reared. Similar effects have since been found to result from the dark-rearing of kittens (Weiskrantz, 1958) and of rats (Liberman, 1962).

Such findings readily suggest the importance of a search for deficiencies in neuroanatomical and neurobiochemical development in higher centers of the visual system. Evidences of defects in the cellular portions of the lateral geniculate bodies of the thalami of kittens deprived of vision for three months following the opening of the eyes have been reported by Wiesel and Hubel (1963). Also, evidences of defects in the fine structure of the striate area of the occipital lobe, the main center within the brain for visual reception, following light deprivation in early life have been reported by several investigators (Gyllesten, 1959; Coleman and Riesen, 1968; Ruiz-Marcos and Valverde, 1969; Valverde, 1967, 1968). Some of these have concerned the branching of the dendrites; those of Valverde and his collaborators at the Cajal Institute in Madrid concern the number of spines on the dendrites of the large apical cells in the striate areas.

Such investigations can be interpreted to mean merely that anatomical maturation of the visual system demands encounters with light. On the other hand, various studies of increasing the variety of objects encountered perceptually with opportunities to manipulate them have been associated with increases in the growth of neuro-anatomical structures. Altman and Das (1964) have reported a greater multiplication of glial cells in the cerebral cortexes of rats reared in environments thus enriched compared to those of litter mates reared in the "impoverished environments" of laboratory cages. Bennett, Diamond, Krech, and Rosenzweig (1964) have summarized their extended series of experiments to show that rats reared in complex environments are not only better solvers of maze problems than litter-mates reared in laboratory cages, but they also show a higher total acetycholinesterase activity and thicker cortexes than their cage-reared littermates. Recently, Volkmar and Greenough (1972) have reported greater branching in the dendrites of the large apical cells in the striate area of the occipital lobes of rats reared in complex environments of enlarged areas with a variety of manipulable objects which were changed regularly than in littermates reared either in pairs or alone in laboratory cages. Since the differences observed were large, and since all the animals in this experiment lived continually in light of about the same level of intensity, the results suggest that the effects of dark rearing may be less a matter of the effects of light, per se, than of decreased informational complexity in the circumstances encountered early in life.

Evidence in this category takes yet another form, namely, that the nature of the circumstances encountered can influence the rate of other developmental achievements commonly attributed to maturation. For instance, Levine and Lewis (1963) have reported that the maturation of resting levels of adrenal ascorbic acid is accelerated in infant rats by handling them during the period after birth during which their eyes are closed. Moreover, Meier (1961) has reported that petting Siamese kittens twice daily for 30 days hastens eye-opening, the development of coloration in the coat, emergence from the nesting box and the onset of EEG patterns.

A fourth line of evidence comes from studies of the effects of several kinds of environmental circumstances on the ages at which various behavioral landmarks appear in human infants and young children. Dennis (1960) has described an orphanage in Tehran where two-thirds of the children in their second year still fail to sit up, and where 84 percent of those in their fourth year still fail to walk alone. In a series of studies of infants reared under controlled conditions at the

Tewksbury State Hospital, White and Held (1966) have demonstrated very substantial effects of enrichments consisting of turning infants onto their stomachs after each feeding, handling some twenty minutes each day, and providing objects for infants to look at, first simple ones and then more complex ones. This work began with a normative study of the development of visual attention and eye-hand coordination in infants being reared under the standard regime. In this normative study, the first landmark of eye-hand coordination, fisted swiping at objects in view, appeared at 65 days of age, and the final landmark, top-level reaching in which the hand moves directly to the object in view and is shaped for the grasping before it arrives to grasp the object, appeared at 145 days of age. In infants who experienced the second enrichment program, the median age at which these two landmarks appeared were, respectively, 55 days and 87 days. If, for purposes of communication, one casts this effect on the age at which top-level reaching appeared into the more familiar terms of the developmental quotient, by making 145 days the norm and equivalent to 100, then the decrease to 87 days amounts to an increase in DQ of 66 points.

Even in the home-reared infants of middle-class families, it seems possible to modify given landmarks and specific functions appreciably. Greenberg, Užgiris, and Hunt (1968) have reported that providing infants with an opportunity to look at objects by placing a stabile over their cribs at 5 weeks of age brought about the blink response to a target dropped from 11.5 inches at an average of 7 weeks of age in a group of 10 infants. In another 10 infants selected to act as controls, whose mothers had agreed to put nothing over the crib until their infants were at least 13 weeks of age, the blink response to a target drop of 11.5 inches did not appear until these infants averaged 10.4 weeks of age. Again, if one casts these findings in the more familiar terms of the developmental quotient, the effect of the opportunity to look at a stabile on the appearance of the blink response represents an increase of nearly 50 points in the rate of development for this particular pattern of behavior. While these advances in eye-hand coordination and the blink response cannot be expected to persist in the absence of encounters with appropriate circumstances, and neither can they be considered of any special import in the development of infants, they do illustrate the possibility of producing substantial variations in rates of functional development; together with these other lines of empirical evidence, they help to justify the separation of the notion of developmental sequence from chronological age. These various lines of evidence also imply that ordinal scales for various branches of development during infancy should be highly useful in investigating the development-fostering capacities of various regimes and programs of environmental encounters for infants.

CHAPTER 4

Hierarchical Organization:
Sources of Sequential Order
and the Issue of Stages

In the history of child psychology, sequential order in the appearance of behavior has been attributed to maturation. Thus, when Shirley (1931) found that the order of appearance of various behavioral landmarks in the development of locomotion in individual children correlated regularly in the upper 90s with the modal order of their appearance, she concluded, and entitled her paper, "a motor sequence favors the maturation theory" (p. 204). Similarly, Gesell (1954) saw in the order that he observed in behavioral development evidence that "the original impulse to growth and a matrix of morphogenesis is endogenous rather than exogenous. The so-called environment, whether internal or external, does not generate the progressions of development. Environmental factors support, inflect and specify; but they do not engender the basic forms and sequences of ontogenesis" (p. 354).

These statements by Mary Shirley and Arnold Gesell were made in the context of the debates over the relative importance of heredity and environment. In this context, the preprogrammed aspect of behavioral development was seen as the domain of maturation controlled by heredity; the modifiable, plastic aspect of behavioral development was seen as learning controlled by environmental encounters. As al-

ready noted in Chapter 3, investigations of the physiological concomitants of various kinds of early experience call into serious question
this separation of maturation from learning in development. Despite
the obvious primacy of heredity in preprogramming species-specific
anatomical maturation, the evidence from these investigations appears
to indicate that anatomical and physiological development, long attributed completely to preprogrammed maturation, can be influenced
by the circumstances encountered just as behavior can be so influenced. The evidence is clear that the rate at which individuals
progress along behavioral sequences varies with the type of circumstances encountered; the fact that in each case a consistent sequence is
maintained, however, need not imply that even sequence per se is
completely preprogrammed. Here, we wish to point out that consistent order in the appearance of behavioral landmarks can stem from
a combination of several sources.

HEREDITY

The first source, of course, is that of heredity. In every vertebrate
species known, for instance, development begins with the head end
and proceeds tailward. Coghill's (1929) cephalocaudal principle is
universal, at least among vertebrates, as is also his proximodistal
principle. This programming undoubtedly extends to other aspects of
development. But even genetically programmed development does
not go on in a vacuum; there are continuous interactions with environmental circumstances. There may be critical periods when certain kinds of encounters with circumstances are maximally effective
in facilitating the acquisition of certain organizations of behavior and
thought (see Scott, 1962). On the other hand, it is entirely too easy to
assume such a state of affairs merely because a number of disconti-
nuities are observed to occur at given ages in the children of a given
culture or social class. Several landmarks of behavioral development
may occur together at a given age merely because the culture brings
the children into encounters with various sets of circumstances in a
given order and at a given rate. In addition, it is likely that genetically
based individual differences may exist in the degree to which even the
rates of progress for various branches of development can be modified

by the circumstances encountered. The greater the hereditary potential, probably the greater the modifiability of rate. Ordinal scales for several branches of development should be highly useful in investigating such matters, for they can best be investigated by systems of interventions in which the circumstances are arranged to foster development. Nevertheless, genetic preprogramming is but one source of order in the development of anatomy, behavior, and thought.

LOGICALLY BUILT-IN ORDER

A second source of order in behavioral development appears in the logically built-in sequence of progress within a system of functioning. In its more trivial form, this source of order is exemplified in all quantifiable achievements, where a higher degree of attainment logically implies all lesser degrees. In addition, whenever one achievement logically presupposes another, their order of appearance in behavioral development is set. This logically given relationship between certain achievements in development has been discussed by Flavell and Wohlwill (1969) as "implicative mediation"; consequently, only a few examples from infant development need be presented.

Fantz (1961, 1963) has ingeniously utilized the methods of testing visual acuity in animals to demonstrate that pattern vision is ready-made in newborn human infants. The blink response to an approaching object, however, is not present. It presumably depends upon the development of visual accommodation which Haynes, White, and Held (1965) have found with the aid of dynamic retinoscopy to be severely limited at birth. The eyes of the human newborn have a fixed focus, but the capacity for visual accommodation develops rapidly during the first three months of life. In the study already mentioned (Greenberg, Užgiris, and Hunt, 1968), we noted that the blink response can be regularly elicited by target drops of 11.5 inches before it can be regularly elicited by drops of 7 inches, and it can be elicited by drops of 7 inches before it can be elicited by drops of 3 inches. Thus, being able to elicit the blink response with a target drop of 3 inches implies being able to elicit it with a target drop of 7 inches and with a target drop of 11.5 inches. Similarly, the accommodation of the looking scheme to moving objects is a progressive affair. When an infant can follow an object through an arc of 180°, he obviously must be able to follow it through lesser arcs. Moreover, even a short-lived search for an object which has moved out of the perceptual field presupposes the ability to follow the object to the point of disappearance. In such cases, and there must be a variety of them, the ordinality of developmental progress is logically built-in even though it need not be specifically genetically programmed.

HIERARCHICAL ORGANIZATION

A third source of order in psychological development derives from the coordination of simpler sensorimotor schemes into more comprehensively organized systems. At the simplest level, visual following over wide arcs depends upon a coordination of eye movements with head movements. At a somewhat more complex level come the sensorimotor coordinations of Piaget's (1936) second sensorimotor stage. Here, arm movements and grasping become coordinated with looking in the visually directed reaching which has been the subject of the ingenious investigations by White (1967) and his collaborators (White, Castle, and Held, 1964), and looking becomes coordinated with listening as things heard become something to look at in the behavior of auditory localization (Piaget, 1936). Here, also, vocalization becomes coordinated with listening as the infant begins to recognize repeatedly encountered sounds and to manifest pseudo-imitation of familiar vocal patterns. During the third and fourth stages, according to Piaget's (1936) observations, these first habitual coordinations become coordinated at a new hierarchical level in various means-ends relationships. Through the exercise of these coordinations, representative central processes become increasingly elaborate and mobile. The result is a hierarchical organization of abilities and motivations for which Piaget's observations and theorizing are but one source (see also Ferguson, 1954; Gagné, 1965; Gagné and Paradise, 1961; Hunt, 1961, p. 109ff.).

This conception of the coordination of increasingly complex systems in a hierarchical organization continues, moreover, in Piaget's (1945) conception of the origin of language. Here, the child coordinates his representative central processes which constitute his knowledge of events, objects, persons, and places (see Furth, 1969) with his imitations of novel vocal patterns. At first, such coordinations involve only idiosyncratic congeries of actions, events, objects, and persons, presumably established in the course of encounters with exciting events and combined with imitative garblings of the vocal signs which were part of those events. In time, such coordinations give rise to pseudowords with sufficient semantic specificity to permit the infant limited communication with those who know well his past experience. Still later, and beyond the sensorimotor period, children appear to achieve a generalized "learning set"—Harlow's (1949) term—that "things have names," with a variety of behavioral consequences.

Although environmental encounters can markedly alter the rate of development in any of these sensorimotor systems, as we have seen in the case of the blink response (Greenberg, Užgiris, and Hunt, 1968) and eye-hand coordination (White and Held, 1966), this does not alter the inevitability of order in the behavioral landmarks for such coordinations. Thus differing regimes of child rearing may diminish the correlation between the rates of development in two relatively independent sensorimotor systems. For instance, in the children of academic families who served as subjects in our experiments, ear-vocal coordinations came typically ahead of top-level reaching in the eye-hand coordination system, but in the infants of the Tewksbury State Hospital who served as subjects in the second enrichment study of White and Held (1966), the appearance of top-level reaching appeared long before ear-vocal coordination marked by pseudo-imitation of familiar vocalizations. Moreover, the appearance of top-level reaching at a median of 87 days in the hospital infants is markedly earlier than the typical age at which behavioral evidence of either ear-vocal or eye-hand coordination appeared in our home-reared subjects from academic families. Such differential modification of the rates of coordination between these relatively independent sensorimotor systems does not alter the inevitability of order deriving from the coordination of such coordinations. It should be noted that no matter how far ahead experience pushes one such coordination or serves to delay the other one, the coordination of such coordinations cannot occur until both are present. This is the essence of the hierarchical conception of psychological development and competence.[1]

[1] It is worth noting the similarity and the difference between the conceptions of hierarchically organized abilities proposed by Gagné (1965) and Gagné and Paradise (1961)

ORDER BASED ON PERSISTENCE
OF REPRESENTATIVE CENTRAL PROCESSES

A fourth source of order in behavioral development is to be found
in the increasing persistence of the representative processes which
grow out of the infant's perceptual and manipulative encounters with
events, objects, persons, and places. Evidence for this source of order
may be found in the orderly sequence of behavioral landmarks marking the construction of the object. Even after the very young infant
has begun to follow objects through 180°, his glance immediately wan-
ders once an object disappears from view. After more living and looking, however, a lingering of his glance implies that his central processes
representative of the object persist and that their persistence guides his
glance and holds it where the object disappeared. At about this point,
the infant will reach for an object that he can see, but once his view of
the object is even partially obstructed by a cover, he ceases to seek it
actively. Later, he will reach for and secure the partially hidden object, but if it is completely covered, he ceases to attempt to find it. We
have discerned 14 steps in the sequence of object construction which,
however, reflect more than just an increase in the persistence of representative central processes. Suffice it to say here that, eventually, the
infants become capable of following an object placed in a container as
the container makes a series of disappearances, and of searching for
the object, first in the container, then in the place where the container disappeared last, and then in all the places where the container
was seen to disappear, thus traversing the path of successive disap-

---

and that proposed here. The notion of a hierarchy is common to both. Gagné comes upon
his view from the standpoint of the abilities involved in adult problem-solving; we come
upon ours from the standpoint of seeing how those adult abilities develop out of the ready-
made sensorimotor organizations of the newborn human infant. Gagné and his followers
proceed from their analysis of what skills and motives are needed for any given performance, such as learning to read, and attempt to teach those skills and motives which they
glean must be missing in their older subjects. We start from the ready-made abilities of the
human infant and attempt to discern branches of development and their new levels of organization. Gagné emerges with a taxonomy of learnings differentiated by their conditions. As will be seen in Part II of this monograph, we emerge with six branches of development and with an epigenetic series of sequential steps in each.

As we see it, these two approaches are equally valid at this stage of history. Gagné's is
probably the more useful for educational efforts with school-age children and even with
those of preschool age involved in compensatory education attempts. Ours is probably the
more useful as an approach to understanding the development of abilities and motives and
may be the more useful for the prevention of retardation and apathy in infancy.

pearances of the container in reverse. The actions of reaching for, seeking, and searching out a desired object are constant across a number of hiding situations. The evidence implying increasing persistence of the central processes which must represent the desired object consists in greater persistence of search behavior in the same hiding situation as well as greater persistence of search when the number of barriers between the infant and the desired object are increased. The critical actions defining each step in the sequence concerned with object construction imply the existence of representative central processes which make the infant less and less dependent upon direct perceptual inputs for his belief in the continued existence of the object.

Similarly, evidence for the limited persistence of representative central processes in young infants may be found in their restricted ability to relate events over time. Several recent studies (Millar, 1972; Ramey and Ourth, 1971; Watson, 1967) have demonstrated that young infants are able to act on the basis of existing contingencies between events only if the events are separated by very short time intervals. It may be that the ordering in terms of difficulty for infants of classical and operant conditioning and of various discrimination learning situations reflects, in part, the limited ability of infants to coordinate action with some representation of prior events arising from the short persistence of their central processes.

ORDER IN THE EPIGENESIS
OF INTRINSIC MOTIVATION

A fifth sequence of definite order in development, one perhaps more hypothetical than the foregoing, is motivational in character (see Hunt, 1965). The newborn human being is essentially a responsive organism. He responds to changes in ongoing input especially through the skin, the nose, the ears, and the eyes. The response to such changes in ongoing input has several aspects. These include the arousal assessed by autonomic indicators and the attention comprising the orienting response and various motor behaviors. The arousal component of the orienting response was originally discovered by Pavlov, but the stimulus-stimulus relationships it implied have been far less commonly investigated than the stimulus-response relationships of classical conditioning (see Berlyne, 1960; Razran, 1961; Sokolov, 1960). The motor elements vary with the intensity and modality of the input. They include sucking in response to a touch on the skin near the mouth (Gunther, 1961; McKee and Honzik, 1962; Ribble, 1944); the Babkin reflex, consisting of wide opening of the mouth and a tendency for the head to turn toward the midline from the tonic-neck reflex position in response to tactile pressure on the palm of the neonate's hand; body movement and sharp alterations in the rate of breathing to changes in olfactory input (Engen and Lipsitt, 1965; Engen, Lipsitt, and Kaye, 1963); and the orienting response, consisting of arousal with motor orientation of the ears and eyes toward changes in auditory and visual input (Sokolov, 1960). We believe the effective elicitor of the orienting response to be change in some characteristic of the ongoing receptor input rather than stimulation, per se, defined as energy delivered at the receptors. We hold this belief because the orienting response and the associated motor activities disappear fairly rapidly with receptor adaptation as input of a given character and level of intensity persists. One exception occurs, of course, when the intensity is painful, but some degree of adaptation may occur even to inputs which are painful (Salama and Hunt, 1964).

Even during the days immediately following birth, these responses of the human infant are highly plastic in the sense that they change with experience (see Lipsitt, 1967, 1969). One kind of change consists of habituation, the name given to the phenomenon of response decrement that occurs as the infant encounters repeatedly a given kind of change in input (Harris, 1943; Thompson and Spencer, 1966). This phenomenon has long been implicitly recognized. It was implicit for instance, in the statement by William James that "one does not hear the clock until it stops." It was more explicitly recognized in the work of Raymond Dodge (1923). Even so, the phenomenon has received relatively little attention from investigators, and most of that quite recently (Sharpless and Jasper, 1956; Thompson and Spencer, 1966). Habituation in human infants to repeated encounters with specified changes in olfactory input have been reported by Disher (1934) and Engen and Lipsitt (1965), to specified changes in auditory input by Bartoshuk (1962), Forbes and Forbes (1927), and by Moreau, Birch, and Turkewitz (1970), to repeated presentations of visual patterns by Friedman, Nagy, and Carpenter (1970), and in somewhat older infants by Cohen (1969) and Fantz (1964), among others. After such habituation of response, altering the nature of the change in ongoing input from that which has been repeatedly encountered brings about a recovery (Bartoshuk, 1962; Bridger, 1961; Cohen, Gelber, and Lazar, 1971; Engen and Lipsitt, 1965; Saayman, Ames, and Moffett, 1964; for a review, see Jeffrey and Cohen, 1971). During these early weeks following birth, variations in receptor input appear to be especially important in the motivation of infants. The habituation that may occur in the absence of such variations is probably responsible in considerable part for the apathy and retardation characteristic of orphanage-reared infants.

Newborn infants show plasticity of their responsive behaviors in other ways. They may be capable of classical conditioning (Marquis, 1931; Kaye, 1965; Lipsitt and Kaye, 1964; Siqueland and Lipsitt, 1966), of a kind of discrimination learning (Lipsitt and Kaye, 1965), and of modification in the capacity of a given change in input to evoke a given response through reward. While demonstration of classical conditioning in newborns has been claimed in several studies, it is still being questioned (Sameroff, 1971). The existence of discrimination learning has been based upon the fact that even such activities as sucking occur more commonly to certain changes in input than to others. Gunther (1961) has noted that nipples of differing shapes vary in their capacity to evoke sucking and that infants differ in their reactiveness to different types of nipples. Lipsitt and Kaye (1965) have also noted that there is a cumulative effect of the capacity of rubber tubing and of an ordinary rubber bottle nipple to evoke sucking that appears with repeated encounters. With repeated trials, the rubber tubing evokes fewer and fewer sucks per given time of contact and the nipple produces more and more sucks per given time of contact. The capacity of the rubber tube to elicit sucking, however, can be markedly increased when each ten seconds of sucking brings a cubic centimeter of dextrose-water solution (Lipsitt, Kaye, and Bosack, 1966). Similarly, Sameroff (1968) was able to alter the two components of the sucking response, expression and suction, by differentially reinforcing one or the other with the reward of milk. Siqueland and Lipsitt (1966) observed that when head-turning results in an opportunity to obtain a taste of dextrose solution by sucking for a few seconds, this reinforcement greatly increases the capacity both of a stroke on an infant's cheek and of a previous sounding of a buzzer for a 5-second period to elicit the head-turning response.

Although these studies indicate that even the newborn's responsiveness can be modified by the reinforcement provided through such inputs as the taste of sweetness (with presumably innate reinforcement value), the infant remains essentially responsive until he begins to act on his own initiative to obtain certain inputs that he anticipates from his own action. Piaget (1936) identified this behavioral landmark in the development of his own three children. He saw its initial manifestation in activities to retain or regain perceptual contact with interesting events and scenes, and he interpreted it to indicate coordination of motor habits with perceptions to form intentional acts. As we see it, the intentionality derives from the fact that the sequential organization of central processes which are presumably inculcated through repeated encounters with a given series of events will run off faster than the events. Such a relationship between the relative speeds of representative central processes and of external events can be made to account readily for classical conditioning as well as for both expectations and intentions (Hunt, 1966, pp. 104–6; 1971a). Where the successive events are merely perceived, the first perceptions come to arouse expectations of those following. Where the successive events involve an action on the part of the infant followed by either a perceptual event or an opportunity for further action, the anticipation of the consequence from the action provides the basis for the intention.

With this landmark in psychological development, what Skinner (1953) calls "operants" come into being (Hunt, 1965, 1971a, 1971b). Piaget (1936) identified this behavioral landmark in the development of his own children during the fifth month, but we have identified what appears to be a form of it as early as the end of the second month (Užgiris and Hunt, 1965, 1970). This form consists of children shaking themselves and kicking their legs in order to see movement of a mobile hung over their cribs. A mobile was so attached to each infant's crib that a shake of the body would cause it to move. When the infants were examined four weeks after the installation of the mobiles, several of them had developed a relationship with their mobiles that appeared to provide them with considerable delight. A similar observation has been recently reported by Watson and Ramey (1969) for two-month-old infants, who were given the opportunity to move a mobile by small movements of the head, following just three days of experience with it. Interestingly, while attempting to condition head-turning in somewhat older infants, Papoušek (1969) noted that the infants appeared to perform the correct response not so much for the sake of the reinforcement provided as for the sake of obtaining a confirmation of their expectation concerning the efficacy of the head-turning action; for example, the infants would not watch the visual reinforcement provided, but they would continue to perform the correct action with signs of delight.

Such observations suggest that during this second phase of motivational development, a new form of reinforcement comes into being. Objects, persons, and places repeatedly encountered appear to give satisfaction. But development is a dynamic process, and the reinforcing nature of these objects and events probably resides in their fulfillment of the infant's anticipations. Hunt (1965, 1971b) has suggested elsewhere that the reinforcing value of recognitive familiarity and expectation may well account for both the repetitive babbling of young infants, in the vocal domain, and the pseudo-imitation of familiar gestures and vocalizations. Moreover, in the course of coming to recognize more and more objects, persons, places, and events, the infant may well develop a kind of generalized learning-set which one might verbalize as "things should be recognizable." Such may be the developmental origins of the recognition and identification of objects which Woodworth (1947) described as the goal and the reinforcement of perceptual activity.

At about this point, a new phase opens with the behavioral landmark of interest in the novel rather than the familiar. In our own experiments, in which three-dimensional mobiles were hung over infants' cribs beginning at four weeks of age, the shift from looking longer at the familiar one of a pair of objects to looking longer at the novel one occurred during the third month (Greenberg, Užgiris and Hunt, 1970; Užgiris and Hunt, 1965, 1970). A similar shift was also observed by Curcio (1969) around the third month; it was dependent both on the length of prior experience with the familiar object and on the age of the infant at the time of familiarization.

Much remains to be learned about the nature of and the basis for this motivational landmark in psychological development. It may well result in considerable part from the boredom that comes as part of the habituation arising from repeated encounters with given objects and events described so well by Hebb (1949). It may also have another causal basis in the development of the generalized learning-set that things should be recognizable. With the development of such a set, one would expect that what is novel and not immediately recognizable would motivate the attempt to recognize by examination and scrutiny. In fact, such a landmark is found as part of the sequence in the development of schemes for relating to objects (Užgiris, 1967; also Chapter 16).

During this phase of interest in the novel, development appears to branch in two directions. On the perceptual side comes a kind of learning-set which one might verbalize as: "If I act, I can find interesting inputs." Inasmuch as the novel regularly becomes the familiar with repeated encounters, this interest in the novel provides a kind of growth motivation (see Hunt, 1965, 1971b). On the side of action comes another learning-set that one might well verbalize as: "If I act, I can find interesting things to do." In Piaget's (1936) observations, this latter branch led to a definite separation of means from ends, wherein certain schemes, such as grasping, become ends and others, such as locomotion, become means. Here one finds in early infant development evidence of the "competence motivation" of R. W. White (1959, 1960). Undoubtedly, landmarks in the development of this motivation inherent in information processing and action (Hunt, 1963a) remain to be identified within the increasing complexity both of eliciting situations and of motor competence.

Although this fifth source of definite order in behavioral development is chiefly motivational in character, it is also cognitive in that it develops out of the infant's informational interaction with his circumstances. The various learning-sets (1) that "things should be recognizable," (2) that "if I act, I can make interesting things happen and can find interesting things to do," (3) that "things have names," and (4) that "things come in sets or classes," all have a cognitive aspect which is fundamental as well as a conative or motivational aspect. Moreover, they have an emotional aspect as well. When expectations and intentions are fulfilled, that fulfillment is a source of satisfaction and reinforcement; when expectations and intentions are unfulfilled, the result is frustrative emotional distress which, we believe, accompanies the disequilibrium which Piaget has conceived to be the ground for the accommodative adaptations in psychological development.

ORDER BASED IN COMPLEXITY

A sixth source of definite order in psychological development resides in the epigenetic, stepwise growth of the appreciation and understanding of relationships implicit in the behavior elicited by situations of increasing complexity. This appreciation and understanding probably has its neural counterparts in the complexity, mobility, and reversibility of the firing systems of the brain, but the appreciation and understanding are also epistemological in character. They show in the development of both gestural and vocal imitation, for the infant cannot imitate a gesture or a vocal pattern whose nature he does not appreciate or understand. It is thus, in part, that he imitates the familiar before the novel. It is also thus that he imitates gestures involving the manipulation of the visible parts of his body before he imitates gestures involving invisible parts. This development of appreciation and understanding of relationships is closely akin, and sometimes dependent upon the development of object permanence, but it extends well beyond the grasp of object permanence to that of object relations in space and to an appreciation of practical causality. Thus, even the rapid alternate glancing at two objects implies at least a crude behavioral appreciation of the difference between their positions in space, at the level of action. The ear-eye coordination implied by a correct localization of the source of a sound with the eyes also indicates an appreciation of spatial relationships. Following the trajectory of a rapidly falling or flying object until it escapes from view and then searching for it after it has become invisible implies both a degree of object permanence and some appreciation of localization within visible space. As a final such example, indicating through words or actions the customary whereabouts of familiar objects and persons indicates not only persistence of the central processes representing those objects and persons, but also an appreciation of their locus in space.

We have made no attempt to coordinate the ordinal scales of cognitive development which we shall describe with the different sources of order in behavioral development. Our purpose in describing these six sources of order has been to show that invariant order in the land-marks of behavioral development need not imply a genetically pre-determined rate or even course of development, but rather that both the rate and the course of development result from the ongoing organ-ism-environment interaction in which an element of hereditary pre-programming participates.

SEQUENTIAL ORDER AND
THE ISSUE OF STAGES

The conception of a definite order in behavioral development and the conception of stages in development are related, but not insepara-ble. Piaget (1947) and his collaborators have used the term *stage* to designate qualitatively different levels of organization. Sometimes, the term stage has been used to refer to each of the four major periods in development: the sensorimotor period, the preconceptual period, the period of concrete operations, and the period of formal operations. Sometimes, discernable levels within each period, namely the level of entrance into a period, the level of transition, and the level of con-solidation have been referred to as stages. Within the sensorimotor period, Piaget (1936, 1937) has identified six levels of development which he has also labeled stages. Recently, however, attempts have been made to clarify criteria for identifying stages in development (Inhelder, 1956; Pinard and Laurendeau, 1969; Piaget, 1960) and to elaborate the theoretical implications of the stage concept. The notion of stage focuses concern on the relationship of simultaneously mani-fested behavioral developments to each other and to the postulated organization of central processes giving structure to that level of devel-opment. With a focus on stages of development, the issue of sequence becomes less central even though a fixed order of stages is assumed.

Our investigation in the course of constructing the six scales to be described in Part II of this monograph has led us to focus on the issue of sequence rather than on stages in development. In part, we saw the identification of sequential achievements within each branch of devel-opment as prior to the study of interrelationships between achievements in different branches. In part, our preliminary results led us to question the inevitable simultaneity of some of the behavioral landmarks which Piaget had used to identify each of the six sensorimotor stages. Furthermore, we began to consider that the notion of stage might be more appropriately applied to the sensorimotor period as a whole rather than to particular levels within it. As a consequence, we have used a variable number of behavioral landmarks as steps in our scales. These numbers range from 7 to 14. Moreover, in separating the question of order in development from the matter of chronological age, we have left open for future investigation the questions of which behavioral landmarks in these several scales appear simultaneously and whether they mark six distinct levels of organization seen by Piaget in his own three children.

Part

I I

The Investigation: Developing the Scales

CHAPTER 5

The Plan and the First Phase:
Selecting the Eliciting Situations
and the Critical Actions

The aim of the present study has been neither to replicate the observations of Piaget on infant development during the sensorimotor period nor to construct a new intelligence test to predict the later abilities of individuals tested as infants. Rather, we have aimed to develop a tool of assessment grounded in the theory that development is an epigenetic process of evolving new, more complex, hierarchical levels of organization in intellect and motivation. We have aimed to develop a tool wherein the actions of infants would serve to indicate directly their level of cognitive organization, a tool which in use can extend our understanding of psychological development. Moreover, we have aimed to develop a tool which would facilitate the study of the influence of various kinds of circumstances on development, a tool which would ultimately help guide the efforts of those attempting to devise circumstances to foster the development of very young children.

THE ORIGINAL PLAN

We saw in Piaget's (1936, 1937, 1945) descriptions of the behavior of his own children in various kinds of situations a source of examples

47

of infant-environment interaction which might be arranged into such an instrument of assessment as we aimed to devise. We envisaged the task of developing the instrument to be one requiring several steps. The first step was to identify the various actions of infants described by Piaget as indicative of new levels of cognitive organization or structure. Moreover, we expected to include those behaviors which Hunt (1963b) has considered indicative of new levels of organization in that kind of motivation inherent in information processing and action (Hunt, 1963a). The second step was to arrange these infant actions and the situations Piaget had used to elicit them into a schedule and to prepare instructions for presenting the situations as well as for observing and recording the infant behaviors. We expected to include a good many unelicited, spontaneous actions of infants as items within this schedule. The third step was to examine in their homes a sample of infants of both sexes selected to represent every month of age from birth to two years. From these examinations we hoped to obtain an empirical basis for selecting the toys and materials to be used in eliciting critical actions from infants and to learn how to structure the situations designed to elicit them. The fourth step was to train a second examiner to use the schedule resulting from step three in order to determine inter-examiner reliability. The fifth step was to use the resulting instrument in a longitudinal study of infant development. From longitudinal studies we hoped to get evidence of whether the hypothesized sequential order is indeed invariant, and whether the invariance will persist through different regimes of child-rearing. We hoped to test the hypothesis once formulated by Lois Murphy (1944) that varying rates of psychological development are a matter of degree of parental concern and amount of parental contact with children during various phases of development. Some mothers especially like little, helpless infants, but find the demandingness of the toddler unattractive and difficult to cope with. Some find the little, helpless infant merely someone to be cared for, but find the initiative and demandingness of the older infant delightful. We hoped originally to examine these clinical observations systematically in a longitudinal study, but found it unfeasible to carry out such a study in the neighboring university towns of Champaign and Urbana because of the high rate of mobility among families with small children.

Actually, the enterprise was carried out in three phases. The first of these phases followed closely the original plan.

PHASE I: SELECTING THE ELICITING SITUATIONS AND THE CRITICAL ACTIONS

The first and probably the most subjective aspect of our investigation entailed selecting which of the many situations described by Piaget in his books *The Origins of Intelligence in Children* (1936) and *The Construction of Reality in the Child* (1937) should be tried out with our first group of infants for possible inclusion in the assessment instrument we aimed to develop.

In this process, we attempted to err on the inclusive side by listing all the situations that Piaget had used to evoke actions illustrative of different levels of psychological organization. We then selected from this list those situations which we thought could be readily reproduced within a restricted setting (indoors) and within a reasonably brief time by an examiner unfamiliar with the infants being examined. In addition, a list of *critical actions* in each of the *eliciting situations* was compiled from Piaget's descriptions. *Critical actions* were defined as those implying that an infant had attained a particular level of functioning in a given branch of development. We then began an exploratory testing of the selected eliciting situations to evaluate their capacity to evoke the specified actions regularly and in a reasonably brief period of time.

In the spring of 1963, a sample of 42 infants of both sexes were presented with these eliciting situations. Six infants were seen a second time after an interval of 1 to 2 months, making a total of 48 separate observations. These infants ranged in age from 1 to 22 months and as already noted, were the children of parents who were connected with the University of Illinois. The actual distribution of these infants in terms of age appears in Table 5:1.

Each infant was examined in his or her home in the presence of one or both parents. The examination session was scheduled for a time when the infant ordinarily would be engaged in play activities (following sleep, feeding, diapering, etc.). It lasted for as long as the infant remained cooperative, usually between one and two hours.

TABLE 5:1   *Distribution of the First Sample of Infant Subjects According to Age*

Age in Months	Number of Subjects	Age in Months	Number of Subjects
1	1	12	6
2	5	13	1
3	4 (2 repeated)	14	0
4	2 (2 repeated)	15	3
5	0	16	2
6	1	17	2
7	4	18	1
8	3 (1 repeated)	19	3
9	3 (1 repeated)	20	0
10	0	21	1
11	5	22	1

Not every infant was presented with every eliciting situation. This was due in part to limitations in time. It was also due in part to the inappropriateness of certain situations for the developmental level of some infants, a point which we shall elaborate below. During this first phase, the presentation of the eliciting situations was modified as the examiner (I.Č.U.) gained experience in their use with infants. Those toys and other materials found suitable for structuring the situations were retained. Those found unattractive to our infants, unsafe, too fragile, or for some other reason unacceptable, were eliminated. In the course of this exploratory work, a fairly consistent order for presenting the situations gradually evolved. This order was based largely on the acceptability of the situations to the infants.

We had planned to utilize a good many spontaneous actions of infants in our assessment. The examining quickly brought out, however, that one must spend long periods of time with an infant in order to get an opportunity to observe any given item of spontaneous behavior. Even then, the parent often had to serve as interpreter of the specific meaning of that behavior. As a consequence, the ratio of critical actions elicited by situations structured by the examiner to actions occurring spontaneously was sharply increased by dropping many of the spontaneous kind. This is not to say that the actions of infants in the prepared situations were always clear and without need of parental interpretation, but the saving in time and the need to increase the probability of having an opportunity to observe the various critical actions were important enough in the construction of an instrument designed for the assessment of infant development to tip the scales sharply in favor of structured situations. Interpretations by parents of the meaning of their infants' actions in our eliciting situations and suggestions by parents for modifying the presentation of the situations were solicited and obtained. The examiner took notes during each session with an infant and from them wrote a narrative record of the actions of each infant immediately following the session.

The experience with this first sample of infants definitely encouraged further work. It was gratifying to note that infants responded to most of the eliciting situations prepared by the examiner with one of the critical actions that Piaget had described. This permitted classifying their actions as indicative of one of his stages of functioning. The examiner used the narrative records to determine the sensorimotor stage which seemed to be most characteristic of each infant. Table 5:2 contains the distribution of infants examined according to Piaget's stages and the mean age of the infants within each stage of development.

TABLE 5:2   *Distribution of the First Sample of Infants According to Piaget's Stages of Development*

Stages of Intellectual Development	Number of Infants	Mean Age in Months and Days
I	2	2 (1)
II	9	3 (5)
III	7	6 (14)
IV	12	10 (18)
V	9	14 (8)
VI	9	18 (26)

This initial classification, made by the same examiner who had observed the infants, depended heavily upon behaviors indicative of the general development of object construction and representation. It was noted that in other branches of development such as imitation or operational causality, the actions of a substantial proportion of the infants seemed typical of a stage either preceding or following that which characterized their general level of functioning defined chiefly by object construction. This observation suggested that perhaps development does not proceed at an even pace in all branches as implied by Piaget's stages. This observation prompted the decision to construct an instrument which would attempt to assess separately the capabilities of each infant along several branches of psychological development.

REVISING THE FIRST VERSION
OF THE INSTRUMENT

Relying on the experience gained in using the first version of the instrument with this first group of infants, the examiner rearranged the eliciting situations into a new schedule and wrote more explicit instructions for their presentation. Those situations which had been most successful in eliciting the critical actions were selected. This basis for selecting situations had to be somewhat modified, however, so that a number of situations appropriate to each stage of development would be retained.

The new schedule was then divided into six sections according to the following Piagetian headings: (1) the general level of representation, (2) the development of recognition, (3) the development of prehension, (4) the development of object permanence (subdivided into: following the trajectory of objects, search for the vanished object, and the construction of the object), (5) the development of imitation (vocal and gestural), and (6) the understanding of causality. We considered that these sections might well constitute separately identifiable branches of psychological development. The directions written for each of these sections contained suggestions for presenting the eliciting situations, for noting specified actions which might occur spontaneously during the course of the examination, and for gaining corroborative information about the occurrence of such behaviors at other times from the parents of the infant. A great deal continued to be left, however, to the discretion and ingenuity of the examiner.

In this second version of the instrument, the critical actions of each infant, either those elicited in structured situations or observed to occur spontaneously, were again to be evaluated in relation to Piaget's stages of sensorimotor development. The critical actions for assigning an infant to a given stage in each of the branches of development were carefully spelled out. The examiner, however, was not only to assign an infant to a given stage, but also to justify this assignment by recording the actual behaviors of the infant which prompted each such assignment.

This second version of the instrument reflected our theoretical approach to assessment. Our aim was to observe an infant's typical manner of interacting with his circumstances and to infer from such observations the presence of the specific capabilities and the specific constructions of reality defining his level of psychological functioning. Consequently, relatively little importance was attached to either the eliciting situation or the materials in the sense of the usual approach to ability testing. Rather, another form of standardization was to be achieved by aiming always for a state of optimal cooperation from the infant and by assuring always that his interest in the test materials extended to manipulating the materials provided in a manner which produced relevant information for the examiner. This meant that the infant was presented with the eliciting situations in his own home, usually on the floor of his living room, rather than in a standardized testing room and in a standardized baby seat. Furthermore, the toys and materials used to structure the various situations were to be varied in accordance with the experience and interests of each infant examined instead of being fixed and unchanged from infant to infant. The order of presenting the eliciting situations was also to be varied in accordance with the interests of each infant. Since the aim was to obtain evidence in the form of clear implications from the infant's actions in the eliciting situations of specific capabilities and of specific constructions of reality rather than to score the presence or absence of particular responses to standardized test items, there were no injunctions against repeating the presentation of an eliciting situation, against postponing it, or against modifying its noncritical aspects. For example, in the development of the object concept (Piaget, 1937) which includes object permanence, an important landmark occurs when an infant begins to search for objects completely hidden under covers or screens. To assess this achievement, it is necessary to determine whether hidden objects continue to exist for an infant. It is not important to determine whether an infant will lift a particular cover to obtain a particular toy. The essential features of the situation for eliciting relevant actions from the infant are the presence of interest in the object, a lack of interest in the cover or screen, and an active desire for the object at the moment it is being covered. Therefore, we felt that in presenting this situation, the examiner should be free to vary other elements of the situation in order to maintain these essential features. Thus, the object to be hidden, the screen under which the object is to be hidden, and the particular moment of presenting the situation to capture the infant's interest may all vary. We believe that the subjectivity resident in reliance on an examiner's judgment regarding the essential features of each eliciting situation will be less damaging to the validity of the information to be gained about the infant's level of development than any attempt to standardize the materials and procedures in a rigid fashion.

This same theoretical approach to assessment was also reflected in our unconcern for devising a scoring system to permit a translation of the evaluation of an infant's actions denoting landmarks of achievement in the several branches of development into a single numerical score. We desired to be able to specify an infant's level of interaction with his surroundings and, eventually, to be able to relate his level of achievement to his previous experiences. For these purposes, instances of unusual actions, unusual in the sense of being unexpected given the level of development implied by the infant's actions in other eliciting situations, or, unusual in the sense of being rare and implying a different mode of traversing some portion of a sequence of development, we considered to be potentially the most useful. It seemed unwise to arbitrarily score such actions as pluses or minuses and thus hide them behind a number. Furthermore, our view of human development was not congruent with treating diverse actions of the infant in substantial fashion as additive for the purpose of obtaining a convenient summary represented by a numerical score.

We considered that if psychological development and competence occurs in such a way that definite behavioral landmarks can be recognized as indicating the transition from one level to another, and if these levels are also characterized by the implicit presence of specifiable epistemic constructions, intellectual abilities, and motivational organizations, it should be possible to obtain evidence of each level of psychological development in a number of situations and under a variety of circumstances. If the circumstances were varied to suit each infant as much as possible, moreover, the accuracy of the assessment should thereby be increased.

Thus, this first phase of our investigation began with a compilation of a list of situations for eliciting achievements in psychological development described by Piaget. This list constituted the first version of our instrument. It continued with a presentation of these eliciting situations to a sample of 42 infants. The experience gained herein led to the development of a philosophy of assessing levels of psychological development. To be sure, in part we started with this philosophy, but our several tentative convictions were both altered and sharpened by the observations made during this phase.

CHAPTER 6

Phase II: Reliability of Assessment
by Sensorimotor Stage with the Second
Version of the Instrument

The examination of infants during the first phase of our work was carried out by a single examiner. This left several aspects of the examining procedure and especially the matter of inter-examiner reliability problematical. It was necessary to determine: (1) whether the instructions for presenting the eliciting situations could be followed by another examiner; (2) whether the eliciting situations could be successfully presented by another examiner; and (3) whether the critical actions elicited by the situations and observed by another person would agree with those observed by the examiner.

In the summer of 1963, Tam Wei joined in the investigation. She participated along with the original examiner (I.Č.U.) in a trial use of the instrument with a new group of infants. She made no attempt to use the instrument with only the help of the written instructions, but rather, she received demonstrations from the first examiner and was observed while she attempted to present the eliciting situations to a small number of infants. After this limited period of training, the second phase of the study was undertaken.

A group of 23 infants was examined in this second phase of the study. They included both sexes, and they ranged in age from 1 to 23 months. This sample of subjects is described in Table 6:1.

Table 6:1   *Distribution of the Second Sample of Infants According to Age*

Age in Months	Number of Subjects	Age in Months	Number of Subjects
1	1	13	0
2	1	14	3
3	0	15	2
4	3	16	0
5	2	17	1
6	2	18	0
7	2	19	0
8	1	20	0
9	1	21	2
10	0	22	0
11	0	23	1
12	1	24	0

Each of the two examiners saw each of these 23 infants separately. The two examinations were scheduled 48 hours apart. This ensured that each infant would be seen during the same portion of the day by each examiner, and would be at approximately the same age both times. One of the examiners saw 12 infants first, the other examiner saw 11 infants first. We wished to determine whether both examiners could use the instrument successfully and whether the infants would show some consistency in their actions within the eliciting situations. We did not expect an infant's capabilities to change over such a short interval as 48 hours, but we did expect his moods and motivations to vary, and we wished especially to determine whether his level of development would be assessed similarly by both examiners. Thus, we imposed a fairly strict test on the consistency of assessment, but the design of the first reliability study confounded three sources of variability: the examiner's techinque, the reliability of observation, and the stability of an infant's actions in the eliciting situations over a period of 48 hours. The results appear in Table 6:2.

As may be seen in Table 6:2, the two examiners did agree well about the sensorimotor stage achieved by each infant in the several branches of psychological development. The specific actions of any infant which the two examiners recorded to justify judging him to be at a given sensorimotor stage in each branch of development varied considerably.

TABLE 6:2　*Agreement of Two Examiners in Assessing the Stage of Development for Infants in the Second Sample*

Branch of Development	Number of Cases Rated by Both Observers	Number of Cases on Which Both Observers Agreed
General Representation	18	17
Prehension	22	20
Permanence of Objects:		
Search for vanished object	16	16
Trajectory of object	17	16
Construction of object	21	19
Imitation:		
Vocal	14	11
Gestural	15	13

After discussing the individual cases, the two examiners agreed that some of the differences were undoubtedly due to the differences in their ways of structuring the eliciting situations and to their individual predilections in noting certain actions rather than others. In an appreciable number of instances, nevertheless, the infant's actions in specific eliciting situations changed over even the short interval of 48 hours between the two observation periods. It was decided, therefore, that the study of inter-examiner reliability should be separated from the study of the consistency of infant actions, and that both needed more careful investigation.

Following this initial reliability study in the second phase, the instrument was revised again to incorporate the suggestions gleaned from having another examiner use the instrument and also from the experience gained by the first examiner in using it with a second group of infants. On the whole, the revisions made were in the direction of greater standardization of the eliciting situations and of more specific and detailed description of the critical actions to be observed. The directions for structuring the eliciting situations were both expanded and clarified. For each of them, all of the infant actions which had been observed repeatedly were listed descriptively on the record sheets as a reminder to the examiner. Nevertheless, provision was made again on the record sheets for recording other or additional actions shown by the infant.

In this second revision of the instrument, we planned also for a basic change in the nature of the quantification to be employed. The observations of the first and second phase made it quite clear that quantification in terms of Piaget's six stages of sensorimotor development failed to reflect the full variety of the actions that infants actually manifest in our eliciting situations. Quantification and scaling in terms of Piaget's six stages were therefore abandoned. We should emphasize, however, that the basic nature of our approach did not change. It remained incumbent upon the examiner to repeat or to modify each eliciting situation until the examiner was reasonably satisfied that an infant did or did not have a particular capability. Similarly, it remained incumbent upon the examiner to record the infant's actions in such a way as to permit inference about the infant's level of functioning. Thus, the examiner's task did not become a mere presentation of a series of stereotyped tests according to stated directions combined with an uncritical marking of the actions observed. Moreover, although each eliciting situation was designed to evoke actions particularly significant for one branch of development, sometimes the actions evoked by a given situation proved to be informative about another branch of development or about two branches of development at the same time. It remained incumbent upon the examiner to record such additional information. Thus, the examiner's task consisted in using each eliciting situation as a means for observing actions which provided information about an infant's level of psychological functioning rather than one of slavishly administering test items.

In this revision of the instrument, moreover, the division into six separate sections under Piaget's stage headings was abolished, but the intent to assess each of several branches of development was retained. The instrument, moreover, was focused more carefully on those eliciting situations with the strongest tendency to evoke actions clearly implying significant transitions between successive levels of sensorimotor development. To achieve this focus, certain situations were eliminated and new ones were added. With these changes, the whole instrument became too long to be administered to an infant within a single session, so the eliciting situations were subdivided into five sets. Each set was chosen to be appropriate for infants from middle class local families of a given age-range: 0 to 4 months, 4 to 8 months, 8 to 12 months, 12 to 18 months, and 18 to 24 months. These age designations were made primarily as labels for these sets, but they also served as guides to the examiner in finding a starting point for the assessment of a given infant. To ensure adequate sampling of critical actions, however, each infant was presented with situations from two or three sets of eliciting situations. This was quite feasible inasmuch as considerable overlap existed among the situations in the adjacent sets. It should be emphasized, moreover, that the eliciting situations to be presented to any given infant were to depend wholly on his actions in them and not on his age. Thus, when an infant had succeeded to manifest implicit evidence of capability through several levels of functioning, this evidence warranted the assumption that he would have shown the appropriate critical actions in situations clearly calling for lesser levels of capability even though these were not actually presented. Similarly, at the upper levels, if a child did not demonstrate the critical actions indicative of understanding at several successive higher levels of functioning this warranted the assumption that he would not act any differently in situations appropriate for even higher levels.

LIST OF ELICITING SITUATIONS
IN SECOND REVISION OF INSTRUMENT
PRESENTED TO THIRD SAMPLE OF INFANTS

The 63 eliciting situations were divided into five sets for the purpose of presentation to infants. Set I was usually appropriate for infants o to about 4 months of age; Set II for infants 4 to about 8 months of age; Set III, for infants 8 to about 12 months of age; Set IV, for infants 12 to about 18 months of age; and Set V, for infants 18 to about 24 months of age. The sets in which each of the 63 situations were included are given in parentheses following the heading for each situation. The heading for each situation is followed by the directions for arranging it, then by a list of the actions most commonly observed, and finally space for describing yet other actions. Here the directions have been somewhat condensed to conserve space.

1. *Following a Slowly Moving Object* (Set I)
    a. Have the infant focus on some object such as the multicolored ring and move it slowly through a lateral arc of 180°.

Does not follow_____
Follows through part of arc with jerky accommodations_____
Follows through part of arc with smooth accommodations_____
Follows through complete arc with jerky accommodations_____
Follows through complete arc with smooth accommodations_____
Other (specify):

b. If the infant does not follow the object, have the mother move her face in a similar manner, and observe.

Does not follow_____
Follows through part of arc with jerky accommodations_____
Follows through part of arc with smooth accommodations_____
Follows through complete arc with jerky accommodations_____
Follows through complete arc with smooth accommodations_____
Other (specify):

2. *Disappearance of a Slowly Moving Object* (Sets I and II)

Have the infant focus on a bright object such as the multicolored ring and move it slowly to one side and away from the infant, making it disappear below the crib or some other surface, always in the same direction.

Does not follow object to point of disappearance_____
Follows, but loses interest as soon as object disappears_____
Lingers with glance on point of disappearance_____
Lingers, then returns eyes to starting point_____
Searches with eyes around point of disappearance_____
Other (specify):

3. *Partial Hiding* (Sets I, II, III, IV, and V)

Interest the infant in a small toy such as the small doll and cover it with a scarf so that only a small portion remains visible.

Loses interest_____
Looks at visible part_____
Tries to grasp toy, but does not succeed_____
Obtains toy_____
Other (specify):

4. *Finding a Special Object—Mother* (Set II)

Have the mother hide her head behind a scarf while holding it within the infant's reach, and observe his reaction.

No interest____
Looks at scarf____
Pulls scarf down____
Other (specify):

5. *Hiding under One or More Single Screens* (Sets II, III, IV, and V)

   a. Interest the infant in some toy such as the necklace or the doll and cover it completely with a scarf.
   Loses interest____
   Looks surprised____
   Frowns and/or cries____
   Fingers screen____
   Obtains toy____
   Other (specify):

   b. If the infant obtains the toy, introduce a second screen, the cloth, and use it to cover the toy in a new location, leaving the first screen in place.
   Searches only under the first screen____
   Searches directly under the second screen____
   Other (specify):

   c. Hide the toy alternately under one of the two screens.
   Loses interest____
   Searches haphazardly____
   Searches directly under correct screen____
   Other (specify):

   d. Introduce a third screen, the pillow, and hide the toy under each of the three screens in random order.
   Loses interest____
   Searches haphazardly____
   Searches directly under correct screen____
   Other (specify):

6. *Hiding with Successive Visible Displacements* (Sets III, IV, and V)

   Take an object in which the infant shows a strong interest and hide it successively under each of the three screens, keeping the toy clearly visible while it is between screens. Leave it under the last screen.
   Loses interest____
   Searches only under the first screen____

Searches haphazardly under all screens_____
Searches correctly under the last screen_____
Other (specify):

7. *Superimposed Screens* (Sets III, IV, and V)

Hide a toy in which the infant shows interest by covering it with all three screens, placing them one on top of the other.

Loses interest_____
Reacts to loss, but does not touch screens_____
Lifts one or two screens and gives up_____
Lifts all screens and obtains toy_____
Other (specify):

8. *Hiding with Invisible Displacements under One or More Single Screens* (Sets III, IV, and V)

a. Take a small object in which the infant shows a strong interest and hide it under a single screen by placing it first in an open box and by using the box as the means for creating the invisible displacement.

Loses interest_____
Reacts to loss by looking around for object_____
Appeals to E_____
Searches only in box_____
Searches in box and then lifts screen_____
Searches directly under screen_____
Other (specify):

b. Hide the toy in the same manner under a second screen, placed in a new location (on the opposite side of the infant), while the first screen remains in place.

Loses interest_____
Searches only in box_____
Searches only under the first screen_____
Searches directly under the second screen_____
Other (specify):

c. Hide the toy in the same manner under two screens alternately.

Searches only under one of the screens each time_____
Searches haphazardly under both screens_____
Searches directly under the correct screen_____
Other (specify):

d. Introduce a third screen, and hide the toy under each of the three screens in random order, using the box to create the invisible displacement.

Searches haphazardly under all screens____
Searches directly under the correct screen____
Other (specify):

9. *Hiding with Successive Invisible Displacements* (Sets III, IV, and V)

a. Interest the infant in a small object which can be covered by the palm of the hand and hide it under each of the three screens in succession, using the hand as the means for creating the invisible displacements. Take the same path in hiding each time and leave the object under the last screen.

Searches only in E's hand____
Searches only under the first screen in the path____
Searches haphazardly under all screens____
Searches successively under all screens in the path____
Searches only under the last screen in the path____
Other (specify):

b. While hiding in the same manner as in (a) above, leave the object under the first screen, but continue the movement of the hand to the last screen.

Searches only under the last screen in the path____
Starts search with the last screen and then retraces the path of
  hiding____
Other (specify):

10. *Hand-Eye Coordination—Hand-Watching Behavior* (Set I)

a. Observe whether the infant watches his hands when they come in front of his eyes at any time in the session.

No____
Yes____

b. Ask the mother whether she has observed hand-watching behavior.

No____
Yes____   Since when?____

11. *Hand-Mouth Coordination* (Set I)

a. Observe whether the infant gets his hand into his mouth at any time during the session.

No____
Yes____

b. Observe whether the infant is able to put the hand back into his mouth immediately when it is removed.

No____
Yes____

c. Ask the mother if she has observed such behavior.

No____
Yes____   Since when?____

12. *Smiling* (Set I)

a. Observe whether the infant smiles upon seeing his mother's face at any time during the session.

No____
Yes____

b. Have the mother stand outside the infant's line of vision and speak softly to the infant. Observe whether he smiles upon hearing her voice.

No____
Yes____

c. Ask the mother whether the infant has been observed to smile at any objects.

No____   Since when?____
Yes____   Which?____

13. *Maintaining an Interesting Spectacle—Secondary Circular Reaction* (Sets I and II)

a. Find some toy which would interest the infant when activated (e.g., musical toy) and hold it so that the infant could activate it accidently by moving his legs.

No reaction____
Smiles____
Intensifies leg movements____
Attempts by kicks to keep toy moving____

Other (specify):

b. Repeat by holding the toy close to the infant's hands.

No reaction_____

Smiles_____

Attempts to hit toy again_____

Repeats hand movements systematically and keeps toy active_____

Tries to grasp toy_____

Other (specify):

14. *Eye-Hand Coordination—Visually Directed Grasping* (Sets I and II)

a. Hold the rattle in front of the infant within reaching distance and observe his reaction.

Looks at toy_____

Reaches_____

Touches_____

Grasps_____

Other (specify):

b. If the infant does not succeed in grasping the rattle, present it so that both his hand and the rattle would be within view simultaneously.

Looks at toy_____

Reaches_____

Touches_____

Grasps_____

Other (specify):

15. *Means and Ends—Dropping One Object to Pick Up Another* (Set III)

Get the infant to hold something in each hand simultaneously (e.g., blocks) and quickly present a third object, more attractive than the other two.

Looks at third object_____

Reaches for third object while holding on to those already in the hands_____

Reaches for third object and drops one already held in the process_____

Quickly drops one or both objects already held and then reaches for third_____

Other (specify):

16. *Means and Ends—Support* (Sets III, IV, and V)

a. Seat the infant next to a table and after getting him interested in some toy, take the toy and place it on a pillow located on the table in such a way that the toy would be out of the infant's reach, but a corner of the pillow would be within reach.

Loses interest in toy_____

Reaches for toy and shows unhappiness_____

Tries to climb onto table to obtain toy_____

Appeals to E or mother_____

Pulls the pillow and obtains toy_____

Other (specify):

b. If the infant *does not* use the pillow as a support, demonstrate that moving the pillow back and forth also moves the object, and observe again.

Loses interest in toy_____

Reaches for toy and shows unhappiness_____

Tries to climb onto table to obtain toy_____

Appeals to E or mother_____

Pulls the pillow to obtain toy_____

Other (specify):

c. If the infant *does* use the pillow as a support, on one trial hold the object a few inches above the pillow and observe whether the infant will still pull the pillow.

Pulls pillow_____

Reaches for toy directly_____

Other (specify):

17. *Means and Ends—Locomotion as Means* (Sets III and IV)

While the infant is engaged in play requiring more than one object (e.g., putting blocks into cup), take the object most essential for the play activity and place it at a distance from the infant, so that he would have to move in order to retrieve it.

Loses interest in toy_____

Reacts to loss, but does not move to retrieve toy_____

Moves to retrieve toy_____

Other (specify):

18. *Means and Ends—String* (Sets IV and V)

a. Seat the infant next to a table and, after getting him interested

in some toy, tie a string around the toy and place it on the table so
that it is outside the infant's reach, but stretch the string out from the
toy to the infant's hands.

Loses interest in toy——

Plays with the string instead——

Reaches for toy and shows unhappiness——

Tries to climb onto table to obtain toy——

Appeals to E or mother——

Pulls string and obtains toy——

Other (specify):

b. If the infant *does not* use the string to obtain the toy, demonstrate
that pulling the string brings the toy closer, and again observe his
behavior.

Loses interest in toy——

Plays with the string instead——

Reaches for toy and shows unhappiness——

Tries to climb onto table to obtain toy——

Appeals to E or mother——

Pulls string and obtains toy——

Other (specify):

c. If the infant *does* use the string to obtain the toy, lower the toy
to the floor and stretch the string up, placing it close to his hands.

Loses interest in toy——

Looks down searching for toy——

Throws down string and cries for toy——

Plays with string instead——

Pulls string, but not enough to get toy——

Pulls string and obtains toy——

Other (specify):

d. If the infant *does not* obtain the toy from the floor by means of the
string, demonstrate that raising and lowering the string moves the
toy up and down.

Loses interest in toy——

Looks down searching for toy——

Throws down string and cries for toy——

Plays with string instead——

Pulls string, but not enough to get toy——

Pulls string and obtains toy_____
Other (specify):

19. *Means and Ends—Stick* (Sets IV and V)

a. Seat the infant next to a table and, after getting him interested in some toy, take the toy and place it on the table outside his reach, but put a small stick within the infant's reach.

Loses interest in toy_____
Reaches and cries for toy_____
Attempts to climb onto table to obtain toy_____
Plays with stick only_____
Hits toy with stick, but gets it no closer_____
Uses stick to obtain toy_____
Other (specify):

b. If the infant *does not* use the stick to obtain the toy, take the stick and demonstrate that one can move the toy closer and further away by means of the stick.

Loses interest in toy_____
Reaches and cries for toy_____
Attempts to climb onto table to obtain toy_____
Plays with stick only_____
Hits toy with stick, but gets it no closer_____
Uses stick to obtain toy_____
Other (specify):

20. *Foresight in Manipulation—Necklace and Container* (Sets IV and V)

Present the infant with a long necklace and a tall container. If the infant does not attempt to place the necklace into the container spontaneously, do so behind your back and show the infant the necklace within the container, as an enticement for him to do the same.

Shows no interest_____
Attempts to put in piece by piece and fails_____
Puts in piece by piece after some failures_____
Adopts a successful method such as holding the container with one
    hand after a failure_____
Foresees the falling of the container and adopts a successful method
    from the start_____
Other (specify):

21. *Foresight Indicated by Recognition of Solidity* (Sets IV and V)

Present the infant with a rod and some plastic rings for stacking,
one of which has been made solid. If the infant does not stack the
rings spontaneously, demonstrate by placing a few rings on the rod.
Move the solid ring close to the infant and observe his behavior.

Does not stack rings____
Tries to stack the solid ring by force____
Tries the solid ring once and avoids it thereafter____
Does not attempt to stack the solid ring____
Other (specify):

22. *Foresight in Manipulation—Nested Boxes* (Sets IV and V)

Present the infant with four of a set of nested boxes and encourage
him to put them together.

Shows no interest in putting them together____
Tries to put larger boxes into smaller ones by force____
Tries to put larger boxes into smaller ones, but readily realizes when
    they do not fit____
Gets the boxes together after groping____
Gets the boxes together without groping____
Other (specify):

23. *Learning a New Task—Opening a Matchbox* (Sets IV and V)

Interest the infant in a small trinket, place it in a matchbox and
present the closed box to the infant, urging him to open it. Observe
his attempts to open the box. If the infant does not succeed, demonstrate.

Shows no interest____
Uses force, but does not succeed____
Opens once accidentally and succeeds thereafter____
Opens after demonstration(s)____   How many?____
Opens immediately____
Other (specify):

24. *Learning a New Task—Putting a Bead on a String* (Sets IV and V)

Show the infant some beads on a string, and after arousing his interest, present him with the beads and string separately. Observe his

attempts to slip a bead onto the string. If the infant does not succeed, demonstrate.

Shows no interest____

Hands a bead and the string to E____

Puts a bead against the string____

Attempts to slip a bead onto the string, but fails____

Slips a bead onto the string after demonstration(s)____

How many?____

Slips a bead onto the string immediately____

Other (specify):

25. *Differentiation of Vocalizations* (Set I)

a. Observe whether the infant vocalizes in any manner other than crying. Ask the mother.

No____ Mother's Report: No____

Yes____ Yes____

b. Observe whether the infant vocalizes repetitive sounds (babbles). Ask the mother.

No____ Mother's Report: No____

Yes____ Yes____

26. *Recognition by Infant of Own Vocalizations* (Set I)

a. Talk to the infant in typical adult fashion and observe his reaction.

No observable reaction____

Stops ongoing activity____

Smiles____

Vocalizes____

Other (specify):

b. Talk to the infant by saying sounds which he has been observed to make frequently.

No observable reaction____

Shows interest____

Smiles____

Makes mouth movements____

Vocalizes____

Vocalizes sounds similar to ones made by E____

Other (specify):

27. *Vocalization—Mutual Imitation* (Set I)

If the infant is observed to vocalize spontaneously, repeat the sounds the infant has just made and stop abruptly.

No observable reaction____
Shows interest____
Smiles____
Resumes vocalizing____
Other (specify):

28. *Vocal Imitation of Familiar Sound Patterns* (Sets II and III)

Ask the mother what sound combinations are frequently vocalized by the infant and say one of them repetitively, when the infant is not vocalizing spontaneously.

a. Examiner as model:
Shows no interest____
Interest____
Vocalizes, but not same sounds____
Vocalizes similar sounds____
Other (specify):
b. Mother as model:
Shows no interest____
Interest____
Vocalizes, but not same sounds____
Vocalizes similar sounds____
Other (specify):
Sound combinations used:____ ____ ____

29. *Vocal Imitation of Unfamiliar Sounds* (Sets II, III, and IV)

Say some sound combinations definitely different from the ones frequently vocalized by the infant and observe his behavior.

a. Examiner as model:
Shows no interest____
Interest____
Vocalizes, but not same sounds____
Vocalizes sounds similar to E's by gradual approximation____
Vocalizes sounds similar to E's directly____
Other (specify):
b. Mother as model:

Shows no interest____
Interest____
Vocalizes, but not same sounds____
Vocalizes similar sounds by gradual approximation____
Vocalizes similar sounds directly____
Other (specify):
Sound combinations used:____   ____   ____

30. *Vocabulary* (Sets IV and V)

a. Ask the infant's mother for her estimate of the total number of words in the infant's vocabulary and for some examples. List up to 10.

1.____   6.____
2.____   7.____
3.____   8.____
4.____   9.____
5.____   10.____
     Total:____

b. Ask the mother whether the infant repeats most new words which he is told.

Does not____
Does____

31. *Immediate and Delayed Imitation of Words* (Sets IV and V)

During the course of the session, name the various objects presented to the infant and observe whether the infant repeats any of these names.

a. Words repeated immediately:

1.____
2.____
3.____

b. Words used at a later time in the session:

1.____
2.____
3.____

32. *Representation Indicated by Verbal Memory* (Set V)

Observe throughout the session whether the infant verbalizes anything about a past event or a person or object not immediately in sight, and list such instances.

1._____
2._____
3._____

33. *Imitation of Familiar Gestures* (Set II)

Note which motor schemes (hitting, sliding, shaking, etc.) the infant exhibits spontaneously and, while he is engaged in some other activity, demonstrate a few.

INFANT'S BEHAVIOR

Gesture Used	No Interest	Looks	Makes a Movement Other than E's	Makes Same Movement as E	Other (specify)
1._____	_____	_____	_____	_____	_____
2._____	_____	_____	_____	_____	_____
3._____	_____	_____	_____	_____	_____

34. *Maintaining an Interesting Spectacle—Hitting* (Sets II, III, IV, and V)

Hit two blocks together in front of the infant several times, and observe his behavior.

Shows no interest_____
Responds with a "procedure"_____
Takes a block from E's hand, but does nothing with it_____
Touches E's hand or a block_____
Gives blocks to E to perform again_____
Takes a block and hits one in E's hand with it_____
Picks up two blocks and hits them together_____
Other (specify):

35. *Imitation of Unfamiliar Gestures* (Sets II, III and IV)

Select several gestures that are likely to be unfamiliar to the infant (bending index finger, scratching a surface, etc.) and demonstrate.

INFANT'S BEHAVIOR

Gesture Used	No Interest	Looks	Makes a Movement Other than E's	Makes Same Movement by Gradual Approximations	Makes Same Movement Directly	Other (specify)
1._____	_____	_____	_____	_____	_____	_____
2._____	_____	_____	_____	_____	_____	_____
3._____	_____	_____	_____	_____	_____	_____

36. *Imitation of Unfamiliar Gestures—Facial Gestures* (Sets III, IV, and V)

Perform each of the following gestures and observe whether the infant will make an attempt to imitate the movement.

INFANT'S BEHAVIOR

Gesture Used	No Interest	Looks	Makes a Movement Other than E's	Makes Same Movement by Gradual Approximations	Makes Same Movement Directly	Other (specify)
1. Opening and closing mouth	___	___	___	___	___	___
2. Blinking eyes	___	___	___	___	___	___
3. Pulling on the earlobe	___	___	___	___	___	___
4. Patting cheek	___	___	___	___	___	___

37. *Maintaining an Interesting Spectacle—"Procedure"* (Sets I and II)

Perform some spectacle in which the infant would be interested, such as making the musical toy ring, making a face, etc. Stop abruptly and observe whether some gesture stands out in the infant's behavior.

Shows interest only during performance___
Reacts with a definite "procedure"___
Touches the toy or E___
Tries to obtain toy___
Other (specify):

38. *Maintaining an Interesting Activity—Familiar Game* (Set II)

Ask the infant's mother to play some favorite game with the infant (e.g., jouncing him on her knee) and have her interrupt the game abruptly. Observe the infant's actions.

Remains passive___
Responds with a "procedure"___

Starts part of the action____
Other (specify):

39. *Maintaining an Interesting Spectacle—Shaking* (Sets II, III, IV, and V)

Take a few blocks, drop them into the plastic container, and shake the container a few times while the infant watches. Set the container down and observe his behavior.

Shows no interest____
Responds with a "procedure"____
Touches E's hand____
Gives container back to E____
Tries to shake container____
Other (specify):

40. *Maintaining an Interesting Spectacle—Spinning Musical Toy* (Sets II, III, IV, and V)

After the infant has played with the musical toy, take and spin it while the infant watches.

Shows no interest after toy stops____
Responds with a "procedure"____
Gives toy back to E for repetition____
Touches toy or E's hand____
Tries to spin toy himself____
Other (specify):

41. *Maintaining an Interesting Spectacle—Mechanical Toy* (Sets IV and V)

Present the infant with a moving mechanical toy after winding it up out of the infant's sight. Observe the infant's attempts to reactivate the toy after it stops. Then, demonstrate the activation of the toy and again observe the infant's behavior.

Withdraws from toy____
Touches toy lightly and waits____
Gives toy to to E to activate____
Attempts to reproduce the action mechanically____
Explores for a way to activate the toy ____
Attempts to activate the toy in the appropriate manner after demonstration____
Other (specify):

42. *Alternate Glancing* (Set I)

a. Hold two target objects such as two checkerboards in front of the infant's eyes and about 8 inches apart. Observe whether the infant will look at both objects by focusing on each alternately for a short period of time.

Looks at one only___

Looks at both, but alternates slowly___

Looks at both in rapid alternation___

Other (specify):

b. If the infant has looked at only one of the objects, move the unnoticed object into the infant's line of vision for a moment and then back again.

Looks at one only___

Looks at both, but alternates slowly___

Looks at both in rapid alternation___

Other (specify):

c. If rapid alternate glancing was observed, see whether the infant will focus on three objects several times in rapid succession (e.g., rattle, E, side of crib, rattle again, etc.).

Looks at two only___

Looks at three in succession once___

Looks at three in succession several times___

Other (specify):

43. *Eye-Ear Coordination—Localization of Sound* (Sets I and II)

Stand outside the infant's line of vision and shake a rattle or some other noise-making object vigorously for a few seconds on the infant's right, then left, etc., to observe whether he turns in the direction of the sound.

Does not turn head in direction of sound___

Turns head in direction of sound to one side only___

Turns head in direction of sound to both sides___

In how many trials?___

Searches for source of sound with eyes___

Localizes source of sound___

Other (specify):

44. *Following a Rapidly Moving Object* (Sets I, II, and III)

a. Interest the infant in a small, light object such as a plastic flower or a piece of crumpled aluminum foil, have him focus on it, and drop it from above the infant's head to both right and left at random, retaining the hand in position after releasing the object.

Does not follow_____

Turns to correct side or follows a short way_____

Follows toy to about where it falls_____

   In how many trials?_____

Other (specify):

b. On a few trials, have the object drop to the floor so that it becomes invisible to the infant.

Searches with eyes around point of disappearance_____

Returns glance to E's hand_____

Leans forward to search for the object in the direction in which it fell_____

Other (specify):

45. *Construction of the Object—Reverse Side* (Sets II and III)

Present the infant with a toy having a clearly different reverse side and, while the infant is reaching for it, flip it around so that the other side of the toy faces the infant.

Grasps toy as if nothing happened_____

Withdraws hands_____

Looks surprised_____

Turns toy around immediately_____

Other (specify):

46. *Construction of the Object—Container and Contained* (Sets III, IV, and V)

Present the infant with some small objects, such as the blocks, and a container. If the infant does not spontaneously place objects into the container, demonstrate dropping of objects into the container and turning the container over to get the objects out.

Does not place objects into the container_____

Places objects in and takes them out one by one_____

Drops objects in and takes them out one by one_____

Drops objects in and turns the container over to get them out____
Other (specify):

47. *Construction of the Object—Building a Tower* (Sets III, IV, and V)

If the infant does not build a tower spontaneously while playing with blocks, demonstrate several times by building a four-block tower in front of the infant.

Scatters tower, does not build____
Approximates two blocks, but does not leave one on top of the
    other____
Builds a tower of at least two blocks____
Other (specify):

48. *Phenomenon of the Fall* (Sets IV and V)

While the infant is sitting off the floor, present him with several small objects and observe his behavior.

Plays with objects____
Drops some objects but does not watch their fall____
Drops objects and observes their fall____
Other (specify):

49. *Orientation in Space—Absence of a Familiar Person* (Set V)

Ask the infant where an absent member of the family is, or to be taken to him, and observe his behavior.

Does not comprehend question____
Goes to look for that person in his usual place in the home____
Indicates knowledge of absence____
Tells something about that person____
Other (specify):

50. *Repertoire of Schemes—Rattle* (Sets I and II)

Place the rattle in the infant's hand or present it to him, and observe his behavior.

Holds for 20–30 seconds____
Brings to mouth____
Brings before eyes____
Looks at hand holding rattle____
Hits toy with hand____

Hits surface with toy_____
Shakes_____
Examines_____
Slides_____
Drops purposefully_____
Throws_____
Shows_____
Other (specify):

51. *Repertoire of Schemes—Doll* (Sets I, II, III, IV, and V)

Place the doll in the infant's hand or present it to him, and observe his behavior.

Holds_____
Brings to mouth_____
Brings before eyes_____
Looks at toy in hand_____
Hits toy with hand_____
Hits surface with toy_____
Shakes_____
Examines_____
Drops purposefully_____
Throws_____
Slides_____
Shows_____
Hugs_____
Makes it "walk"_____
Names_____
Other (specify):

52. *Repertoire of Schemes—Aluminum Foil* (Sets I, II, III, IV, and V)

Place a piece of foil in the infant's hand or present it to him, and observe his behavior.

Holds_____
Brings to mouth_____
Brings before eyes_____
Looks at toy in hand_____
Hits toy with hand_____
Hits surface with toy_____

Waves____
Shakes____
Crumples____
Examines____
Drops purposefully____
Throws____
Tears____
Slides____
Shows____
Other (specify):

53. *Repertoire of Schemes—Musical Toy* (Sets II, III, IV, and V)

Present the infant with the musical toy and observe his behavior.
Holds____
Brings to mouth____
Looks at it____
Hits toy with hand____
Hits surface with toy____
Shakes____
Examines____
Drops____
Throws____
Shows____
Other (specify):

54. *Repertoire of Schemes—Necklace* (Sets II, III, IV, and V)

Present the infant with the necklace and observe his behavior.
Holds____
Brings to mouth____
Looks at it____
Hits toy with hand____
Hits surface with toy____
Shakes____
Examines____
Drops____
Throws____
Wears____
Shows____

Names____
Other (specify):

55. *Repertoire of Schemes—Toy Animal* (Sets II, III, IV, and V)

Present the infant with the toy animal and observe his behavior.
Holds____
Brings to mouth____
Looks at it____
Hits toy with hand____
Hits surface with toy____
Shakes____
Examines____
Drops____
Throws____
Slides____
Hugs____
Shows____
Names____
Other (specify):

56. *Repertoire of Schemes—Car* (Sets II, III, IV, and V)

Present the infant with a toy car and observe his behavior.
Holds____
Brings to mouth____
Looks at it____
Hits toy with hand____
Hits surface with toy____
Shakes____
Examines____
Drops____
Throws____
Spins wheels____
Makes it go on floor____
Shows____
Names____
Other (specify):

57. *Repertoire of Schemes—Blocks* (Sets II, III, IV, and V)
Present the infant with six blocks and observe his behavior.
Holds_____
Brings to mouth_____
Looks_____
Pushes around on surface_____
Hits with hand_____
Hits surface with toy_____
Shakes_____
Examines_____
Drops_____
Throws_____
Hits two blocks together spontaneously_____
Shows_____
Builds_____
Names_____
Other (specify):

58. *Repertoire of Schemes—Familiar Toy* (Sets II and III)
Ask the mother for one of the infant's own favorite toys and present it to him.
Holds_____
Brings to mouth_____
Looks at it_____
Hits toy with hand_____
Hits surface with toy_____
Shakes_____
Examines_____
Drops_____
Throws_____
Plays appropriately_____
Shows_____
Names_____
Other (specify):

59. *Repertoire of Schemes—Cup* (Sets III, IV, and V)
Present the infant with a plastic drinking cup and, after a while, introduce several small objects. Observe his behavior.

Holds____
Brings to mouth____
Looks at it____
Hits cup with hand____
Hits surface with cup____
Shakes____
Examines____
Drops____
Throws____
Puts other objects into cup____
Demonstrates drinking from cup____
Shows____
Names____
Other (specify):

60. *Repertoire of Schemes—Cotton* (Sets III, IV, and V)

Present the infant with a ball of cotton and observe his behavior.
Holds____
Brings to mouth____
Looks at it____
Rubs on surface____
Examines____
Drops____
Tears____
Shows____
Other (specify):

61. *Repertoire of Schemes—Doll's Shoe* (Sets III, IV, and V)

Present the infant with a doll's shoe and observe his behavior.
Holds____
Brings to mouth____
Looks at it____
Hits toy with hand____
Hits surface with toy____
Shakes____
Examines____
Drops
Throws____

Gets a doll to put it on____
Points to own shoes____
Shows____
Names____
Other (specify):

62. *Representation Indicated by Action* (Sets IV and V)

Observe throughout the session whether the infant behaves toward objects or toys in an "as if" manner, indicating through his actions knowledge of another use of the object (e.g., seeing the pillow, puts head down as if to sleep for a second, looks up and smiles).

    1.____
    2.____
    3.____

63. *Recognition of Objects Indicated by Naming* (Sets IV and V)

Observe during the course of the session whether the infant responds to any of the toys presented to him or to other objects in his surroundings by naming them spontaneously. List such instances.

    1.____   4.____
    2.____   5.____
    3.____   6.____

CHAPTER 7

Phase III: Inter-examiner Reliability and
Inter-session Stability of Infant Actions
in the Eliciting Situations

Phase III began with the examining of a third sample of infants with this second revision (third version) of the instrument. The original purposes of this phase were two: (1) to determine the inter-examiner reliability for infant actions in the various eliciting situations, and (2) to determine the inter-session stability (or test-retest reliability) of the infants' actions in the various eliciting situations. When a longitudinal study of the sort originally contemplated became unfeasible, however, the observations from this third phase were also employed (3) as the basis for dividing the instrument into six series or scales, and (4) to determine the scalability of the infants' actions in the eliciting situations included within each of these six scales. Thus, the behavior of the infants in this third sample also provides the evidence to be reported from our study for the ordinality of the scales to be described.

METHOD

Two examiners, working together, saw each of the infants in this third sample twice. One served as the examiner and presented the eliciting situations. The other acted as an observer. Thus, each served as the examiner and the observer, in rotation, with each infant. The examiner and the observer both recorded their observations during every session, but each recorded his or her own without knowledge of that of the other. This made possible two separate observations for inter-observer reliability. The successive examining sessions for each infant were separated, in nearly all cases, by 48 hours. The results from the two sessions permitted an evaluation of the stability of infant actions over this short interval according to the recorded observations of each of the two examiners.

EXAMINER TRAINING

Three pairs of examiners, including four separate individuals, participated in this third phase of the study. All of the examiners were between 20 and 30 years of age. Three were women (Ina Č. Užgiris, Tam Wei, and Melissa Galloway Kaplan) and one was a man (Donald K. Heil). Mr. Heil and Mrs. Kaplan entered the study during this phase. Each new examiner received training in presenting the eliciting situations and in recording the actions of the infants by an experienced examiner. This training consisted of having the beginner observe a number of demonstration examinations of infants varying across the age span, and then, of attempting to present the appropriate situations while being observed by an experienced examiner. Afterward, the presentation of the eliciting situations and the infant's actions were thoroughly discussed. Finally, the beginner examined a number of infants varying in age, while the experienced examiner served as observer, and both recorded the actions of each infant. This part of the training was continued until a high level of agreement between the two examiners was reached. Each new examiner began to participate in the data collection for this third phase of the study only following such training.

SUBJECTS

This third sample of infants numbered 84. They were examined during the fall of 1963 and throughout 1964. They included both sexes. Inasmuch as our investigative concerns minimized the importance of the representativeness of our sample of infants, we used again those most readily available. They came largely from graduate student and faculty families at the University of Illinois who responded to a written invitation to participate in the study. The sample was so selected that at least four infants represented each month of age up to one year, and at least four infants represented each two months of age between one year and two years. The number of infants of each sex observed at each age level appears in Table 7:1.

TABLE 7:1 *Distribution of Infants in the Third Sample According to Age and Sex*

Age in Months	No. of Boys	No. of Girls	Total
1	1	3	4
2	3	4	7
3	3	1	4
4	3	2	5
5	2	3	5
6	2	2	4
7	4	1	5
8	0	4	4
9	3	2	5
10	4	3	7
11	4	1	5
12	1	1	2
13	0	3	3
14	1	2	3
15	1	1	2
16	2	0	2
17	0	2	2
18	4	0	4
19	0	1	1
20	1	1	2
21	1	2	3
22	2	0	2
23	0	3	3
24	0	0	0

PROCEDURE: EXAMINING

These infants were examined in their own homes during an hour of the day when each was expected to be most alert and playful by his mother. The mother was usually present during the examination sessions, but arrangements were made to have siblings away from the room during the examinations.

Each pair of examiners saw about one-third of the infants in this sample. The first pair (I.Č.U. and T.W.) saw 20 infants. The second pair (I.Č.U. and D.H.) saw 31. The third pair (D.H. and M.G.K.) saw 33 infants. The infants observed by each pair of examiners were scattered throughout the whole age-range of the sample.

PROCEDURE: CODING

The records of the actions elicited from these infants constituted the data for a further evaluation of the instrument. As a first step to all subsequent analyses, we devised a way of coding the recorded behavior elicited by each situation in terms of a number of component actions. The records of each infant were then coded for the presence or absence of each of these component actions. This process undoubtedly added a further measure of selection and subjectivity, but it was necessary to permit handling the substantial number of new behaviors that were seen by the examiners in this larger sample of infants, which had not been included in the lists provided for each eliciting situation described above in Chapter 6 and which were recorded by the examiners in their own words under "other actions." Since a given behavioral component, such as evidence of groping prior to the critical action, was treated as a new component action in the eliciting situation in which it appeared, a total of 261 separate component actions were scored for each infant. We also worked out a numerical code to differentiate (1) the actions in situations actually presented to an infant, (2) the assumed actions in those eliciting situations which were appropriate only to a much lower or to a much higher developmental level, and (3) those few instances in which no behavior in the situation was recorded due either to omission or to error on the part of the examiner. We then prepared an explicit coding-guide, and two experienced examiners (M.G.K. and I.Č.U.) used it to code the records of each of these 84 infants. Before starting to code the 336 records (4 for each infant), they independently coded 20 sample records. When they registered agreement on most of the items coded, we felt justified in sharing the coding; spot-checks on agreement throughout the coding yielded agreements ranging from 98 percent to 99 percent for independently coded records. We then punched these coded protocols into IBM cards and used an IBM 7094 computer to calculate the inter-observer agreement and the inter-session stability for the various actions in the eliciting situations.

INTER-OBSERVER AGREEMENT

Overall, the inter-observer agreement was high. Those instances where both observers noted the presence of a given behavior and those instances where both observers indicated the absence of a given action were counted as agreements. Those instances where one observer noted the presence of a particular action and the other failed to note its presence were counted as disagreements. Such counts were made only for the various component actions in those eliciting situations which had actually been presented to any given infant. Thus, the calculated percentage of inter-observer agreement for the various actions is based on a varying number of infants, and this is always fewer than the 84 comprising the total sample.

The percentage agreement for the two observers of infant actions in each eliciting situation was calculated separately for the first and for the second examination session. Since the inter-observer agreement for the first session matched very closely that for the second session, and since neither session yielded consistently higher agreement than the other, the two percentages of agreement for each infant action were averaged. Appendix A presents the mean percentage of agreement for each action elicited by the various situations presented both for infants in each of the five age-groups separately and for the total sample of infants to whom the given eliciting situation was presented Since few investigators have reported inter-observer reliabilities for infant behaviors in response to individual test items (Werner and Bayley, 1966), we have considered it worthwhile to report this information for the actions observed in this study even though Appendix A is of considerable length. Appendix A contains, however, no percentages of agreement for the actions elicited by situations 4, 6, 23, 24, 31, 38, and 58 of the list given in Chapter 6 because these situations were presented too seldom to permit confidence in the percentages of agreement computed.

Inasmuch as Appendix A is so very long, we have summarized here the evidence in a distribution of the averaged percentages of agreement for the 157 infant actions in those eliciting situations for which adequate evidence is available, based on the total sample of infants presented with those situations. Although, in three instances, the averaged percentages of inter-observer agreement fall at 80 or below, the cumulative arrangement of these averaged percentages of agreement in Table 7:2 shows that they were above 90 for 87 percent of the 157 infant actions. The mean of these average percentages of inter-observer agreement for all 157 actions was 96.1. Thus, the evidence indicates that the actions of even very young infants in these situations can be noted and recorded by different observers with a high degree of agreement when these observers are well trained.

TABLE 7:2 *Distribution of the Averaged Percentages of Inter-observer Agreement for the 157 Infant Actions in Eliciting Situations for Which Adequate Evidence Is Available for the Total Sample of Infants*

Averaged Percentages of Agreement	Number of Infant Actions	Percentage of Infant Actions	Cumulative Percentage of Infant Actions
100	26	16.56	16.56
99.9–98	26	16.56	33.12
97.9–96	42	26.82	59.94
95.9–94	17	10.83	70.77
93.9–92	19	12.10	82.87
91.9–90	7	4.46	87.33
89.9–88	5	3.18	90.51
87.9–86	8	5.12	95.63
85.9–84	4	2.52	98.15
83.9–82	–		
81.9–80	1	.63	98.78
79.9–78	–		
77.9–76	–		
75.9–74	1	.63	99.41
73.9–72	1	.63	100.04
Total	157		

The instances of low inter-observer agreement for certain infant actions appear to have been due to inadequate guidance in the directions provided. When actions other than those specifically listed were elicited, one observer was likely to note and describe the action under "other actions," while the other attempted to subsume the action under one of those already specified but with the addition of some qualification. Some of these notes and added qualifications by observers served as the basis for subdividing some of the originally specified actions into two separate ones. In our study of inter-observer reliability, agreement was scored only if both observers had added precisely the same qualification. The result from the analysis of the actions from this larger sample of infants has been a more complete listing of typical infant actions for the various eliciting situations. This new, more complete listing can be expected to lead to even higher inter-observer reliabilities.

While Table 7:2 gives only the distribution of percentages of inter-observer agreement for the 157 infant actions based on the total sample studied, the inter-observer agreement for any given action is probably best indicated by the range of agreements obtained for infants in the various age-groupings. It should be remarked that an examination of Appendix A shows that the percentages of inter-observer agreement, while still high, tend to be lowest for that age-grouping in which many infants manifest and many fail to manifest a particular criterion action. For those age groupings in which practically none of the infants show the criterion behavior for a given eliciting situation, or in which practically all infants do show it, inter-observer agreement tends to be very high. This may result in part from observer expectations. It may result also from the fact that well-established actions are usually more easily identified than ones on the brink of development. The fact that both observers were in the same room in the infant's home while the eliciting situations were being presented must also be considered. In order not to make the whole interaction completely unnatural, the examiner did make verbal comments to the infant and to the infant's mother about the situations being presented. These comments were by no means an evaluation of the infant's performance, but they undoubtedly contained clues to the examiner's perception of some of the actions shown by the infant, and these verbalized clues may have influenced the observer. Since such comments were unsystematic, however, while inter-observer agreements were consistently high, one must conclude that these infant actions are easily recognized and therefore lend themselves to agreement between observers.

Overall, the variation in percentages of inter-observer agreement with variations in the age of the infants examined was rather small. For all the actions elicited by the situations from the infants in each of the five age groupings, the mean percentages of inter-observer agreement ranged from a low of 93.1 for infants in the 4 to 7 month group to a high of 96.9 for infants in the 18 to 24 month group. The age of the infants examined thus appears to be a rather insignificant factor in determining inter-observer agreement compared to such factors as the nature of the eliciting situation, the disposition of the infant, and the training of the observers.

We have also made an attempt to evaluate observer differences. We have computed the percentages of agreement for the various infant actions for each pair of observers separately. The differences between the various pairs in percentage of agreement were negligible and inconsistent. Each of the pairs of observers did debate, from time to time, whether being an active examiner or a passive observer provided the better opportunity to note the behavior shown by infants. The position of examiner provided the advantage of being close to the infant and, thus, of being better able to detect nuances of expression, minimal actions, and verbalizations. On the other hand, the needs to keep the session going and to record hurriedly in order not to lose rapport with the infant were seen as disadvantages of being the examiner. The position of being the observer was seen as providing opportunity for more leisurely recording, but this position had the disadvantage of not being able to repeat a presentation or to vary an eliciting situation when the meaning of a particular infant action was perceived as unclear. It was concluded, therefore, that the best way to assess inter-observer reliability was to have two observers present at each session in addition to an examiner and to compare the records of the two observers, but that the way to make inferences about an infant's level of functioning with most confidence was to serve as examiner and to arrange the eliciting situations.

INTER-SESSION STABILITY

The stability of infant actions in the eliciting situations over a 48-hour period was evaluated in terms of percentages of inter-session agreement or consistency. We have defined inter-session consistency or test-retest reliability as occurring whenever an observer recorded a particular action as either present or as absent in both examinations. Inter-session disagreements occurred whenever a particular infant action was recorded as present in one examination and as absent in the other. We originally calculated the percentages of consistency for each infant action separately for the two observers. Inasmuch as the percentages of consistency for particular actions were found to be highly similar for both observers, however, the two percentages of consistency for each action were averaged.

This procedure of evaluating the stability of infant actions in our eliciting situations was confounded by whatever unreliability of observation existed and also by change in the person of the examiner from the first examination to the second. Nevertheless, considerable consistency in the infant actions appears, and this is especially high for well-established actions. The averaged percentages of inter-session consistency for the actions elicited by the various situations are given in Appendix B. There, the average percentages of consistency are given both for the individual age-groupings and for the total sample of infants presented with each eliciting situation.

We have summarized in Table 7:3 most of the evidence to be found in Appendix B. Table 7:3 gives the distribution of averaged percentages of inter-session consistency for the 157 infant actions, based on the total sample of infants studied. Although averaged percentages of inter-session consistency occasionally fell to 50 or below, Table 7:3 shows that these percentages were above 70 for about 80 percent of the 157 infant actions. For all actions, the mean of the averaged percentages of inter-session consistency was 79.9. The variation in percentages of inter-session consistency with variations in the age of the infants examined was very slight, ranging from a low of 79.0 for the 4 to 7 month group to a high of 81.9 for the group aged between 18 and 24 months.

A somewhat more precise evaluation of the consistency of the particular infant actions may be obtained by examining in Appendix B the range of consistencies across the several age-groupings of infants. Infants appear to be more consistent in manifesting those actions which characterize their highest, well-mastered level of functioning in

TABLE 7:3 *Distribution of Averaged Percentages of Inter-session Consistency for the 157 Infant Actions in Those Eliciting Situations for Which Adequate Evidence Is Available for the Total Sample of Infants*

Averaged Percentages	Number of Infant Actions	Percentage of Infant Actions	Cumulative Percentage of Infant Actions
100–96	8	5.05	5.05
95.9–92	15	9.52	14.57
91.9–90	13	8.27	22.84
89.9–86	21	13.37	36.17
85.9–82	11	7.00	43.17
81.9–80	10	6.37	49.54
79.9–76	24	15.28	64.82
75.9–72	18	11.46	76.28
71.9–70	6	3.82	80.10
69.9–66	12	7.64	87.74
65.9–62	5	3.18	90.92
61.9–60	1	.64	91.56
59.9–56	3	1.91	93.47
55.9–50	4	2.54	96.01
49.9–46	3	1.81	97.82
45.9–42	3	1.81	99.63
Total	157		

relation to any given eliciting situation. The type of eliciting situation also appears to be a factor. Those situations which rely most heavily on inducing a particular motivation in the infant, as is the case with both imitation and the "problem solving" situations, appear to produce the greatest inconsistency.

The evidence here of substantial consistency and stability in the actions elicited by given situations over a period of 48 hours serves again to call into question the widespread belief that infant tests are unreliable. Even though scores (especially DQs or IQs) based on tests given before 2 years predict later performances very poorly, the tests show high contemporary reliability. Our findings on inter-session consistency tend to confirm the earlier results reported by Bayley (1940) which indicated that infant tests are highly reliable for repeated performances at any given age. Bayley got a reliability coefficient of +.94 by correlating scores derived from the odd and even items in a combination of tests given to her sample of infants at the ages of 7, 8, and 9 months. Moreover, the combined scores on these three testings correlated $+.81$ with scores obtained from such testings as much as three months later. More recently, Werner and Bayley (1966) have reported the stability of reactions of 28 eight-month-old infants to items from Bayley's Revised Scale of Mental and Motor Development over the period of one week. They report high stability of reactions to items dealing with object permanence and with vocabulary and low stability of reactions to items requiring close interaction with the examiner.

Our findings, based on a sample of infants covering a broader age range, correspond quite closely to those of Werner and Bayley (1966). As shown in Appendix B, of the 36 infant actions for which the percentage of inter-session consistency for the total sample of infants was 90 or above, 13 are actions shown in situations designed to elicit behavior indicative of the infant's grasp of object permanence, 11 are actions indicative of the construction of object relations in space, 6 are actions shown in situations designed to elicit evidence of means–ends differentiation, and 4 pertain to verbal behavior, including spontaneous naming of objects and vocabulary size. On the other hand, of the 31 infant actions for which the percentage of inter-session consistency was 70 or below, 9 are actions shown in situations designed to elicit imitation of the examiner, another 9 are actions shown in situations designed to elicit behavior indicative of the infant's grasp of causal relations by having the infant attempt to reproduce some event, and 5 are actions in problem-solving situations designed to elicit anticipation and planning of outcomes. To generalize, infant actions with high inter-session consistency seem to be shown in relation to objects in those situations where the infant's intentions have a high probability of corresponding with the examiner's intentions, because either the situation offers few likely alternatives (e.g., a sound presented out of the infant's sight), or the presentation of the eliciting situation hinges on such correspondence (e.g., the hiding of an object which the infant desires to possess), or because there are numerous opportunities for the action to be manifested (e.g., naming an object). Infant actions with relatively low inter-session consistency seem to occur in situations where a correspondence between the examiner's and the infant's intentions is less likely, at least in both sessions (e.g., imitation, reproduction of a spectacle), and where such correspondence depends much more heavily on the infant's motivational inclinations of the moment and his relationship with the examiner (e.g., contrast imitation of a sound made by the examiner and search for a hidden desired object).

An infant's failure to act in an eliciting situation in any of the ways which the examiner finds relevant and critical is especially important for the question of the stability of behaviors. Infants do act while being presented with each of the eliciting situations in some manner. Such actions as leaving the room, turning to mother, starting to play with something else, crying, and vocalizing to the examiner, however, fail to match the expectations of the examiner based on what the examiner considers to be relevant to the examination and are, therefore, recorded as "no response" or "no interest." While such behaviors may indicate that the infant finds the examination too much and is unable to cope with the situation presented, this should not be an automatic conclusion; the same behaviors sometimes reflect excellent foresight and a clever use of persons as means to attain goals important to the infant. If the reaction of "no interest" is due to transitory moods or the like, short-term instability of infant actions is to be expected. A great many of the eliciting situations used in this study may be said to be particularly dependent upon inducing the infant to approach each situation in the manner desired by the examiner. In situation number 19 of those listed at the end of Chapter 6, for example, the infant is supposed to see that the stick is for obtaining an object out of reach rather than an implement for hitting the examiner. Items appearing in the usual infant tests, however, are not independent of this problem. Thus, we wish to stress our conviction that an examiner must constantly attempt to make inferences about an infant's capabilities from his behavior rather than remain content to record the presence or absence of particular infant actions.

Aside from reliance on the experience and ingenuity of examiners, a partial solution to this problem may lie in devising several situations for eliciting the same critical actions or even in presenting the eliciting situations on consecutive days in order to minimize the chance of misinterpreting the reaction of "no interest" which may be due more to a lack of coordination between the intentions of the infant and the intentions of the examiner than due to a lack of capability on the part of the infant. It may also prove worthwhile to record the examiner's judgment of the infant's apparent goal in each situation in addition to the infant's actions to help weight the actions when making inferences about the infant's level of development.

CHAPTER 8

Revision of the Instrument:
The Six Series with Evidence
of Their Reliability and Stability

From the presentation of our eliciting situations to the third and largest sample of infants has come evidence that observations of infant actions in these situations as well as judgments of their cognitive implications can be made with a high level of inter-observer agreement and that a substantial degree of consistency or stability exists in the way in which infants act in these situations, at least over a period of 48 hours. Moreover, the experience of Phase III brought new information about the various eliciting situations. This new information provided the basis for yet another revision of the instrument. First of all, for many of the eliciting situations with low inter-observer agreement, the lack of agreement could obviously be attributed to failure to anticipate some of the actions shown by infants in these situations and to alert the observers to them. This finding suggested the enumeration of additional infant reactions both in the directions given and on the recording-sheets. Second, the experience of Phase III made it clear that some of the eliciting situations evoked behavior on which it was extremely difficult for observers to agree. This lack of agreement suggested omitting those few eliciting situations which evoked actions that observers interpret with special difficulty. Third, certain of the eliciting situations were so highly dependent upon moment-to-moment motivation and quality of the infant's relationship with the examiner that stability over even 48 hours was low, especially when there was a change of examiner. Prudence suggested omitting such situations, except in those cases where the reactions elicited by these situations were especially pregnant with implications of developing abilities, motive systems, and constructions of reality. Fourth, the experience of having two examiners who differed present the eliciting situations to this third and relatively large sample of infants and get different reactions demonstrated that some of the situations were hard to structure in a fashion that dependably elicited relevant actions from the infant. Again, unless the actions elicited by these situations have especially important diagnostic significance, the suggestion is that they be eliminated. Fifth, in a few instances, the actions elicited by certain situations appeared to lack clear relevance for any developing ability. Again, the resulting suggestion is to eliminate such situations from the instrument.

REVISION OF THE INSTRUMENT

On the basis of these five criteria, we again revised the instrument. The revised instrument retains, nevertheless, the preponderant majority of the eliciting situations used with the third sample of infants. The directions and the recording-sheets have been modified to specify all of the relevant infant actions that we have now identified. The instructions for arranging certain of the situations have been altered with the intent of improving the dependability with which relevant actions are elicited from the infants and to facilitate the task of structuring the situation for the examiner. The result is a new set of directions and a new set of recording-sheets. These are described in Part III of this monograph.

It should be clear that these new directions and procedures for recording have not yet been tried out on a new sample of infants.[1] It should be noted also that our third sample of 84 infants came almost entirely from middle-class families, so that the lists of actions in our

[1] The newest version of the scales has been made available to several investigators prior to publication, and information regarding the usefulness of the scales with different populations of infants will be forthcoming.

eliciting situations given in the directions and on the recording-sheets may still omit some actions that will occur in samples of infants from other backgrounds. This report, we must repeat, is one of progress toward ordinal scales of psychological development in infancy.

DIVISION INTO SIX SERIES

In Phase III, we had discarded our earlier classification of eliciting situations with respect to various branches of development. The experience of Phase III, however, made it intuitively clear that these eliciting situations should be grouped according to the specific branches of development to which the actions evoked by them are relevant. Thus, in this third revision of the instrument, eliciting situations have been grouped into six series or scales. We first called these series, and then, as evidence of a sequential order of the actions of infants in these situations was obtained, we have come to call them scales, *ordinal scales*.

The first of these six scales concerns development in the concept of object, including progress in visual pursuit and the permanence of objects. The second concerns development in means for obtaining desired environmental events. The third series, concerned with imitation, is actually two: development in vocal imitation and development in gestural imitation. The fourth series concerns development in operational causality. The fifth concerns development in the construction of object relations in space. The sixth concerns development in schemes for relating to objects.

For each of the six series of eliciting situations, we selected certain infant actions as indicative of significant steps in the course of that branch of psychological development. We attempted to find a set of actions which could be taken as critical indicators of the attainment of each sequential step, to be elicited in at least one, and sometimes in several situations. Usually, only one action elicited by each situation was considered to be a critical indicator of a step in that branch of development, but this was not invariably so. Constructing the sequences of steps for each branch of psychological development was a process involving several criteria. The primary considerations were the relevance of the attainment to a branch of development having, at least intuitively, psychological unity, and the maintenance of a sequential progression based upon the logical implications of the infant's actions in the eliciting situations arranged for him. While Piaget's ideas regarding the sequence of development in the sensorimotor period were part of our general orientation, an additional guide in constructing the sequences was the relative difficulty of each step in the series for the 84 infants in the third sample. Here relative difficulty was conceived as the inverse of the proportion of infants who performed each particular action at each month of age.

In what follows, we shall describe each of the six series, and then present in tabular form the sequences of steps comprising the six series. In the tables, we shall give (1) the generalized description of each step which represents our conceptualization of the step warranting its particular placement in that series, (2) the situation which was actually used to elicit the set of actions considered to be a critical indicator for the attainment of that step, and (3) the critical actions implying the attainment of that step in development within the branch. We recognize fully that the particular situation we use to elicit the actions considered critical for inferring the attainment of each step need not be the only one which could be used. It is possible and even likely that for infants with differing backgrounds of experience, these particular situations may fail to elicit actions critical for inferring the achievement of the step of development in question, and that quite different eliciting situations, especially with other materials, may have to be devised. If the basic outlines of the six sequences of steps turn out to be a reasonable description of progress in each of these branches of development, a number of alternative eliciting situations may eventually be constructed from which one appropriate to any given infant could be selected as necessary.

To save space in the tables which follow, the situations are numbered rather than described in detail. The number following each situation identifies its description in the list given at the end of Chapter 6. We include within the table for each series also the mean percentage of inter-observer agreement and the mean percentage of inter-session stability for each of the infant actions, as well as the age by which the majority of those infants tested showed each critical action. These ages by which the various steps in the sequences were attained by a majority of infants in our sample are given simply in order to indicate that an orderly progression of achievement along the several series was observed with increases in chronological age. These ages, however, *should not be interpreted as typical for infants in general* or even for infants of similar backgrounds as the ones in our sample. We have observed too few infants at any given month of age to establish even rough age-norms. Moreover, the infants who have served as subjects for our work constitute a highly unrepresentative sample of the population as a whole. In certain instances, where there was no month of age at which the majority of infants manifested the behaviors critical for inferring the achievement of a given step in a sequence, the span of ages from the month when one or some few of the infants showed the actions in question to the month when all of the infants did is presented.

1. VISUAL PURSUIT AND THE PERMANENCE OF OBJECTS

This series focuses on what Piaget (1937, ch. 1), has termed the construction of the object. It concerns the development of the concept of objects of independent existence. This development begins with the ready-made scheme of looking. The orienting response and looking behavior may be elicited in a situation which presents the infant with a change in his ongoing visual input. First accommodative changes in the looking scheme are manifest in the visual pursuit of slowly moving objects. Development proceeds through progressive accommodative changes in the looking scheme to permit following objects moving faster and faster, through wider and wider arcs. In this development of visual pursuit, a certain degree of ordinality is logically built in, for pursuit through a full arc of 180°, which requires a coordination between looking and head-turning, clearly implies the ability to follow through lesser arcs. Even when an infant becomes able to follow an object through 180°, however, there is a period when his gaze immediately leaves the place where the object has disappeared. When, later, the infant begins to hold his gaze at the point of disappearance, this holding of gaze implies that the representative central processes which have presumably developed out of his repeated visual encounters with the objects and his visible surroundings begin to endure. The fact of visual following and of holding the gaze at the point where an object has disappeared implies some desire for continuing contact with the object. At a later point in psychological development, this desirability becomes even more obviously indicated by the coordination between visual following and reaching for the object (Hunt, 1963b). Then comes a point when the infant responds as if to the whole object from seeing but a small portion of it, and this is manifest in his efforts to reach for and to grasp with his hands desired objects which have been partially hidden. Infants will reach for a desired object, partially covered, however, when that same object totally covered elicits no effort whatever on their part. Later, however, they search for and remove the covers from desired objects which have been covered completely, and thereby completely removed from view. This implies the beginning of object permanence and of the persistence of central processes allowing a limited construction of perceptually absent events. A little later, the fact that infants will persist in their search for desired objects long enough to remove several covers implies an increased endurance of these central processes. In each of these eliciting situations, termed *visible displacement,* the examiner places a cover directly over an object for which the infant has demonstrated a desire, while it is in full view of the infant. Still later, infants manifest a higher level of object permanence by following desired objects through *invisible displacements.* Here the eliciting situation is elaborated further: the examiner places the desired object into a container of some sort (a box, a cup, or the hand) and then places the container under a cover, releases the object, and withdraws the container empty. Following an object through such an invisible displacement implies a new level in the central processes representing the object which must permit the infant to consider the object separately from the container and to infer the location of the object from observing the displacements of the container. Even later, infants follow an object through a series of such invisible displacements. The eliciting situation consists of having the examiner place the desired object in the container and then hide the container under several covers in a sequence. At one level, infants search for the desired object under the several covers in the order in which the container was placed under them. Eventually, infants are able to reverse the order of search and start their search under that cover where the container disappeared last, then next to last, etc. This reversal in the order of search implies central processes which can run off in the opposite as well as in the same direction as the sequence represented. The sequence of steps for this series is given in Table 8:1.

TABLE 8:1   *Sequence of Steps in the Development of Visual Pursuit and the Permanence of Objects*

(*Mean percentages of inter-observer agreement, mean percentages of inter-session stability, and the month of age by which the majority of infants of that age showed the actions indicative of each step in the sequence.*)

Sequence of Steps	Inter-observer Agreement	Inter-session Stability	Month of Age[a]
1. Momentary perceptual construction of an object is implied by a sustained attempt to follow an object visually. Situation 1[b]: Follows a slowly moving object through a complete arc of 180° with smooth accommodations.	100.0%	93.3%	1
2. A momentary organization of central processes to include a perceptually absent object is implied by maintenance of orientation in the direction in which an object was last seen. Situation 2: Lingers with glance on the point where a slowly moving object disappeared.	91.0%	86.3%	2
3. Some guidance of behavior by central processes which incorporate perceptually absent objects is implied by reconstruction of a whole object on the basis of a small visible portion of the object. Situation 3: Searches for a partially hidden object.	98.6%	93.8%	4–5
4. Guidance of behavior by central processes which differentiate somewhat the organization of actions from constructions of perceptually absent objects is implied by turning of the glance in the direction from which a presently absent object has appeared before. Situation 2: Returns eyes to starting point when a slowly moving object disappears.	87.7%	73.6%	5–8
5. Guidance of behavior by central processes which differentiate the constructions of perceptually absent objects from actions previously directed at them is implied by search for a perceptually absent object. Situation 5: Finds an object hidden under a single screen.	98.5%	92.7%	7
6. Guidance of behavior by more differentiated constructions of objects is implied by correct search for a perceptually absent object in the face of potentially confusing cues.			

[a] These data on age are given only because they are repeatedly requested. They are intended to have no normative value.

[b] The numbers refer to the situation numbers in Chapter 6 where these situations are described.

TABLE 8:1 (*continued*)

Sequence of Steps	Inter-observer Agreement	Inter-session Stability	Month of Age
Situation 5: Finds an object hidden under one of two screens by searching directly under the correct screen.	99.2%	87.6%	7
7. Guidance of behavior by constructions of objects differentiated from their previous spatial locations is implied by correct search for a perceptually absent object in the face of a greater number of potentially confusing cues.			
Situation 5: Finds an object hidden under one of three screens by searching directly under the correct screen.	99.2%	92.0%	7
8. Greater persistence of central processes pertaining to constructions of objects is implied by maintenance of search for a perceptually absent object when a single action does not reveal the object.			
Situation 7: Finds an object hidden under a number of superimposed screens.	97.9%	84.0%	9–10
9. Further persistence and differentiation of central processes pertaining to constructions of objects is implied by ability to deduce the location of an object from observing the spatial displacement of a container with the object.			
Situation 8: Searches in box top and then under the screen for an object hidden by an invisible displacement under a single screen.	96.5%	78.5%	11–13
10. Increasing persistence of the constructions of objects is implied by ability to deduce the location of an object from observing the spatial displacement of a container with the object in the face of potentially confusing cues.			
Situation 8: Searches in box top and then directly under the correct screen for an object hidden by an invisible displacement under one of two screens.	100.0%	78.7%	13
11. Persistence of the constructions of objects and guidance of behavior by these differentiated constructions is implied by ability to deduce the location of an object from observing the spatial displacement of a container with the object to different positions in space.			
Situation 8: Searches in box top and then directly under the correct screen for an object hidden by an invisible displacement under one of two screens alternately.	100.0%	81.0%	14

TABLE 8:1 (*continued*)

Sequence of Steps	Inter-observer Agree-ment	Inter-session Stabil-ity	Month of Age
12. Guidance of behavior by enduring constructions of objects differentiated from their spatial locations is implied by ability to deduce the location of an object from observing the spatial displacement of a container with the object to a greater number of different positions in space. Situation 8: Searches in box top and then directly under the correct screen for an object hidden by an invisible displacement under one of three screens.	95.4%	80.2%	14
13. Even greater persistence of the differentiated constructions of objects is implied by continued guidance of behavior by these constructions in the face of a number of *successive* displacements of an object within a container, when only the container is seen to be displaced, and the concomitant displacements of the object have to be inferred. Situation 9: Finds an object hidden by a series of successive invisible displacements by searching along the path that the container with the object was observed to take.	95.4%	74.9%	17
14. Persistence of the constructions of objects and their mobility is implied by ability to infer the spatial displacements of the object hidden in a container in reverse of the order in which the displacements were observed. Situation 9: Finds an object hidden by a series of successive invisible displacements by searching under the last screen first and then retracing the path of the container.	94.5%	76.2%	21-22
Mean for all critical actions:	96.7%	83.8%	

The ground for this sequence of steps in the development of visual pursuit and the permanence of objects appears to us to be especially firm. Where an infant follows an object through an arc of 180°, for instance, he must obviously be able to follow it through lesser arcs. Moreover, when an infant follows an object through an arc of 180° and holds his glance at the point where the slowly moving object has disappeared, the central processes which include some construction of the object must have acquired greater stability and permanence than is the case when the infant's glance departs immediately from the point where the object disappeared. And to continue searching for and removing the cover from an object which has been completely covered implies central processes which are more independent of present inputs than those implied by searching merely for an object that is partially covered. And finally, reversal in search implies central processes which are more mobile than search through a series of invisible displacements in the order in which those displacements took place.

On the other hand, it is also clear that the distances between certain of the successive steps in this series are much smaller than those between others. Probably, the smallest distances are between steps 6 and 7, 10 and 11, and 11 and 12. While their placement represents a logical ordering, only longitudinal studies can determine whether these steps constitute an invariant ordinal sequence, or are achieved without a specific order.

Nevertheless, development along this sequence may be said to imply increasing persistence of representative central processes, increasing differentiation of central processes allowing for separation of the constructions of objects from, first, the action and, then the spatial contexts in which they are embedded, and increasing mobility of central processes leading up to representational thought.

II. Development of Means for Obtaining Desired Environmental Events

The eliciting situations in this series are directed mainly at what infants do to cause events or obtain objects which they have come to desire. In such situations, they combine the use of one behavior pattern as means with another as end or goal. One of the most rudimentary of such coordinations is hand-watching activity wherein the infant appears to move his hands about in order to make an interesting spectacle for his eyes. Hand-watching, as Dennis (1941) has noted, is autogenic in character inasmuch as infants can and do obtain this self-stimulation at will. Hunt (1965, 1971b) has contended that hand-watching is probably motivated by the interest of infants in what has become or is becoming recognitively familiar. A further differentiation of the means-end relationship appears in the attempts of infants to maintain or regain perceptual contact with interesting environmental events by use of well-developed action schemes. This level of differentiation is followed by the use of well-developed action schemes in somewhat novel circumstances where some accommodative modification of these schemes is required to achieve the perceptual or motor end. Such accommodative modifications are usually evidenced by overt groping, and this accommodative groping contributes to the development of new sensorimotor organizations. Finally, foresightful behavior appears. In foresight the accommodative groping is implicit, and the appropriate means are chosen directly even in novel circumstances. Piaget (1936) has contended that such implicit groping appears along with that level of object construction in which toddlers follow objects through hidden displacements, but only longitudinal investigations will verify such an hypothesis.

Table 8:2 presents the sequence of steps in this series concerned with the development of means for obtaining desired environmental events. This table also shows the mean percentages of inter-observer agreement, the mean percentages of inter-session stability, and the ages by which the majority of our infants manifested the actions critical for each step in the sequence.

We are less confident about the invariance of the sequence of 13 steps in this series concerned with the development of means for achieving desired environmental events than we are about the invariance of the sequence of 14 steps in the series concerned with the development of visual pursuit and the permanence of objects. Each successive step here does appear, however, to call for more in the way of autonomy and central control on the part of the infant than the foregoing step. Thus, grasping a toy with only the toy in view calls for more representational organization on the part of the infant than grasping a toy when both hand and toy are in view. Again, using a string tied to an object to obtain it while the object is not in the direct line of sight calls for more constructive activity on the part of the infant, including some attribution of permanence to objects, than using a string to obtain an object which is directly within view. Increasing differentiation of actions-as-means from actions-as-ends, increasing determination of means by the envisioned end leading to subordination of means to ends, and increasing anticipation regarding the appropriateness of particular means seem to characterize progress along this sequence. Our lack of confidence in the invariant nature of this

TABLE 8:2   *Sequence of Steps in the Development of Means for Obtaining Desired Environmental Events*

(*Mean percentages of inter-observer agreement, mean percentages of inter-session stability, and the month of age by which the majority of infants of that age showed the actions indicative of each step in the sequence.*)

Sequence of Steps	Inter-observer Agreement	Inter-session Stability	Month of Age
1. Coordination between two schemes permits a rudimentary differentiation of means and ends as evidenced by commencement of eye-hand coordination leading to visual exploration of the hand.			
Situation 10: Hand-watching behavior is observed.	86.7%	73.3%	2
2. Some differentiation of means and ends is implied by immediate repetition of schemes which accidentally produce an interesting result.			
Situation 13: Attempts to keep a toy in motion by repeated hand or leg movements.	93.0%	77.0%	3
3. Greater differentiation of means and ends is implied by the singling out of a scheme as means for multiple ends, evidenced by progress in achieving visually directed grasping.			
Situation 14: Grasps toy when both hand and the toy are in view.	100.0%	100.0%	3-4
4. Further progress in the use of a scheme as means for multiple ends is evidenced by attainment of visually directed grasping.			
Situation 14: Grasps toy with just the toy in view.	97.0%	94.1%	4
5. Some anticipatory differentiation of means and ends is implied by execution of one scheme preparatory to the execution of another.			
Situation 15: Quickly drops one or both objects already held in the hands before reaching for a third.	96.4%	46.8%	8
6. Some anticipatory adaptation of means (particular actions) to ends is implied by exploitation of perceived relationships between objects for desired ends.			
Situation 16: Pulls a support to obtain a toy with or without demonstration.	100.0%	89.0%	8
7. Further anticipatory differentiation of means and ends is implied by use of common behavior patterns as means for multiple ends.			
Situation 17: Uses some form of locomotion to retrieve a toy needed in play.	93.7%	71.0%	9
8. Further anticipatory adaptation of means (particular			

TABLE 8:2 (*continued*)

Sequence of Steps	Inter-observer Agreement	Inter-session Stability	Month of Age
actions) to ends is implied by more discriminate exploitation of relationships between objects.			
Situation 16: Resists pulling the support when the object does not rest directly on it.	96.0%	58.5%	10
9. Some anticipatory construction of alternate means for a given end is implied by exploitation of perceived characteristics of a situation in order to obtain a desired object.			
Situation 18: Uses a string tied to an object to obtain the object on a horizontal surface with or without demonstration.	95.9%	75.8%	12
10. Further progress in anticipatory construction of means adapted to an end is implied by the use of an extension of an object as means while the object (the end) is not directly in view.			
Situation 18: Uses a string tied to an object to obtain it while it is not in the direct line of sight, pulling the string vertically with or without demonstration.	100.0%	71.9%	13
11. Additional progress in anticipatory construction of means adapted to an end is implied by exploitation of other objects as extensions of one's body.			
Situation 19: Uses a stick to obtain a toy out of reach on a horizontal surface with or without demonstration.	96.4%	78.8%	15–18
12. Anticipatory coordination of an end and appropriate means is implied by evidence of foresightful behavior in the face of a problem situation.			
Situation 20: In the problem of putting a long necklace into a tall container, foresees the likely fall of the container and adopts a successful approach from the start.	97.4%	56.9%	19–20
13. Perceptual recognition of hindrances toward an end implies representation of the end, of the means, and of the applicability of specific means.			
Situation 21: Does not attempt to stack a solid ring mixed in among other rings onto a peg.	97.6%	88.2%	22
Mean for all critical actions:	96.2%	75.5%	

sequence of steps in the development of means for achieving desired environmental events depends in considerable part upon the fact that each step upward in the sequence involves a different eliciting situation. In the case of the series concerned with the development of object permanence, for instance, steps 9, 10, 11, and 12 involve a progression of critical actions in one situation (situation number 8). On the other hand, with three exceptions, each of the steps in this series concerning the development of means utilizes a different situation. When sequences are dependent upon differing situations, one might expect that extending experience with any given situation would enable the critical actions elicited by that situation to precede those elicited by other situations. Such a possibility would seem more likely if the distance between two adjacent steps is small and their achievement is derived from the same structural organization of competence. Only longitudinal investigation of infants developing under environmental circumstances which differ substantially can determine the inevitability of these sequences despite variations in the nature of the infant's experience.

III. DEVELOPMENT OF IMITATION

The situations utilized to elicit imitative behaviors are subdivided into a series pertaining to vocal imitation and a series pertaining to gestural imitation. The series for vocal imitation begins with the ready-made scheme of vocalizing. Perhaps the first differentiation of this scheme occurs when, in addition to distress vocalizations, the infant begins to engage in playful vocalizations: cooing and various types of voice play. As the infant hears given patterns of vocalization repeatedly, as vocalized by himself or by others, they presumably become familiar and recognizable. At this point in development, if an adult imitates either an infant's vocalization or the sounds he most commonly vocalizes instead of talking to him in the usual adult fashion, the young infant typically responds with widening of the eyes and pupils, with mouth movements, and even with returns of the vocalizations. It is apparently the attractiveness of such newly recognized patterns of input, either visual (Hunt, 1963b, 1965, 1970, 1971b; Užgiris and Hunt, 1970) or auditory (Friedlander, 1970), which are becoming recognitively familiar that probably motivates such actions.

The familiarity of the vocal patterns heard by the infant probably also motivates the imitation of familiar sound patterns which Piaget (1945, p. 19ff.) has termed "pseudo-imitation." Later, with the development of interest in novelty, infants also imitate progressively more unfamiliar sound patterns. At first, they do this by a process of gradual approximation and, later, they do it directly. The infant progresses to the imitation of words and phrases, first those which he has heard repeatedly and which are within his vocabulary, and then he begins to systematically repeat practically all simple new words and short phrases.

The series concerned with gestural imitation follows a similar sequence. Infants begin by imitating simple gestures which are well within their behavioral repertoires, i.e., the earliest of their motor schemes. Later, they imitate more complex actions which utilize familiar schemes, but which include some demands for their accommodative modification. Infants then progress to the imitation of unfamiliar gestures which they can see themselves perform and, finally, they proceed to the imitation of unfamiliar gestures which they cannot see themselves perform except with a mirror, i.e., the facial gestures. This imitation of facial gestures invisible to infants appears to imply the capacity for some representation of the face and its features.

Table 8:3 presents the sequence of steps in the development of imitation, first vocal, and then gestural. We give again for each step the mean percentages of inter-observer agreement, the mean percentages of inter-session stability, and the month of age for each step by which the majority of infants of that age in our sample showed the critical actions.

We feel quite confident of the sequences of steps in both the series for vocal and for gestural imitation. On the other hand, it should be noted that both the average percentages of inter-observer agreement and the average percentages of inter-session stability were relatively low for certain of these steps. Nondistressful vocalizing or cooing, for instance, has relatively low inter-session stability because it depends upon the moment-to-moment motivation of the infant. Pseudo-imitative vocalizing also has low inter-session stability because motivation for it depends in part upon the relationship a particular examiner establishes with the infant. Even inter-observer agreement is relatively low, because it is not always easy to determine whether the

TABLE 8:3   *Sequence of Steps in the Development of Imitation*
(*Mean percentages of inter-observer agreement, mean percentages of inter-session stability, and the month of age by which the majority of infants of that age showed the actions indicative of each step in the sequence.*)

Sequence of Steps in Vocal Imitation	Inter-observer Agreement	Inter-session Stability	Month of Age
1. Some differentiation of the vocalizing scheme is implied by instances of non-distress vocalization. Situation 25: Cooing is observed.	86.6%	60.0%	1
2. Some rudimentary standard for infant's own vocalizations is suggested by apparent recognition of "own" sounds. Situation 26: Increases mouth movements and/or smiles upon hearing "own" sounds.	96.4%	66.2%	1
3. Further facility in recognition of familiar sounds is implied by matching own vocalizations to the familiar ones just heard. Situation 26: Vocalizes similar sounds upon hearing "own" sounds.	96.6%	76.6%	3
4. Recognition of familiar sound patterns is implied by vocal response to such sound patterns. Situation 28: Vocalizes some sounds upon hearing "own" sound patterns (babbling).	88.5%	66.2%	4
5. Further facility in recognition of familiar sound patterns is implied by matching own vocalizations to the familiar patterns just heard. Situation 28: Vocalizes similar sound patterns upon hearing familiar ones.	73.7%	73.7%	9
6. Inability to accommodate to a novel sound pattern is implied by vocalization of familiar sound patterns in response to novel ones. Situation 29: Vocalizes, but not similar sounds, upon hearing novel ones.	91.5%	64.8%	12
7. Some accommodation to novel sound patterns is implied by approximation of the novel sounds through repeated attempts. Situation 29: Vocalizes sounds similar to novel ones presented through gradual approximations.	96.1%	75.1%	12–14
8. Further plasticity of the vocalizing scheme is implied by reproduction of novel sound patterns without overt groping. Situation 29: Vocalizes novel sound patterns directly.	96.9%	78.0%	14
9. Greater plasticity of the vocalizing scheme is implied by direct repetition of new words. Situation 30: Repeats most simple new words.	100.0%	93.1%	14–17
Mean for all critical actions:	91.8%	72.6%	

TABLE 8:3 (*continued*)

Sequence of Steps in Gestural Imitation	Inter-observer Agree-ment	Inter-session Stabil-ity	Month of Age
1. Some recognition of a familiar body movement is implied by a selective response to it. Situation 33: Makes a gestural response upon seeing a familiar gesture.	88.7%	43.3%	4
2. Further facility in recognition of familiar body movements is implied by matching of own movements to the ones presented. Situation 33: Makes the same gesture upon seeing a familiar gesture.	95.8%	63.3%	7
3. Inability to accommodate to a novel body movement is implied by only partial imitation of such movements. Situation 34: When shown the gesture of hitting two blocks together, responds by hitting a block on the floor or in the examiner's hand.	97.0%	80.9%	8
4. Some accommodation to novel body movements is implied by imitation of such movements through gradual approximations. Situation 34: Imitates the hitting of two blocks together after overt groping.	97.1%	84.0%	9
5. Further plasticity of motor schemes is implied by immediate imitation of a novel body movement. Situation 34: Imitates the hitting of two blocks together directly.	96.4%	79.0%	10
6. Facility in accommodating to novel body movements which the infant can see himself perform is implied by immediate imitation of such novel movements. Situation 35: Imitates several novel gestures which he can see himself perform.	96.9%	77.5%	11
7. Inability to accommodate to novel body movements which require representation of own body parts is implied by failure to reproduce "invisible" gestures. Situation 36: Responds with some movement, but does not succeed in imitating a facial gesture.	96.8%	63.0%	14
8. Representation of own body parts is implied by imitation of an "invisible" gesture. Situation 36: Imitates at least one facial gesture.	96.6%	69.0%	14–17
9. Increased facility in accommodating to novel body movements and in representation of own body parts is implied by ready imitation of "invisible" gestures. Situation 36: Imitates more than one facial gesture.	96.6%	69.0%	14–20
Mean for all critical actions:	95.7%	70.0%	

infant is initiating the vocalization in response to the model presented by the examiner, or whether the vocalization is in response to some other aspect of the situation. Similarly, the imitation of various gestures depends heavily upon the infant's momentary relationship with the examiner. Thus, the low average percentage of inter-session stability probably reflects primarily the variation in the quality of the relationship with the infant from day to day.

IV. The Development of Operational Causality[2]

A primordial appreciation of causality appears early as infants actively begin to anticipate events. This anticipation is apparently based upon the fact that the central processes established through repeated perceptual encounters with events run off faster than do those events. On the subjective side, such elementary appreciation of causality hardly can be imagined to be more than a diffuse feeling of anticipation as the perception of a repeatedly encountered event evokes the expectation of others, or more than a diffuse feeling of efficacy as the infant begins to follow objects with his eyes and to seek out the sources of sounds. In neither of these cases has the implication of even operational causality, as distinct from what will much later become conceptual causality, any clearly observable basis. With the appearance of hand-watching and the grasping of interesting objects, however, infants begin to show some overt control through their hand-movements of what they see with their eyes. Later, infants make active attempts to regain interesting perceptual inputs. These self-initiated actions that anticipate an outcome have been termed "procedures" by Piaget (1936, ch. 3). These "procedures" appear to be generalizations of particular repetitive actions to circumstances other than the ones in which they originated. Thus, after watching the examiner put a toy penguin in motion by pulling a string dangling from it, infants who have learned to shake their legs to cause certain events, will shake their legs in an apparent effort to get the examiner to repeat the

---

[2] We are using the term *operational* in the sense of "practical" or "effective" to contrast with conceptual understanding of the same causal principles. This use should not be confused with that in operational thought.

spectacle. Such "procedures" as the leg-shaking presumably feed back to the infant's feelings of effort which become associated in time with obtaining such interesting inputs as the movement of a stationary object.

At this level, the source of causality appears to lie entirely within the infant. Somewhat later, infants begin to show an appreciation of centers of causality outside themselves. They show this appreciation of external causality by attempting to act directly upon the source of the interesting event. Thus, after hearing a musical sound from a toy clown which the examiner has produced by striking the clown, infants will often extend their hands and touch the examiner's hand or even the clown as if to start the musical sound again. Still later, infants begin to show an appreciation of the causal powers of older persons to produce interesting events. Thus, for instance, when the infants' own efforts fail to get such interesting events as the musical sound from the toy clown, they hand the toy clown back to the examiner with a gesture of request to make it sound again. Still later, infants begin to examine the objects which yield interesting spectacles for objective causes of those spectacles, and they try various objective means to get the toys to repeat the interesting actions. The appropriateness of these efforts, of course, depends upon something akin to mechanical knowledge of the objects or their mechanisms. The critical actions, however, are the attempts to find objective causes and not their appropriateness.

The sequence of seven steps in the development of operational causality, along with the mean percentages of inter-observer agreement and mean percentages of inter-session stability for each of the critical behaviors, appears in Table 8:4. Despite the abstract nature of the steps in this scale, the mean percentages of inter-observer agreement are high, and, except for step four, the mean percentages of inter-session stability are very respectable. Again, certain of the distances between steps, especially those between steps 2 and 3, and between steps 3 and 4, appear to be much smaller than those between other steps, e.g., between steps 4 and 5, and between steps 5 and 6. This series, like that for the permanence of objects, constitutes a series of landmarks in the construction of one of the categories of reality.

TABLE 8:4 *Sequence of Steps in the Development of Operational Causality*
(*Mean percentages of inter-observer agreement, mean percentages of inter-session stability, and the month of age by which the majority of infants of that age showed the critical actions indicative of each step in the sequence.*)

Sequence of Steps	Inter-observer Agreement	Inter-session Stability	Month of Age
1. Momentary control over a source of input is made possible by coordination between two schemes. Situation 10: Hand-watching behavior is observed.	86.7%	73.3%	2
2. More definite control over a source of input is made possible by immediate repetition of efficacious actions. Situation 13: Immediate repetition of an action resulting in an interesting input is observed.	93.0%	78.1%	3
3. Generalization of efficacious actions is implied by evidence of "procedures." Situation 37: Cessation of an interesting spectacle evokes a "procedure."	87.0%	67.6%	4
4. Some appreciation of centers of causality outside the self is implied by direct action on such centers. Situation 34: Touches the examiner's hand after demonstration of hitting two blocks;	92.4%	71.9%	5
or Situation 39: Touches the examiner's hand and/or container after demonstration of shaking an object in a container;	97.8%	86.2%	5
or Situation 40: Touches the examiner's hand or the toy after a demonstration of spinning it.	89.7%	55.3%	5
5. Further appreciation of centers of causality outside the self is implied by substitution of request for direct action on another person. Situation 40: Hands the toy back to the examiner after a demonstration of spinning it;	98.2%	69.2%	12–15
or Situation 41: Hands a mechanical toy to a person to be started again after it stops.	94.0%	69.0%	12–15
6. Further objectification of causality is implied by behavioral recognition of direct ways for activating objects. Situation 41: Attempts to activate a mechanical toy himself after a demonstration.	100.0%	66.9%	18
7. Greater objectification of causality is implied by spontaneous behavioral construction of direct ways for activating objects. Situation 41: Attempts to activate the mechanical toy himself directly.	98.2%	74.8%	21
Mean for all critical actions:	93.7%	71.2%	

V. The Construction of Object Relations in Space

This fifth series concerns the developmental transformations in infants' implicit appreciation of and construction of object relations in space. Implicit behavioral recognition that objects differ in their position in space is manifest very early in the slow alternate glancing at two objects. Somewhat later, this alternate glancing becomes more rapid, suggesting an active comparison of inputs achieved through one scheme of action. Later yet, as infants coordinate the scheme of looking with that of listening, they begin to localize sounds and their sources. Thus, things heard become things to search for with the eyes and to look at.

In our group of infants, the coordination of the scheme of looking with that of grasping was observed somewhat later, as they began to reach for and to grasp seen objects. White, Castle, and Held (1964) have uncovered a whole series of steps in the development of such visually directed reaching. In this scale of the construction of object relations in space, we use only an approximation of their top-level reaching, an action in which infants extend their hands directly to the visible target object and shape their hands in anticipation of grasping it.

Another aspect of the construction of object relations in space depends upon the accommodation of the looking scheme to objects moving rapidly through the visual field. At first, infants are unable to reconstruct the trajectories of rapidly moving objects. Later, they begin to reconstruct those trajectories of objects where a simple extension of the glance forward along the trajectory permits the infant to locate the object. Still later, infants reconstruct the trajectory which a falling object must have taken even when only a portion of that trajectory was visible. This development appears to depend in part upon the achievement of a degree of object permanence, but it also appears to depend upon the ability to extrapolate the trajectory. Once it has appeared, infants can hunt for an object in an area where it must have fallen.

Progress in the development of central processes which can represent objects is shown in the recognition of a reverse side of objects and in the understanding, at least on the behavioral level, of such relationships as that of the container and the contained, of equilibrium, and

TABLE 8:5 *Sequence of Steps in the Construction of Object Relations in Space* (*Mean percentages of inter-observer agreement, mean percentages of inter-session stability, and the month of age by which the majority of infants of that age showed the critical actions indicative of each step in the sequence.*)

Sequence of Steps	Inter-observer Agreement	Inter-session Stability	Month of Age
1. Some accommodation to two loci of input in space is implied by successive shifting of the glance between two objects. Situation 42: Alternates glance slowly between two visual targets.	93.3%	80.0%	2
2. Some anticipation of two loci of input in space is implied by rapid alternation between two objects. Situation 42: Alternates glance rapidly between two visual targets repeatedly.	93.3%	86.7%	3
3. Further construction of loci of input in surrounding space is implied by correct localization of perceived inputs. Situation 43: Localizes source of sound correctly.	96.6%	90.0%	3-5
4. Further accommodation to distances in surrounding space is implied by accurate approach to near objects. Situation 14: Grasps an object directly when within reach.	97.0%	94.1%	4-5
5. Construction of the movements of objects in surrounding space is implied by following of rapidly moving objects. Situation 44: Reconstructs the trajectory of a falling object and directs the eyes to about where it must have come to rest.	98.2%	92.7%	6
6. Further construction of the movements of objects in surrounding space is implied by localization of rapidly moving objects even when portions of their trajectories are obstructed from view. Situation 44: Leans forward to search for a dropped object in the direction in which it fell.	99.0%	86.4%	7
7. More complete construction of three-dimensional objects is implied by appreciation of their rotation in space. Situation 45: Recognizes the reversal of an object.	96.2%	86.2%	9
8. Construction of some interrelationships between objects in space is implied by behavioral utilization of these relationships. Situation 46: Uses one object as a container for another.	96.0%	76.4%	9

TABLE 8:5 (*continued*)

Sequence of Steps	Inter-observer Agree-ment	Inter-session Stabil-ity	Month of Age
9. Further construction of the interrelationships between objects in space is implied by behavioral anticipation of natural forces acting on objects. Situation 47: Builds a tower by placing one block in equilibrium over another.	100.0%	90.0%	15
10. Further construction of the surrounding space is implied by behavioral anticipation of the effects of natural forces acting in it. Situation 18: Uses a string as an extension of an object vertically, compensating for gravity.	100.0%	71.9%	13–15
11. Representation of familiar space is implied by memory of the usual locations of objects or persons in it. Situation 49: Indicates knowledge of usual whereabouts of familiar persons and recognizes their current absence.	96.4%	76.6%	18
Mean for all critical actions:	96.9%	84.6%	

of gravity. Finally, a representation of familiar objects in familiar space is constructed. Such representation is implied by various actions such as the ability to indicate the usual whereabouts of persons or objects absent at the time, and to make detours to get to objects which have disappeared behind barriers.

The sequence of 11 steps in the series on the construction of object relations in space along with the mean percentages of inter-observer agreement and mean percentages of inter-session stability for the critical actions in each step, as well as the month of age at which the majority of our infants achieved them appear in Table 8:5.

The percentages of inter-observer agreement are consistently high for the actions critical for these 11 steps. Moreover, the percentages of inter-session stability are also above those for most of the other series. It is likely, however, that the circumstances encountered by infants can alter the order in which certain steps in this sequence appear. For instance, whether localizing sounds correctly with the eyes comes before or after grasping an object within reach may be largely a matter of whether the circumstances encountered have supported ear-eye coordination more or less than eye-hand coordination. On the other hand, such relatively simple coordinations of two schemes must regularly appear before the child can achieve the complex coordination involved in constructing interrelationships between objects in order to accommodate his actions to such interrelationships in advance, which is indicated, for example, by using a long string to pull an object up from the floor.

A careful analysis of the competencies involved in pulling up objects or in tower-building coupled with observation of the coordination of these competencies in development would undoubtedly uncover several additional steps in this series between those depicted as steps 6, 7, and 8, on the one hand, and steps 9 and 10, on the other hand. The full story of the developmental transitions involved in the construction of object relations in space is undoubtedly much more intricate than the landmarks that we have thus far identified and utilized in this series.

VI. The Development of Schemes for Relating to Objects

Unlike the sequences in the construction of object permanence, the construction of operational causality and the construction of object relations in space, this series concerns the ways through which infants interact with objects, consisting mainly of relatively common toys. The development of these activities may be described as a series of peaks in the tendencies for certain ways of interaction. Given behavior patterns make their appearance, become characteristic of an infant's relating to objects, and then these behavior patterns are gradually replaced by others which often incorporate the earlier ones. At first, objects serve chiefly to elicit various schemes already present within the infant's repertoire of actions. Infants appear to be intent upon exercising these familiar schemes regardless of the characteristics of the eliciting objects. They appear to pay little attention to the characteristics of the objects as such, for the manipulative schemes in the repertoires of very young infants are applied to objects indiscriminately. Gradually, however, accommodation of such schemes as hitting, shaking, waving, and so on to particular characteristics of different

TABLE 8:6 *Sequence of Steps in the Development of Schemes for Relating to Objects* (*Mean percentages of inter-observer agreement, mean percentages of inter-session stability, and the month of age by which the majority of infants of that age showed the critical actions indicative of each step in the sequence.*)

Sequence of Steps	Inter-observer Agreement	Inter-session Stability	Month of Age
1. Incidental use of objects in the exercise of a scheme. Situation[a]: Mouthing.	93.7%	72.3%	2
2. Appearance of momentary attention to the object involved in the exercise of a scheme. Visual inspection.	84.3%	63.0%	3
3. Systematic use of objects in the exercise of schemes. Hitting.	93.9%	81.5%	4
4. Beginning of differentiation of schemes as a result of interaction with different objects. Shaking.	90.2%	75.8%	5
5. Shift of attention from the exercise of schemes to investigation of the properties of objects. Examining.	90.2%	74.4%	6
6. Selective application of schemes depending on the properties of objects. Differentiated schemes.	92.6%	77.1%	7
7. Acquisition of new schemes as a result of studying various properties of objects. Dropping and throwing.	94.3%	81.6%	8–9
8. Beginning of appreciation of the social uses of objects. Socially instigated behaviors.	96.7%	84.2%	10
9. Beginning of the representation of objects is implied by reference to them in a shared interaction. Showing.	97.2%	88.0%	14
10. Representation of objects in a symbolic system is indicated by verbal expressions of recognition. Naming.	96.7%	91.8%	18
Mean for all critical actions:	93.0%	79.0%	

[a] Situations 50, 51, 52, 53, 54, 55, 56, 57, 59, 60, and 61 were used to elicit schemes for relating to objects.

objects seems to contribute to the development of new schemes, on the one hand, and to interest in objects for themselves, on the other.

The acquisition of the scheme of examining objects, which consists of looking at objects while manipulating them, stands out as a turning point in this sequence. The infants begin to show an interest in the particular characteristics of various objects, and their manipulative schemes begin to be applied selectively. Moreover, a rapid differentiation of schemes occurs, and this differentiation takes into account not only the physical characteristics of objects, but their social significance as well. Thus, behaviors such as showing objects to a person, indicating appreciation of their usual function, naming them, and other socially instigated ways of relating to objects come to dominate the actions of the infants in regard to the objects they encounter.

The sequence of steps in the development of schemes for relating to objects with the mean percentages of inter-observer agreement, the mean percentages of inter-session stability, and the months of age at which the majority of the infants in our sample showed the critical actions for each step appear in Table 8:6.

The mean percentages of inter-observer agreement are consistently high for the critical actions for the 10 steps in this series. The mean percentages of inter-session stability are all above 70 except that for the second step concerned with the appearance of momentary attention to the object itself.

The first five steps in this sequence are essentially motor and manipulative in character. Their developmental course of appearance, dominance of the infant's action, disappearance, and integration into or coordination with new systems of action appears to correspond closely to the development of locomotor behaviors described by Mary Shirley (1933) and to some of the branches of motor development in infants described by Myrtle McGraw (1943). Inasmuch as the object encountered has little to do with the elicitation of one of these motor patterns rather than another through the first half year of life, it might suggest that this sequence is probably essentially preprogrammed. Whether it is the same for nearly all infants is a matter of question; there may be individual differences. As we shall see, the scalogram analysis of the critical behaviors in this series shows the lowest level of ordinality of any of the six series which comprise our ordinal scales of psychological development in infancy.

The detailed instructions for arranging the eliciting situations and for recording the critical actions for all the steps in these six series comprising the final version of the instrument appear in Part III of this book beginning with Chapter 10.

CHAPTER 9

The Scalability of the Six Series
and Some Intercorrelations

It may be argued that if all the critical actions forming the developmental landmarks in a series are elicited from a cross-sectional sample of infants, these may then be subjected to a scalogram analysis to yield an indication of the ordinality of the sequence obtained. We believe this approach is impossible in practice, especially when the successive steps in the sequence involve reorganizations of the mode of functioning rather than simple accretions of elements. Our observations make it evident that unless infants are made to shift their level of functioning through stress, fatigue, or some other unusual process, they will not exhibit certain of their earlier patterns of action once these earlier patterns have been incorporated into higher-order organizations of actions. For instance, any infant who has objectified causality sufficiently to indicate an appreciation of centers of causality outside himself will not use the self-based "procedures" to make interesting events reoccur, except under very special circumstances. Similarly, infants who have passed through the phase of hand-watching and have attained top-level reaching in their eye-hand coordination will not engage in hand-watching behavior except under such unusual circumstances as numbness of a hand. Neither will they revert to the cruder levels of eye-hand coordination in reaching when a target for grasping is put within their view. Thus, once an infant has achieved higher levels of organization in his actions elicited by our situations, it becomes very difficult to get those situations to elicit the earlier, cruder patterns of behavior. Again, at the upper limits, tasks which exceed in their demands an infant's current capacity for accommodative modification tend to evoke frustration and anger. With such tasks, it becomes first difficult and then impossible to maintain the infant's interest and cooperation. An infant who does not have representative central processes which endure long enough to permit him to obtain an object hidden under a single screen, for instance, will not remain attentive and unfrustrated through a number of more elaborate hidings of the object. Such examples can be multiplied indefinitely. Considerations of this nature suggest that attempting to elicit all of the critical actions in such sequential series from every infant is unfeasible with a cross-sectional sample of infants varying in age.

Consequently, when we realized that it would not be possible to observe a new sample of infants longitudinally within the limits of the present investigation,[1] we decided to attempt a tentative evaluation of the ordinal nature of each of our six series of steps with the data already available. Since the infants had not been presented with every eliciting situation included in each of the six series, it was necessary to assume an existing or earlier capacity for some of the critical actions to those situations which were judged to be clearly below an infant's current range of functioning and, thus, were not presented. Similarly, at the upper limits of an infant's capacity, it was necessary to assume his lack of capacity for critical actions above those in the series for which he had already exhibited behaviors implying a lower level of functioning.[2] In most instances, these assumptions could be made without any qualms for the reasons given. It seems certain, for instance, that infants over four months of age who are able to follow an object

---

[1] Since this was written, preliminary reports on the sequential order of acquisition of the steps in several of these scales and the interrelationships among them have been published (Užgiris, 1972, 1973). Schickedanz and Hunt are using four of these scales in a longitudinal study to assess the effects of a mothers' training program on the rate of infant development. The sequences of achieving the steps of object permanence appear from inspection of the data from this still-incomplete study to confirm their ordinality. Hunt is also using these scales to assess the effects of various interventions in the rearing practices in a Tehran orphanage. Again, inspection indicates that the sequence of achieving the steps in the scale of object permanence confirms the ordinality uncovered by the cross-sectional study. For the other scales, the impressions from inspection of still-incomplete data are less clear.

[2] No assumptions were made about actions in those situations which were not presented to any given infant due to examiner error or due to uncooperativeness on the part of the infant. Such instances were omitted from the analysis.

moving steadily to a point of disappearance and search for that object with their eyes around the point of disappearance would have had the capacity to follow the same object through an arc of 180° had we presented that eliciting situation to them. This is an instance where the necessary observation could have been made. Probably several such occurrences of infants tracking the movements of a toy being put back into the examiner's briefcase or the movements of his mother moving across the room were actually available to be observed, but they were not recorded systematically, because only analyses of the data for reliability and stability had been originally planned. Similarly, we felt we could assume with complete confidence that those infants under four months of age who did not reach out and pick up a partially hidden object would also have failed to reach out for an object covered completely by one, or several screens.

On the other hand, certain of these assumptions were made with less confidence. We assumed that all infants over four months of age had watched their hands at some earlier time, that all infants over eight months of age had tried to replicate an interesting spectacle produced by accidental movements of a limb, and that all infants over 12 months of age who had shown higher order schemes for relating to objects must have shown mouthing, hitting, and shaking previously. These actions would have been hard or impossible to elicit at the later age. An examination of which eliciting situations were actually presented to the infants in each age grouping in either Appendix A or Appendix B provides an indication of what assumptions had to be made and of their frequency. It should be borne in mind, however, that many of the infants were actually presented with eliciting situations from the preceding and following groupings. Almost never, for instance, did an infant who did not obtain a partially covered object fail to get the chance to search for one completely covered. Whenever actual observations were available, of course, no assumptions had to be made.

THE SCALOGRAM ANALYSIS

Four recordings of each infant's actions in these eliciting situations were available. We considered performing a scalogram analysis for each set of records separately and using the finding of the same or similar sequence with each analysis as evidence of both reliability and scalability. Because we would have had to discard the data for a larger number of infants due to missing observations, however, we decided against this approach. In the analyses of scalability, the four records of each infant's actions in the eliciting situations were combined according to the following rules: (1) the majority judgment was followed where possible, i.e., when three of the four records agreed, the majority observation was accepted; (2) a seniority rule was followed when the observers agreed with themselves over the two sessions, but did not agree with each other on both occasions, i.e., the record of the more experienced observer was accepted; (3) the infant was scored at the higher level of functioning observed when the split was between the successive examinations. A somewhat higher proportion of infants performed at a higher level on one of the series during the second than during the first examination (19 versus 14 percent on the average), but this difference was small. Moreover, if no observation had been recorded to a given situation during one of the examinations, the record of the other examination was used.

In the scalogram analysis of the series concerned with the development of schemes for relating to objects, the following special criteria were used for scoring the presence of a given scheme: (1) infants under four months of age were scored as showing a particular scheme if it was observed in regard to one of the three objects presented to them; (2) infants over four months of age were scored as showing a given scheme only if it was observed in regard to two of the eight objects presented them, or, in the case of infants over eight months of age, in regard to two of the ten objects presented to them.

In constructing the six series of eliciting situations for these sequences of psychological development, we attempted to arrange a logical sequence of steps for each of the six branches studied and to find a critical action in an eliciting situation for each step. Sometimes, however, several of the situations would elicit actions indicating the attainment of a given step. As a rule, only one action in each eliciting situation was selected as critical, but this rule was not invariably followed. The selection of the steps for the sequences in each of the six branches of development was based on several factors. Of primary consideration was a logical progression with psychological unity, but the experience of observing infant actions in the various situations was utilized, and the relative difficulty of each step for the 84 infants in our third sample served as an additional guide in ordering each sequence.

The scalogram analysis was performed in order to determine whether these series do, in fact, represent ordinal scales. Insofar as each infant's pattern of achievements corresponds to the proposed pattern embodied in each of these six series, a sequential order of progression along the series is suggested, making each of the series ordinal in character. A modification of Guttman's scalogram analysis, suggested by Green (1956), uses summary statistics appropriate for the data available. Green states that a set of items for which his index of consistency (I, a coefficient of reproducibility corrected for chance reproducibility) is above .50 may be considered to form a scale. With a perfect scale, any individual's sequence of achievements could be completely reproduced from knowledge of the highest item scored. The number of this item is the individual's scale score.

The results of these scalogram analyses appear in Table 9:1. The table presents the number of steps in each of the scales, the number of subjects involved, and Green's Index of Consistency (I) for each series. Because there are two series for imitation, one vocal and one gestural, there are seven such analyses.

TABLE 9:1   *Scalogram Analysis of Actions Comprising Each of the Proposed Series*

Series	Number of Items	Number of Subjects	Green's Index of Consistency
Visual Pursuit and the Permanence of Objects	14	82	.97
Development of Means for Obtaining Events	13	84	.81
Development of Imitation, Vocal	9	84	.89
Development of Imitation, Gestural	9	83	.95
Development of Operational Causality	7	82	.99
Construction of Object Relations in Space	11	82	.91
Development of Schemes for Relating to Objects	10	84	.80

According to the criteria specified by Green (1956), all seven of these series may be considered to form ordinal scales. Green's I approaches perfection for the series concerned with visual pursuit and the permanence of objects and for that concerned with operational causality. The former series includes a number of steps in which ordinality is logically built into the sequence. This is true especially for steps 5, 6, 7, and 8, since finding an object hidden under one of several screens presupposes the ability to find an object hidden under a single screen, and finding an object hidden under a number of superimposed screens presupposes the ability to find an object hidden under just one screen. Similarly, success with step 12 in this series implies the ability for step 11; step 11 implies the ability for step 10; and step 10 implies the ability for step 9.

The series concerned with the development of operational causality shows the highest index of consistency (.99). Because this series contains but 7 steps, as compared with 14 in the sequence concerned with visual pursuit and the permanence of objects, the index might be expected to be high. The series of steps in the developmental shift for sources of causality from within the self to sources of causality outside the self in other persons and in inanimate objects exemplifies a progressive course in the construction of reality which is not reversible. Yet, one can hardly say that the ordinality among these steps is logically built into them.

The indices of consistency for the two series concerned with imitation and that concerned with the construction of object relations in space are all of the order of .9. The steps in the series concerned with imitation appear to be based upon what Hunt (1965, 1971b) has termed "the epigenesis of intrinsic motivation." The series on the construction of object relations in space appears to be based in part upon the construction of the object and in part upon the development of central processes representing the organization of familiar space.

The lowest indices of consistency occur for the development of means for obtaining desired environmental events and for the development of schemes for relating to objects. It is interesting to find the lowest indices of consistency for these two series because the sequences of the steps in them may well be less a function of environmental encounters than are those in any of the other scales. It is these two sets of sequences which appear most likely to be a matter of preprogrammed maturation. This is another bit of suggestive evidence against the contention that the existence of a definite order in the landmarks of development implies a genetically preprogrammed control of development.

The evidence of ordinality in these seven series, representing six branches of development, should not be taken to imply that the sequences of steps found here need be invariant or inevitable. Whether these sequences appear in repeated examinations of the same infants followed longitudinally when the infants encounter differing programs of circumstances remains to be determined. The infants of the Tewksbury State Hospital whom White and Held (1966) provided with enriched opportunities showed the level of eye-hand coordination implied by top-level reaching earlier than our home-reared infants, while our infants showed the ear-vocal coordination epitomized in responding vocally to vocalizations which resemble those in their own repertoire earlier than did the infants at Tewksbury. It is clear from this fact that the order in which such simple coordinations occur can be modified appreciably. As we noted in Chapter 3, however, any coordination of such a pair of simple coordinations in the hierarchical organization of competencies must depend upon their both being present for the coordination to occur. Such hierarchical organization, however, is only one basis for a definite sequential order in the landmarks of psychological development. Another basis, epitomized best perhaps in the series concerned with the construction of the permanent object is the acquisition of central processes representative of events, objects, persons, and places. Still others reside in the landmarks of organization of motivation and of skills. At this stage of knowledge, however, the tie between the theory of the various bases for order in development and the empirical evidence of order in these six branches of development is but tenuous.

CORRELATIONS WITH AGE

By noting the highest step in each scale achieved by an infant, it is possible to assign to that infant a score for that branch of development. As would be expected, the age of infants correlates very highly with their scale scores for each of these sequences. The correlations of the

TABLE 9:2   *Correlations of Infants' Scores on Each of the Scales with Their Ages*

Scales	Number of Subjects	Pearson's r with Age
Visual Pursuit and the Permanence of Objects	82	.94
Development of Means for Obtaining Events	84	.94
Development of Imitation, Vocal	84	.88
Development of Imitation, Gestural	83	.91
Development of Operational Causality	82	.86
Construction of Object Relations in Space	82	.91
Development of Schemes for Relating to Objects	84	.89

scores for the infants in our sample on each of the seven scales with their ages appear in Table 9:2.

The coefficients represent the correlation of scores on these various scales with age under what one would expect to be the relatively similar conditions existing within the middle-class, academic culture. Had the circumstances encountered by some groups of infants within our sample differed markedly, one could expect these correlations to be lower.[3] The more homogeneous the circumstances encountered by the infants in any given sample, the higher would we expect such correlations with age to be.

INTERCORRELATIONS AMONG THE
SCALE SCORES FOR OUR SAMPLE OF INFANTS
ON THE VARIOUS SCALES

Piaget's theory of stages would suggest high correlations among scores on these several branches of psychological development. Moreover, inasmuch as progress along these several branches cannot be completely independent for the reasons already given, it is of interest

[3] Subsequent investigations have indicated that the ages of achieving the behavioral landmarks of the steps on these scales will vary greatly with differing conditions of rearing (Paraskevopoulos and Hunt, 1971). For instance, the mean age of achieving top-level object permanence has been found to range from 73 weeks, for 8 consecutive infants born to the parents from the poverty sector who participated in the program of the Parent and Child Center of Mt. Carmel, Illinois, to an estimated mean of 182 weeks for infants who developed in the Municipal Orphanage of Athens, Greece, where the infant-caretaker ratio was about 10 to 1 (Hunt et al., 1975). The Mt. Carmel infants, however, had the advantage of a program of intervention designed to foster their development.

TABLE 9:3 *Intercorrelations between Scale Scores on the Seven Sequences* (*Age Not Partialed Out*)

	Object Permanence	Development of Means	Vocal Imitation	Gestural Imitation	Operational Causality	Construction of Object Relations in Space	Development of Schemes
Object Permanence	—	.92	.82	.91	.84	.92	.90
Development of Means		—	.83	.89	.85	.93	.88
Vocal Imitation			—	.81	.80	.84	.81
Gestural Imitation				—	.81	.88	.86
Operational Causality					—	.89	.87
Construction of Object Relations in Space						—	.93
Development of Schemes							—

to examine the intercorrelations among the scores achieved by our infants. These intercorrelations between scale scores for our sample of infants are given in Table 9:3.

Because the scores on all these scales show very high correlations with age (see Table 9:2), we have computed intercorrelations among the seven sets of scale scores with age partialed out. This procedure has both advantages and disadvantages. On the one hand, since development takes place in time, leaving age in as a variable would be expected to contribute to an artificially high correlation between any two developing competencies. On the other hand, a matrix of intercorrelations with age partialed out portrays an artificial condition in which a major source of possible parallelism in the development of two competencies, the maturational or preprogrammed component, is artificially removed. Moreover, the inequality of the developmental distances between successive steps along these scales would also tend to lower the correlations. The intercorrelation matrix for scores on the seven scales with age partialed out is presented in Table 9:4.

Although the correlations given in Table 9:4 may be judged spuriously low for reasons already given, they seem to be considerably lower than one would expect from Piaget's (1936) stage theory of sensorimotor development.[4] All of these intercorrelations but one fall below .61; all but two fall below .51. These facts suggest that there may be more independence in development along the several branches than a stage theory encompassing all of early psychological development would require.

---

[4] The relationships among levels of development achieved along the several scales is also subject to substantial variation through differing conditions of rearing. The various sets of rearing conditions represented in the two orphanages and the sample of homes in Athens, Greece, resulted in a correlation between vocal imitation and object permanence of +0.86 (Paraskevopoulos and Hunt, 1971). For this high correlation, age was not partialed out. Užgiris (1973) reported low intercorrelations among achieved levels in the several branches at various ages, as have King and Seegmiller (1973) for a sample of infants from Harlem, New York City. Furthermore, the intervention at the Parent and Child Center of Mt. Carmel advanced the mean age (73 weeks) at which these infants from families of poverty achieved top-level object permanence nearly six months ahead of that (98 weeks) at which it was achieved by the infants from predominantly middle-class families of Worcester, Massachusetts (Hunt et al., 1975), but did not advance the age at which the Mt. Carmel infants achieved top-level vocal imitation. In fact, this particular program of intervention left the mean age at which the Mt. Carmel infants achieved top-level vocal imitation some three months behind that for the Worcester infants (Hunt, Schickedanz, and Užgiris, in preparation).

TABLE 9:4 *Intercorrelations between Scale Score on the Seven Sequences with Age Partialed Out*

	Object Permanence	Development of Means	Vocal Imitation	Gestural Imitation	Operational Causality	Construction of Object Relations in Space	Development of Schemes
Object Permanence	—	.32	-.03	.41	.17	.42	.39
Development of Means		—	.04	.26	.24	.51	.30
Vocal Imitation			—	.07	.20	.16	.12
Gestural Imitation				—	.13	.29	.26
Operational Causality					—	.50	.46
Construction of Object Relations in Space						—	.61
Development of Schemes							—

Although highly tentative, the pattern of correlations among these seven sets of scores suggests some interesting interrelationships among the various branches of development. One cluster of related branches appears to be concerned with actions pertaining to objects taking place in the surrounding space. This cluster is indicated by the correlations ranging from .42 to .61 between the construction of object relations in space with the development of schemes for relating to objects, with the development of means for obtaining desired environmental events, with the development of operational causality, and with the development of visual pursuit and permanence of objects. A lesser constellation exists in the correlations of the development of means for obtaining desired environmental events with the development in object permanence and in gestural imitation, and of the correlation of object permanence with gestural imitation. This constellation may be related to the development of representation for motoric acts. Vocal imitation stands out by being least related to development along the other branches. This may reflect either a relatively independent course for the development of vocalization, or, a relatively small number of situations which can elicit auditory-vocal coordination and provide the grounds for inference concerning the infant's interaction with his circumstances through the auditory channel.

Another way of examining the course of development in the various branches tapped by our seven scales is to consider progress along the scales in relation to Piaget's stages. On the basis of specific criterial achievements, the 84 infants in our third sample were classified as demonstrating a level of development characteristic of one of Piaget's six stages of general intelligence in the sensorimotor period. This classification was carried out at the time when the original records were coded for the reliability analyses and was almost perfectly consistent across the four records available for each subject (average percentage of agreement was 97). The scale scores of infants classified within each of Piaget's stages suggest somewhat different trends in progress along the different branches, both in terms of rate of progression and in terms of the spread of individual achievements.

The results presented in Table 9:5 have to be considered with caution. It must be remembered that the several scales vary in the total number of steps and that the distances between steps on these

TABLE 9:5   *Mean Scale Scores and Average Deviations from the Mean for Infants Classified within Each of Piaget's Sensorimotor Stages*

Piaget's Stage of Sensorimotor Development	N[a]	Mean and Average Deviation	MEAN SCALE SCORES AND AVERAGE DEVIATIONS ON:						
			Object Permanence	Development of Means	Vocal Imitation	Gestural Imitation	Operational Causality	Construction of Object Relations in Space	Development of Schemes
II	9	X̄	1.77	1.33	2.44	0	1.00	1.11	1.55
		AD	.74	.89	.49	0	.66	1.03	.84
III	16	X̄	2.56	3.06	3.69	.62	2.80	3.31	3.75
		AD	.94	1.05	1.23	.70	.91	1.27	1.31
IV	26	X̄	7.76	6.50	4.77	4.11	4.24	7.19	6.77
		AD	1.64	1.38	1.34	1.89	.40	1.07	1.10
V	12	X̄	9.08	7.66	6.17	5.41	4.50	8.00	7.41
		AD	2.41	1.86	1.19	1.94	.58	1.36	.95
VI	20	X̄	12.88	10.84	8.50	7.89	5.95	10.50	9.35
		AD	.74	.97	1.15	1.11	.67	1.10	.84

[a] One infant was classified within Stage I.

scales are as yet indeterminate. Furthermore, while there were few infants who achieved the top step on each of the scales, some ceiling effect may have been operative. With these limitations in mind, however, several trends stand out. There is an increase in the mean scale score on each of our scales at each higher Piagetian stage. This fact suggests that the developmental progression posited by Piaget is being reflected in our scale sequences. Nevertheless, it is clear that the gestural imitation scale reflects achievements characteristic of Piaget's later stages, especially in comparison with the vocal imitation scale, and that the rate of progress along the scale for the development of means is not as rapid as along the scales for object permanence, construction of object relations in space, or development of schemes for relating to objects with each higher Piagetian stage. This again implies that progress in the various branches of development is somewhat independent. The small number of infants tested at any one month of age does not allow an adequate examination of the fit between the obtained results and the different models for relationship between different developmental sequences elaborated by Wohlwill (1973). Nevertheless, some indication of the variability of scale scores with development is provided in Table 9:5. It may be seen that the dispersion of scale scores around the mean (as indicated by average deviation) at each stage is considerable and varies with the stage and branch of development. While the absolute dispersion of scale scores at any stage is clearly a function of the sample of infants examined, the dispersion of scores on one scale compared to another does reflect the congruence between achievements in the various branches of development. In partial agreement with the correspondences suggested by the correlational analysis, dispersion of scores on the scales of object permanence, gestural imitation, vocal imitation, and the development of schemes shows a similarity in following the pattern of increasing dispersion and then a definite reduction in dispersion at the higher stages. On the other hand, the dispersion of scores on the development of means scale increases throughout, and the dispersion of scores on the scale for construction of object relations in space and possibly on the scale for operational causality shows a narrowing of dispersion at stage IV followed again by an increase. While these trends are extremely tentative, they suggest that the interrelationships between achievements in these various branches vary and merit closer study.

CONCLUSION

Despite the still-provisional character of these scales, we believe we have sufficient evidence of their ordinality to justify their use in investigations as ordinal scales. It is always wise to attempt to elicit actions critical for some two or three successive steps beyond the one for which the infant fails to show the critical actions, but the top step for which an infant manifests the critical actions can be used as his score on any given scale. Such scores permit one to describe an infant's psychological development in the several branches concretely. The scores do not depend for meaning upon comparison with the scores of other infants, or upon the position of the infant in some standardization group of infants. Similarly, the scores do not depend upon some rough correlation with age. They have direct functional significance, or what one might call intrinsic validity. We hope they may be useful to ascertain the kinds of circumstances required to promote succeeding steps in development.

Even so, scores on these scales permit comparisons of infants. Mean scores, moreover, permit the comparison of groups of infants. When either scores or mean scores are employed in conjunction with age, they permit comparisons regarding advancement or retardation. Such comparisons for random groups of infants of a given age living under differing circumstances can, moreover, provide one with evidence of which set of circumstances is more effective in fostering development in the several branches.

One may use these scales, moreover, to assess the degree to which development along a given branch is a function of encounters with particular kinds of circumstances. This can be done by determining the average ages at which infants living under differing kinds of circumstances achieve given levels of development on the several scales. If, for instance, one wishes to determine the effects of given circumstances on the development of object permanence, one can present the appropriate eliciting situations and observe which infants reach for and find a desired object that is partially covered; which infants reach for and find a desired object completely covered by a single screen; and which find a desired object completely covered by several screens. Success with finding a desired object completely covered by a single screen and failure to find it when covered with several constitutes a level of development of object permanence and these actions have direct functional significance. Their interpretation does not depend upon the rank of an individual's score in the scores from some group nor upon a rough correlation with age. The critical actions mark levels of psychological development and permit one to make repeated testings at regular intervals, and then to compare groups of infants in terms of the distribution of ages at which they achieve a given landmark, and to relate the means and dispersions of age for the groups of infants studied to the characteristics of the environmental circumstances under which they are being reared.

In a similar fashion, one can assess the development-fostering capacity of differing kinds of circumstances by comparing the time required by infants living under these differing circumstances to move from one landmark of psychological development to another. Thus, again, in the concrete case of object permanence, one can compare the times required for infants to move from finding a desired object completely covered by one screen to finding a desired object which is hidden by means of a single invisible displacement. Again the method can be based on repeated testings at regular intervals and on an evaluation of the actions of the infants at each testing.

Such uses are independent of any conventional standardization. Yet, although it would be a tremendous task, conventional standardization is entirely feasible. It would be feasible, for instance, to have distributions of ages for infants in representative samples of the population for the achievement of each landmark of the several scales. If, as we guess, great plasticity exists in the ages at which infants achieve these various landmarks according to the environmental circumstances which they encounter, however, it is doubtful if such conventional standardization will ever be of much value.

Nevertheless, because of their provisional character, these scales and the approach to the assessment of development which they reflect should themselves become subjects of further investigation.

Part
III

Arranging the Eliciting Situations
and Recording the Critical Actions
for the Various Steps
in Each of the Scales

CHAPTER 10

General Directions and Description of Materials

A number of considerations enter into arranging the examination situation for infants of different ages. Certain conditions must prevail throughout the examination of all infants and may be attained in various ways, depending on the age and mood of the infant. Those conditions apply to all the various scales and eliciting situations. Other considerations are more applicable to particular types of eliciting situations. Directions for establishing these more general conditions, and descriptions of the materials to be used in arranging the eliciting situations are the subject matter of this chapter.

1. With young infants, the administration of these scales is feasible and valid only when the infant is fully cooperative. Therefore, it is best to pick a time for presenting the eliciting situations when the infant is neither hungry nor sleepy nor wet, and is or would be expected to be engaged in play activities anyway. Infants under one year can be expected to cooperate under these circumstances for about 30 to 40 minutes, while infants over a year can be expected to cooperate for about one hour.

2. Sometimes an infant is disturbed by the fact that the examiner is a stranger. This occurs most often with home-reared infants at about six months of age and again at about eighteen months of age. In such a case, it is best not to approach the infant directly and not to try to overcome the reticence forcefully. The younger infants normally overcome their concern over the examiner's presence in a few minutes if allowed to stay close to their mothers, and the presentation of the

eliciting situations may be undertaken in the usual manner. The few older infants who become disturbed over a stranger's presence may take considerably longer to become accustomed to the examiner. It is very important not to create an unusual situation by silently watching the infant and waiting for him to overcome his shyness. If the examiner carries on a conversation with the infant's mother, stays at a distance from the infant, and really pays very little attention to him while allowing him to get used to the examiner's presence, the infant frequently begins to look for some object to play with; then, he may accept a toy offered by the examiner. In such circumstances, it is desirable to start with a situation which does not demand too much interaction with the examiner. Once the infant becomes involved in playing with the toys, the reluctance to interact with the examiner usually vanishes.

3. To increase the likelihood of maximal cooperation on the part of the infant, it is desirable to present the eliciting situations in a room in the infant's home or in a testing room equipped to resemble a living room, in which the infant could be allowed to move around, but which would not contain too many distractions. A table, several chairs, a sofa, or an arm chair, a high chair which comes up flush to the table, an infant seat for young infants, and a rug to cover at least a part of the floor in the room facilitate presentation of the eliciting situations. Unneeded toys or other children frequently become distractions.

4. There is no need to present the six scales in a single session or in sequence. On the contrary, it may be desirable to intermingle the situations from several scales in order to keep the infant's interest and attention. The infant may be given a chance to engage in play activities of his own in between eliciting situations for the same reason. If an infant does not cooperate in a situation of a particular type (e.g., imitation or search), a different activity should be interposed, and the remaining situations of the same type should be presented at a later time.

5. Certain toys are suggested for each situation. However, these suggestions are meant to serve only as guides. If an infant shows no interest in the particular toy suggested, another may and should be substituted; otherwise, a lack of response may indicate merely a lack of interest. Toys which are not being used in a particular situation should be removed from the infant's sight. It is generally better to

offer the infant a new toy or object before attempting to store away the one used previously.

6. The directions for each situation state that it should be repeated a given number of times. These instructions should serve only as suggestions to the examiner. It is much more important that the range of an infant's actions in each situation would be clear to the examiner than that it would be repeated a specific number of times. Therefore, whenever the implications of an infant's behavior in any situation are equivocal, the situation should be repeated either immediately or at a later time, even when the directions do not call for a repetition.

7. As suggested in Chapter 9, one need not make use of all the scales. While for many purposes it may be desirable to present all of the situations constituting a particular scale, it is perfectly sensible (given the ordinal nature of these scales) to use specified steps in particular scales to investigate the effects of given kinds of circumstances on development. It is always necessary, however, to ascertain the infant's level of development by presenting situations appropriate for eliciting the critical actions for several consecutive steps on the scale. One identifies a given level of development in a given branch by observing the infant act in a way that allows inferring the achievement of a particular step, and then, observing the infant act in a way which indicates the lack of achievement of the next several steps in the same scale.

8. The specific directions for arranging the eliciting situations appropriate for each step are given separately for each of the scales in Chapters 11 through 16. These directions specify: (1) the position of the infant and the nature of the physical space around the infant, helpful in presenting the situation; (2) the object or objects suggested for use in the situation; (3) the instructions for actions to be carried out by the examiner; (4) the suggested number of times the situation is to be repeated; and (5) the various actions an infant may be expected to show in the situation. Our experience suggests that pairs of observers achieve higher reliability when they are alerted to the kinds of infant actions that may be expected in each situation. Infants being reared in other cultures or in settings other than homes may well exhibit actions not listed. If the full range of actions in each situation is under investigation, a place for noting *others* should be provided in the record. Specific considerations pertinent to the setting up

of each particular situation or to observing the infant's actions in it are given in the form of a note to the examiner in addition to directions in the usual format.

The situations are generally listed in the order of the steps in each scale. However, there is no one-to-one correspondence between situations and scale steps; infant actions shown in a number of situations are relevant for more than one step. Although the order of presentation for these situations may be varied, it is desirable or at least convenient to present certain situations in sequence. These situations are grouped together under identifying headings marked by capital letters. All situations appropriate for each scale are numbered consecutively, irrespective of such groupings.

The letters before the descriptions of infant actions which are considered critical for inferring the achievement of a step in each scale are in italics. Those actions which have been used to judge the level of an infant's development for the scaling analyses of this investigation are marked with an asterisk. It is possible that other infant actions may be observed regularly and appear to belong in a particular sequence; however, if these actions were not considered critical for the steps delineated in the present study, they are not italicized or marked with an asterisk.

9. Sample *examination record forms* for each scale are given in Chapter 17. Each record form may be simplified or expanded, depending on the use that is to be made of the information obtained. For example, if the results are not to be used to study the range of behaviors in a particular situation, or their orderly change during development, only two categories of infant actions may need to be designated: the critical action category and one for recording all other behaviors. On the other hand, if the infant's range of behaviors is to be the focus of the study, the record form may need to be expanded to allow recording of all the actions shown during each presentation of the situation, their sequence, possibly their duration, and so forth. Investigators may also wish to vary the extent to which the instructions to the examiner are reproduced on the record form.

10. Sample *summary record forms* for each of the scales are also given in Chapter 17. These forms list the sequence of steps which were scaled in phase III of the present study (described in Chapter 8) and

are meant to allow a quick evaluation of the level of development achieved by an infant.

11. A list and description of materials needed to present the eliciting situations follows.

SUGGESTED MATERIALS

1. **Aluminum Foil** Pieces 4 x 6 inches in size, of commercially sold aluminum wrapping foil.
2. **Ball** Colorful child's ball about 4 inches in diameter.
3. **Bell** A small, brass bell, with a handle, about 2 inches in diameter and 4 inches high and making a clear sound.
4. **Blocks** Ten one-inch-square wooden blocks, usually sold commercially with letters or numbers painted on them in different colors.
5. **Bottle** A commercially sold baby bottle of whitish plastic.
6. **Box** A plain cardboard box, about 5 x 4 inches and 4 inches deep. The box is completely unimportant in itself as long as it is not attractive to the infant, is big enough to make a small toy invisible when it is lowered into the box, and is still small enough so that it can be turned over while completely covered by one of the screens.
7. **Car** A small red car or truck (about 5 inches long) which can be operated by friction.
8. **Cardboard** A piece of neutral-colored heavy cardboard, 6 x 8 inches in size, to be used to construct an incline.
9. **Checkerboards** Two 4-x-4–inch cards with half-inch checkered squares taped on with plastic tape, yellow and red on one, and yellow and blue on the other.
10. **Container** A tall container (about 6 inches high), narrow at the bottom and widening at the top, made of unbreakable material, such as plastic. It is im-

portant that it would be unsteady enough so that a piece of the necklace draped over its rim would topple it.

11. **Cotton**   A ball of cotton as sold commercially.

12. **Cup**   A regular plastic drinking cup (3 inches high) with a handle, and pale in color.

13. **Doll**   Two different dolls: (a) a plastic baby doll, about 5 inches high, which does not squeak, and has eyes that close; (b) a miniature boy or girl doll, about 3 inches high, with a vinyl head and pliable arms and legs, dressed in appropriate clothes.

14. **Jumping Jack**   A 5-inch wooden toy with movable joints, in the shape of a man, a bird, or an animal, painted in bright colors and activated by pulling a string.

15. **Mechanical Toy** A 4-to-6–inch toy in the shape of an animal (duck, bunny, squirrel) that moves on the floor in a characteristic way when wound by an unobtrusively located key.

16. **Multicolored Ring**   A brightly colored ring made up of about 16 plastic snap-together beads, each about 2 inches long, of several shapes and colors.

17. **Musical Clown** A roly-poly toy in the shape of a clown that makes a musical sound when shaken. It consists of a ball, about 5 inches in diameter, topped by a smaller ball with the features of a face and a hat. It is weighted to return to an upright position when pushed from side to side.

18. **Musical Rattle** A colorful plastic cylinder, about 4 inches high, attached to a slender handle, which makes a musical sound when moved.

19. **Necklace**   A long single-stranded necklace made of fairly small, shiny, pale-color beads with several larger, darker beads interspersed at 3-inch intervals. The necklace should be at least 32 inches long so that it would easily go over the head of the infant. It is extremely important that the

string used would be very strong and that the beads would be made of hardy material, *not* glass, so that they could not be broken and swallowed by an infant.

20. **Pillow** A square 12-x-12–inch decorator pillow, covered with corduroy or some other sturdy material, and neutral in color (rust, olive, mustard) so that it would not be attractive in itself.

21. **Pinwheel** A plastic brightly colored pinwheel about 4 inches in diameter attached to a rod.

22. **Plastic Animals** Several kinds of plastic animals: (a) a 5-inch animal (fish, duck) made of soft vinyl in white or yellow, making a sound when squeezed; (b) a 5- or 6-inch animal (duck, porpoise) made of hard vinyl designed to be a floating bathroom toy and, thus, with a flat, undecorated bottom side; (c) several 2-inch animals (cow, dog, lamb, horse) made of hard vinyl, sold commercially in farm animal sets.

23. **Plastic Flower** Commercially sold artificial flower blossom, 2 inches in diameter.

24. **Pull-Toy** A wooden toy on wheels, in the shape of an animal, about 5 inches high, designed to be pulled along by a toddler.

25. **Rattle** A small plastic baby rattle, with two round balls at each end and a slender, easy-to-grasp center.

26. **Screens** Several pieces of cloth used to cover objects. It is important for them to be unattractive in themselves, nontransparent, and large enough to be bunched over the object covered in a fashion which completely avoids revealing its shape. An 18-x-18–inch white scarf, a similar piece of cotton material in a small print, and one in a drab color are appropriate.

27. **Shoe** A white doll's shoe made of rubber, about 2 inches long, with a strap.

28. **Slinky** A coiled wire toy which flips over on a step.

29. **Spool**   A wooden spool with the thread taken off, with a stripe painted around the center in red.

30. **Stacking Rings**   A set of five flat plastic rings of equal size (about 2¾ inches in diameter and about 1 inch thick) that fit over a rod which is 6 inches long and unconnected to anything. Each of the rings used is of a different color. One of the rings is made solid by taping over its hole with tape of the same color, after stuffing it with cotton.

31. **Stick**   A round, wooden dowel, about 18 inches long.

32. **String**   Seven feet of strong wrapping string.

33. **Stuffed Animal** Two different-sized toys: (a) a furry, stuffed animal (dog or cat) in a sitting position, about 4 inches high; (b) a smaller, also furry animal in an upright position, about 2 inches high.

34. **Walking Toy**   A plastic weighted animal (dog, cat) about 2 ½ inches high, designed to move by itself on an incline.

CHAPTER 11

Scale I: The Development of Visual Pursuit and the Permanence of Objects

A. VISUAL PURSUIT OF SLOWLY MOVING OBJECTS

✓ 1. FOLLOWING A SLOWLY MOVING OBJECT THROUGH A 180° ARC

Location: The infant may be supine on a flat surface, in an infant seat, or sitting up by himself.

Object: Any bright object that attracts the infant's attention, but does not make a sound when moved, e.g., the multicolored ring.

Directions: Hold the object about 10 inches in front of the infant's eyes, until he focuses on it. With a young infant it may be necessary to shake the object lightly in order to attract attention or to vary its distance from the infant's eyes, to find the optimal focal distance. If an older infant tends to focus on the examiner rather than on the object, stand behind the infant. Once the infant has focused on the object, move it slowly through a lateral arc of 180°.

Repeat: 3–4 times.

Infant Actions: a. Does not follow object.
                     b. Follows object through part of arc with jerky accommodations.
                     c. Follows object through part of arc, with smooth accommodations.
                   *d. Follows object through the complete arc smoothly.[1]

2. NOTICING THE DISAPPEARANCE OF A SLOWLY MOVING OBJECT

Location: Same as in situation 1, but not on the floor.
Object: Same as in situation 1.
Directions: Once the infant has focused on the object, move it slowly to one side and away from the infant, making it disappear below the edge of the infant's seat or the surface on which he is placed. After a few moments, bring the object back in front and slightly above the infant's eyes from the opposite side (i.e., move the object behind the infant). Always move the object in the same direction and have it disappear at the same point.
Repeat: 3–4 times.
Infant Actions: a. Does not follow object to point of disappearance.
                     b. Loses interest as soon as object disappears (eyes begin to wander and then focus on any interesting object within view).
                   *c. Lingers with glance at the point where the object has disappeared.
                   *d. After several presentations, returns glance to the starting point or the point of reappearance (slightly above normal eye level) before the object has reappeared.
                     e. Searches with eyes around the point where the object has disappeared.[2]

[1] As noted on p. 146, an italic letter before the description of an infant action indicates that the action is considered critical for achievement of a step in the scale. An asterisk indicates an action which has been used to judge the level of an infant's development for the scaling analyses of this investigation.

[2] This action appeared too seldom to be included in the scaling analysis so the asterisk

Note: If a tendency of the infant to move the head to one side and to keep it there is suspected in the course of the presentation, repeat the whole procedure at a later time, making the object disappear on the opposite side.

B. SEARCH FOR SIMPLY HIDDEN OBJECTS

3. FINDING AN OBJECT WHICH IS PARTIALLY COVERED

Location: The infant must be in a sitting position with both hands free to manipulate objects. A young infant may be propped up in an infant seat or on a sofa using pillows. An older infant may be seated in a high chair or on a rug on the floor. A working surface must be available in front of and to the side of the infant; it may be provided by placing a board across the infant seat, by pushing the high chair against a table, or by using the rug-covered space around the infant, if he is sitting on the floor. An infant feeding-table is also suitable.

Object: Any object which the infant demonstrates interest in by reaching for it; and, for a cover or screen, a white nontransparent scarf. It is important that the object be unitary, and that no portion of the object should look equivalent to the whole. A plastic doll or animal may be used, but an object such as a necklace would be unsuitable. Use of a white non-transparent scarf for the screen helps to minimize the interest of infants in the screen.

Directions: To ascertain that an infant desires the object, place it on the surface and observe that the infant reaches for it. Take the object, while making sure the infant is focusing on it, place it on the surface within his

is omitted even though "searching with the eyes around the point where the object disappeared" may appear to be equivalent to a "lingering of the glance" in implying the beginnings of object permanence. The term "searching" is an interpretation. It implies movement of the eyes, and the meaning of such motion in this situation is still empirically unclear.

reach, and cover it with the screen in such a way that a small portion of the object remains visible (the feet of the doll, the tail of the animal, etc.). If, in his attempts to obtain the object, the infant covers it up completely, start a new presentation. If the infant's interest in the object becomes doubtful, interpose a presentation in which the object is left uncovered on the surface to determine if he will still reach for it.

Repeat: 3 times.
Infant Actions: a. Loses interest in the object once it is partially covered.

b. Reacts to the loss of the object, but does not reach for it and does not obtain it once it is partially covered.

*c. Obtains the object by pulling it out from under the screen or by removing the screen and picking up the object.

4. FINDING AN OBJECT WHICH IS COMPLETELY COVERED

Location: Same as in situation 3.
Object: Any object in which the infant shows a strong interest and which is small enough to be completely covered by each of the screens without bulging too conspicuously may be used. A necklace has been very popular, but a small doll, car, and plastic flower have also been used. Use the same white, nontransparent scarf used in situation 3 as the screen.
Directions: Ascertain that the infant desires the object by holding it out to him and observing whether he reaches for it. If the infant starts to reach for the object, place it on the surface within his reach and cover it completely with a screen, before the infant grasps the object. Do not stretch the scarf flat, but bunch it up so that the contours of the object do not show through the screen. If the infant succeeds in obtaining the object on the first presentation, shift the work

area to one side of the infant (left or right) and make all subsequent presentations on the same side. It is important here to differentiate the search for the hidden object from pulling at the screen out of a desire to play with the screen itself. In general, if the infant has demonstrated a desire for the object before it was hidden and reaches for it either while lifting the screen or immediately afterwards, one may assume that the infant is searching for the hidden object. On the other hand, if the infant lifts the screen and holds it for a considerable length of time before reaching for the now exposed object, possibly even looking at and handling the screen, one may assume that the infant has lifted the screen for its own sake.

Repeat: 3 times.

Infant Actions: a. Loses interest in the object once it is completely covered.
                b. Reacts to the loss of the object, but does not search or obtain it from under the screen.
                c. Pulls the screen, but not enough to uncover the object, and does not obtain the object.
               *d. Pulls the screen off and obtains the object.

5. FINDING AN OBJECT WHICH IS COMPLETELY COVERED WITH A SINGLE SCREEN IN TWO PLACES

Location: Same as in situation 3. It is important to work on a sound-absorbing surface or to use a soft toy so that the noise created in putting the object down does not serve as an additional clue to the object's location.

Object: Same as in situation 3. Use as the second screen a piece of nontransparent cloth of a dull color different from that of the scarf.

Directions: If the infant obtains the object covered by a single screen on two successive presentations, place the second screen on the opposite side of the infant during the last covering of the object with the first screen, making sure both screens are within the infant's reach. Then, hide the object in the same manner under the second screen. Make sure that both screens are bunched rather than flat. To repeat the presentation, hide the object under the second screen two more times, and then switch to hiding the object under the first screen, counting the last hiding as the second presentation of this situation.

Repeat:			2 times.

Infant Actions:		a. Loses interest in the object once it is hidden under the second screen.

			b. Searches for the object where it was previously found, i.e., under the first screen on the first presentation.

			c. Searches for the object where it disappeared, i.e., under the second screen, on the first presentation.[3]

6. Finding an object which is completely covered with a single screen in two places alternately

Location:		Same as in situation 5.

Object:			Same as in situation 5.

Directions:		Hide the object under each of the two screens alternately, covering the object completely with the screen each time.

Repeat:			3–5 times.

Infant Actions:		a. Becomes perplexed and loses interest in the object.

			b. Searches haphazardly under one or both screens.

			*c. Searches correctly under each of the screens.

---

[3] Action *c* carries no asterisk here because the actions in this situation were not included in the scaling analysis. They are included here intuitively. Even though this situation may elicit actions which duplicate those in Situation 6, this situation would appear to put somewhat lesser demands on flexibility in dissociating objects from actions previously directed at them.

7. Finding an Object Which Is Completely Covered with a Single Screen in Three Places

Location: Same as in situation 5.

Object: Same as in situation 5. Use the pillow or a third non-transparent cloth, discriminable from the other two, as the third screen and place it directly in front of the infant, within his reach.

Directions: Hide the object under each of the three screens, selecting the screen to be used on each presentation at random.

(Sample order: 2d, 1st, 3d, 1st, 1st, 3d, 2d)

Repeat: 5–7 times.

Infant Actions: a. Loses interest in the object.

b. Searches haphazardly under some or all screens.

*c. Searches directly under the screen where the object disappeared.

Note: In most cases, it is best to present situations 3–7 in succession. It is extremely important that the infant have a strong interest in the object chosen for these situations. It is permissible to change objects at any point, but it should be recognized that loss of interest may also signify that the task is becoming too difficult.

If the examiner suspects that the infant is losing interest due to the difficulty of the task, the same object should be hidden in a simpler way (i.e., a way that the infant was previously able to handle) to see whether the infant will then search for the object. If the infant is still interested in the object, he will usually search for it in the easier situation.

The constant disappearance of a desired object often proves frustrating to young infants. When it seems that the loss of interest in the situation may be due to frustration, the infant may be permitted to play with the object for a short while without interference in an attempt to restore his cooperation and his interest in it. On the other hand, if the need to relinquish the object after each trial appears to be causing frustration, it is best to pick up the object as soon as the infant removes the screen and is reaching for it, without permitting the infant actually to hold the object each time.

Since these situations are presented to infants varying considerably in age, certain adjustments in procedure are helpful with younger and older infants. The younger infants tend to become frustrated, and it is necessary to check their interest in the object being used as well as their attention to the task. Conversely, older infants tend to become bored with the simple hidings, and, if this basis for their behavior is clear, it is often desirable to cut the number of presentations of the simple hidings to a minimum required for assurance of competence in order to prolong their cooperation. The cooperation of older infants may also be secured by helping them see the situations as a game and by permitting them a turn at hiding the object, if they so desire.

C. SEARCH FOLLOWING MORE COMPLEX HIDING

8. FINDING AN OBJECT AFTER SUCCESSIVE VISIBLE DISPLACEMENTS

Location:　　　　　Same as in situation 5.

Object:　　　　　　Same as in situation 7.

Directions:　　　　Hide the object successively under each of the three screens located around the infant by moving the hand holding the toy in a path from left to right or from right to left so that the object becomes hidden under one of the screens, then reappears in the space between the screens, and again becomes hidden as the hand passes under another screen. Make sure the infant attends to the complete hiding procedure, the complete series of object appearances and disappearances. Check for position preference by reversing the direction of hiding after a few presentations. Check for screen preference by changing positions of particular screens after a few presentations.

Repeat:　　　　　　3–5 times.

Infant Actions:　　a. Does not follow the successive hidings.

　　　　　　　　　b. Searches only under the first screen under which the object disappeared.

　　　　　　　　　c. Searches under the screen where the object was found on the previous presentation.

    d. Searches under all screens haphazardly.

    e. Searches under all screens in the order of hiding.

    f. Searches directly under the last screen in the path (the one under which the object disappeared last).[4]

Note: If the infant fails to attend to the whole series of successive hidings, he may have to be moved back from the screens during the hiding and then moved closer again to within reach of the screens once the hiding is completed.

9. FINDING AN OBJECT UNDER THREE SUPERIMPOSED SCREENS

Location: Same as in situation 5.

Object: Same as in situation 7.

Directions: Ascertain that the infant is interested in the object and place it in front of him within his reach. Cover the object with one screen, then take a second screen and cover the first screen with the second, and so on. Arrange the screens in such a way that the infant cannot remove all of them with one swipe (e.g., use the pillow as the middle screen).

Repeat: 2–3 times.

Infant Actions: a. Loses interest in the object.

                b. Lifts one or two screens, but gives up before finding the object.

           *c. Removes all screens and finds the hidden object.

Note: When multiple screens are used, an infant sometimes begins to pull all screens in sight without paying much attention to the displacements of the object. The examiner may check for this by going through the hiding procedures and retaining the object so that it is clearly visible to the infant, instead of leaving it under a screen. If the infant still persists in searching under screens, his behavior is no longer a valid indication of his construct of the object which is here of interest to the examiner. In such an instance, it is desirable to interrupt the

[4] Actions (e) and (f) in this situation carry no asterisks because there were too few to be included in the scaling analysis. These actions may point to more than one step between steps 7 and 9 which may reflect increasing flexibility in the spatial localization of the object constructs as well as greater persistence of the central processes representing the objects.

presentation of this sequence and to intersperse other activities or a period of free play. In general, it may be advisable to introduce a break after each group of situations in order to minimize the occurrence of indiscriminate removal of all screens.

D. SEARCH FOLLOWING AN INVISIBLE DISPLACEMENT

10. FINDING AN OBJECT FOLLOWING ONE INVISIBLE DISPLACEMENT WITH A SINGLE SCREEN

Location: Same as in situation 5.

Object: Use a small object which would readily fit into the box to be used to hide the object in order to produce the invisible displacement (e.g., miniature doll, small stuffed animal, small car, etc.). Use a cardboard box, without a cover, which is deep enough to make the object invisible to the infant once it is lowered into it. Use as a screen a piece of nontransparent cloth which is large enough to allow the examiner to invert the box under it without exposing the object.

Directions: While the infant watches, lower the object into the box and then hide the box under the screen. Turn the box over under the screen, leaving the object hidden, and remove the empty box. If the infant hesitates, show him that the box is empty. If the infant appears to lose interest in the object, check on the difficulty of the task by hiding the same object under the screen directly.

Repeat: 3 times.

Infant Actions: a. Loses interest in the object.
                  b. Reacts to the loss of the object, but does not search for it.
                  c. Searches only in the box for the hidden object.
                 *d. Checks the box and proceeds to find the object under the screen where the box disappeared.
                 *e. Searches for the object directly under the screen where the box disappeared.

11. FINDING AN OBJECT FOLLOWING ONE INVISIBLE DISPLACEMENT WITH
    TWO SCREENS

Location: Same as in situation 5.
Object: Same as in situation 10. Use as the second screen
                 another piece of cloth differing from the first in
                 either color or pattern.
Directions: Place the second screen to the side of the infant op-
                 posite to that of the first during the last presentation
                 of situation 10. Hide the object in the same manner
                 (using the box to produce the invisible displace-
                 ment) under the second screen. To repeat the
                 presentation, hide the object under the second screen
                 two more times and then switch to hiding the ob-
                 ject under the first screen, counting this last hiding
                 as a second presentation of the situation.
Repeat: 2 times.
Infant Actions: a. Searches only in the box.
                  b. Searches under the screen where the object was
                     previously found.
                 *c. Searches correctly under the screen where the
                     box disappeared.

12. FINDING AN OBJECT FOLLOWING ONE INVISIBLE DISPLACEMENT WITH
    TWO SCREENS ALTERNATED

Location: Same as in situation 5.
Object: Same as in situation 10.
Directions: Hide the object, using the box to produce the in-
                 visible displacement, under one of the two screens,
                 alternating on each presentation. Place the empty
                 box in the center between the two screens.
Repeat: 3 times.
Infant Actions: a. Loses interest in the object.
                  b. Searches haphazardly under the two screens.
                 *c. Searches directly under the screen where the
                     box disappeared.

13. FINDING AN OBJECT FOLLOWING ONE INVISIBLE DISPLACEMENT WITH THREE SCREENS

Location: Same as in situation 5.
Object: Same as in situation 10. Use as the third screen the pillow or an obviously different piece of cloth. Place it to the other side of the first screen.
Directions: Using the box to create the invisible displacement by first lowering the object into it, make the box disappear under one of the three screens at random on each presentation, leaving the object hidden under the screen each time.
Repeat: 5–7 times.
Infant Actions: a. Loses interest in the object.
                 b. Searches haphazardly under all three screens.
                *c. Searches directly under the correct screen where the box disappeared.

E. SEARCH FOLLOWING SUCCESSIVE INVISIBLE DISPLACEMENTS

14. FINDING AN OBJECT FOLLOWING A SERIES OF INVISIBLE DISPLACEMENTS

Location: Same as in situation 5.
Object: Same as in situation 13. The object should be small enough to fit in the palm of the hand since it is more convenient to produce the invisible displacements by hiding the object in the palm of the hand.
Directions: While the infant watches, place the object in the palm of one hand and hide it by closing the hand. Move the hand in a path in one direction (e.g., from left to right), making the hand disappear under the first screen then reappear between the first and second screens, disappear again under the second screen, and so on. Do not open the hand between screens. Leave the object under the last screen in the

path and show the infant that the hand is empty.
Repeat the presentations by following the path in
the same direction each time.

Repeat: 4–6 times.

Infant Actions:
a. Searches only in the examiner's hand or around
the room.
b. Searches only under the first one or two screens
in the path and does not obtain the object.
*c. Searches under all screens in the path in the
same order as followed by the examiner's hand
and finds the object under the last screen.
*d. Searches directly under the last screen on at
least two successive presentations following success in finding the object there.

15. FINDING AN OBJECT FOLLOWING A SERIES OF INVISIBLE DISPLACE-
MENTS BY SEARCHING IN REVERSE OF THE ORDER OF HIDING

Note: Present this situation only to infants who search directly under
the last screen at least twice in situation 14, and only immediately subsequent to situation 14.

Location: Same as in situation 5.

Object: Same as in situation 14.

Directions:
Immediately following the presentation of situation
14, having established an expectation that the object is to be found under the last screen, move the
hand in which the object is hidden in the same manner *and in the same* direction as in situation 14, but
leave the object under the first screen in the path.
Continue the movement of the hand to the second
and third screen, then show the infant that it is
empty. In order to remember to stop momentarily
under the last screen, open the now empty hand
there also. This situation can be repeated only by
repeating situation 14 first, and then presenting the
"trick" of situation 15. To check for position preference, repeat situation 14 by moving the hand in
the opposite direction, thus making the screen which

was previously first, last. To check for preference for specific screens, rearrange the order of the screens in the path, without changing direction of hiding.

Repeat: 2 times.

Infant Actions:
    a. Searches only under the last screen and gives up.
    b. Searches haphazardly under all three screens.
   *c. Searches systematically from the last screen through the middle screen to the first, following an inverse of the order used in hiding.

Note: It is important in step 15 that the behavior of the infant imply clearly that he holds a reversible image of the whole series of places where the hand holding the object disappeared. Only if he goes to the middle screen in the reversed series without the object having been hidden there is such an image implied, for before such a reversible image has been developed, he may learn through experience to find the object under any of the three screens where he may already have found it.

CHAPTER 12

Scale II: The Development of Means for Obtaining Desired Environmental Events

A. DEVELOPMENT OF EYE-HAND COORDINATION

1. APPEARANCE OF HAND-WATCHING BEHAVIOR

Location: The infant may be supine on any flat surface such as the table or the sofa, or in his own crib. There should be no other visually attractive objects within sight.

Object: None.

Directions: Observe whether the infant engages in hand-watching activities, i.e., whether he attempts to keep his hands within view and follows them with his eyes as they move out of sight. Allow a few minutes for this observation. Supplement it with any evidence of hand-watching that may be observed during the rest of the examination.

Infant Actions: a. Hand-watching behavior is not observed.

*b. Hand-watching behavior is observed.

2. ACHIEVEMENT OF VISUALLY DIRECTED GRASPING

Location: The infant may be supine or propped up in a sitting position, as long as both arms are free to reach out.

Object: Use a small bright object such as a rattle. Make sure at least a portion of it is small enough for the infant's hand to close around.

Directions: Hold the object about 12 inches in front of the infant's face for at least 30 seconds. If the infant does not succeed in grasping the object, move it slowly toward the infant's hand, so that by following the object with his eyes he will come to see both the object and his hand at the same time. Hold the object a few inches from the infant's hand for at least 20 seconds.

Repeat: 3 times.

Infant Actions: a. Reaches toward the object, but does not grasp it.

*b. Grasps the object when both object *and* hand are in view simultaneously.

*c. Grasps the object when it is visually presented by bringing the hand up to contact the object.

d. Grasps the object when it is visually presented and opens the hand in anticipation of contact with the object.[1]

B. DEVELOPMENT IN DIFFERENTIATION OF MEANS AND ENDS

✓ 3. REPETITION OF ACTIONS PRODUCING AN INTERESTING RESULT

Location: Any position suitable for eliciting a "secondary circular reaction" from the infant, usually a sitting position in an infant seat or a high chair.

Object: An object which can be activated by one of the earliest motor schemes, such as hitting, and which provides visual and auditory input when so activated

[1] No asterisk is provided for this action because it was noted too infrequently and, thus, was not included in the scaling analysis. The investigations of B. L. White (1967) on visually directed reaching and grasping would clearly imply that opening the hand in anticipation of contact with the object should be a satisfactory criterion of success for the fourth step on this scale.

has been found to be most effective. For example, a
brightly colored musical toy in the shape of a clown,
a musical rattle in the shape of a cylinder attached to
a handle, and a set of multicolored discs on a chain
have been used with success.

Directions: The presentation of this situation depends on finding some object on which the infant will act and,
through his action, produce a result which he finds
interesting. After selecting such an object, hold it
within easy reach of the infant's preferred hand, but
in a way that discourages grasping (i.e., either the
part of the toy closest to the infant should be too
large for grasping or the toy should be held securely
at a height where it can be touched but not grasped).
If the infant does not contact the toy within 15
seconds, strike the toy against the infant's hand once,
allowing the infant to see that the toy moves and
makes a sound, then hold the toy in position again.

Repeat: 2 times.

Infant Actions: a. Shows interest in the object by looking at it.
b. Intensifies arm movements in the direction of
the object and activates it occasionally, but not
regularly.
*c. Repeats arm movements systematically and
keeps object active consistently.
d. Only tries to grasp object.

4. LETTING GO OF AN OBJECT IN ORDER TO REACH FOR ANOTHER

Location: The infant should be propped in a sitting position
or may sit in an infant seat or high chair, as long as
both arms remain free to reach out.

Object: Two small objects which the infant can hold, one
in each hand (e.g., small plastic animals, or blocks),
and a more desirable third object (e.g., a cookie, a
watch, etc.) are needed.

Directions: Get the infant to hold an object in each hand simultaneously by offering the two objects, one to each

hand if necessary. Once the infant has both hands full, quickly offer a third attractive object by holding it up in front of the infant, barely within his reach. The infant may accidentally drop one of the objects he holds. It is necessary to observe his actions closely and to repeat the situation until it becomes clear that the infant regularly and purposefully releases one of the objects to free his hand to reach for the more attractive one.

Repeat: 3 times.

Infant Actions: a. Reaches toward the third object while still holding the others in his hands.

b. Reaches for the third object with a filled hand, but in the process of reaching, the first object slips out from the hand.

*c. Drops one of the objects he already holds and *then* reaches for the third object with an empty hand.

5. USE OF LOCOMOTION AS MEANS

Location: It is easiest to present this situation if the infant is seated on the floor, but it may be presented anyplace where the infant is free to crawl or move about.

Object: Several pairs of objects which are often used jointly in play, e.g., blocks and cup, spoon and cup, doll and shoe, and so forth are needed.

Directions: Present the objects to the infant and wait for him to begin using them in play. If the infant does not start any play using several of the objects, demonstrate an activity such as dropping blocks into the cup. Once the infant is actively engaged in such play, remove the most necessary object for the play (e.g., the cup) and place it to the side of the infant, out of reach, yet still visible to him. If the infant appears to treat the removal of the object as prohibition, it may be necessary to encourage him to go

.after the object and then to present the situation again at a later time.

Repeat: 2 times.

Infant Actions: a. Continues play and makes no attempt to re-
                   trieve the object.

                   b. Indicates desire for the object (looks at it re-
                   peatedly, whimpers), but does not try to re-
                   trieve it.

                   *c. Moves to regain the object and resumes play
                   using it.

C. DEVELOPMENT IN THE USE OF OBJECTS AND THE RELATIONSHIPS BETWEEN OBJECTS AS MEANS

6. USE OF THE RELATIONSHIP OF SUPPORT

Location: It is easiest to present this situation if the infant is
                   seated in a high chair which comes flush against the
                   table. However, it may be presented with the infant
                   seated anywhere, as long as he can be restrained
                   from moving and can have a working surface ex-
                   tending well beyond his reach.

Object: Any object in which the infant shows a strong in-
                   terest (e.g., stuffed animal, doll) and a larger ob-
                   ject, such as a pillow, to act as its support.

Directions: Interest the infant in an object and, while he is play-
                   ing with it, place the support barely within the in-
                   fant's reach. Take the object from the infant and
                   place it on the center of the support, thus making it
                   beyond the infant's reach. Encourage the infant to
                   obtain the object, but do not allow the infant to
                   climb out of the chair. If the pillow is used as sup-
                   port, point a corner of the pillow toward the infant,
                   making the pillow easier to grasp. Wait at least 20
                   seconds. Repeat by taking the object off the sup-
                   port and, after ascertaining the infant's continued

interest (usually indicated by reaching), replace the object on the support. If the infant still does not attempt to grasp and pull the support, demonstrate the fact that the object moves with the support by pushing the support a short distance toward the infant and then pulling it back twice. Encourage the infant again to get the object.

Repeat: 2 times.

Infant Actions: a. Reaches for the object on the support and indicates desire for it.

                 b. Tries to climb out and, thus, to reach the object.

                 c. Appeals to another person to get the object for him.

            *d. Pulls the support and obtains the object after demonstration.

            *e. Pulls the support and obtains the object without demonstration.

7. Understanding of the relationship of support

Location: Same as in situation 6.

Object: Same as in situation 6.

Directions: *If the infant obtains the object by pulling the support in situation 6*, either at once or after the demonstration, repeat the presentation once more, but instead of placing the object on the support, hold it about 4 inches above it. Hold the object from behind, so that your hand would not obscure it for the infant.

Repeat: 1–2 times.

Infant Actions: a. Pulls the support expecting to obtain the object.

                 b. Pulls the support while reaching for the object and looking at it and/or the examiner.

            *c. Does not pull the support, but points, reaches, or looks at the object, or asks the examiner to give it to him or to put it down upon the support.

8. Use of string horizontally

Location:	Same as in situation 6.
Object:	Any toy in which the infant shows a strong interest (e.g., stuffed animal, doll) and some sturdy string.
Directions:	Once the infant has demonstrated interest in an object, tie one end of the string securely around it. Place the object way beyond the infant's reach (2–3 feet away) although in full view, and extend the other end of the string toward the infant's hands. Encourage him to get the object, but do not allow the infant to climb toward it. Wait at least 20 seconds. Repeat by picking up the object, bringing it closer to the infant in order to ascertain his interest in it, and then returning it to the out-of-reach position. If the infant still does not use the string to obtain the object, demonstrate by pulling the string, making the object move closer to the infant, pushing it back, pulling the string again, and so forth, two to three times. Encourage the infant again to get the object.
Repeat:	2 times.
Infant Actions:	a. Reaches for the object and indicates desire for it.
	b. Manipulates the string, but does not pull it enough to obtain the object.
	*c. Obtains the object by pulling the string after demonstration.
	*d. Obtains the object by pulling the string without demonstration.

9. Use of string vertically

Location:	Same as in situation 6.
Object:	Same as in situation 6.
Directions:	With one end of the string tied around the object, slowly lower it to the floor on one side of the infant's chair, calling the infant's attention to the

process. Locate the object on the floor so that it is visible to the infant, if he leans down to look for it. Extend the other end of the string up to the infant's hands, draping it across his chair in front of him. Encourage the infant to obtain the object. Wait about 20 seconds. Repeat by lifting the object to the level of the table and, after ascertaining that the infant still desires the object (usually indicated by reaching for it as it gets closer), lower it again as before. If the infant still does not use the string to obtain the object, demonstrate by slowly lifting the object to the level of the infant's hands by means of the string and then lowering it to the floor several times.

Repeat: 2–3 times.
Infant Actions: a. Indicates desire for object by leaning to look at it, reaching toward it, and so on, but does not use the string to obtain it.
        b. Drops string to the floor and becomes unhappy.
        c. Plays with the string itself.
        d. Pulls the string, but not sufficiently to get the object.
     *e. Obtains the object by pulling the string after demonstration.
     *f. Obtains the object by pulling the string without demonstration.

10. Use of stick as means

Location: Same as in situation 6.
Object: Any toy in which the infant shows a strong interest (e.g., stuffed animal, doll) and a stick.
Directions: Place the object in which the infant is interested on the table, out of the infant's reach, and place near the infant's hand a stick which is long enough to reach behind the object and bring it toward him. Encourage the infant to obtain the object. If the infant fails to notice it, call attention to the stick.

Wait at least 20 seconds. Repeat by picking up the object, ascertaining the infant's interest in it, and returning it to the out-of-reach position. If the infant fails to use the stick to obtain the object, demonstrate the use of the stick by taking the stick and using it to push the object closer to the infant and back again several times. Place the stick next to the infant's hands again.

Repeat: 2 times:

Infant Actions:
    a. Plays with stick and loses interest in the object.
    b. Reaches for or attempts to climb toward object, disregarding the stick.
    c. Plays with stick and object, without getting the object any closer (hits object with stick, knocks it off table, etc.).
  *d. Obtains the object by means of the stick after demonstration.
  *e. Obtains the object by means of the stick without demonstration.

D. FORESIGHTFUL PROBLEM SOLVING

11. FORESIGHT IN THE PROBLEM OF THE NECKLACE AND THE CONTAINER

Location: Have the infant seated on the floor, in a chair, or at a feeding table, with working surface available around him.

Object: Use a long necklace (item 19 in Chapter 10) of small, shiny beads, to maximize its attractiveness to the infant, and a tall, narrow container. The problem is created by the length of the necklace and the unsteadiness of the container due to its dimensions.

Directions: Present the infant with the necklace all stretched out and with the container placed next to the necklace. If the infant does not spontaneously attempt to place the necklace into the container, take both swiftly away, put the necklace inside the container behind your back, and show the infant the spectacle of the beads inside the container. If the infant appears interested, remove the necklace from the container and present both to the infant as before. Encourage the infant verbally, if it seems necessary, and carefully note how the infant goes about trying to get the necklace into the container.

Repeat: 2–4 times.

Infant Actions:
a. Does not attempt to put the necklace into the container even after demonstration.
b. Attempts to put in the necklace piece by piece without holding the container steady and fails.
c. Succeeds in putting the necklace in after several attempts resulting in failure.
d. Invents a method which takes into account the unsteadiness of the container after a previous failure (one or two), such as holding the container with one hand while stuffing in the necklace, and succeeds in putting the necklace in on subsequent attempts.[2]
*e. Adopts a method which takes into account the unsteadiness of the container from the first attempt, such as rolling the necklace up before trying to put it in, dangling it in, and so on.

12. Foresight in the Problem of the Solid Ring

Location: Same as in situation 11.

Object: Use a set of plastic rings which can be stacked on an unmounted rod, one of the rings having been made solid by filling the hole.

Directions: Spread the rings in front of the infant. Place the solid ring in a position where it is unlikely to be picked up first, in order not to discourage the infant. Take the rod and slip one ring over it. Encourage

[2] No asterisk is provided for this action because it was not included in the scaling analysis. It may reflect the invention of an appropriate means through repeated experimentation and thereby point to an additional step in this scale.

the infant to stack the remaining rings. If necessary, hold the bottom of the rod to make it steady for the infant, since the infant's manual dexterity is not at issue. If the solid ring remains as the last one and the infant does not stack it spontaneously, do *not* suggest that he stack it. Instead, remove all the rings and repeat the presentation, maneuvering the solid ring into a position closer to the infant's hands, so that it has a high probability of being picked up, if the infant is going to stack it, and has to be deliberately avoided, if he is not.

Repeat: 2–3 times.

Infant Actions:
   a. Plays with rings, but does not stack them.
   b. Uses force in his attempts to stack the solid ring and attempts to stack it repeatedly.
   c. Attempts to stack the solid ring once and avoids it subsequently.[3]
  *d. Sets aside the solid ring without attempting to stack it.

[3] No asterisk is provided here because this action was not included in the scaling analysis. Like (d) for Situation 11, it may reflect the invention of an appropriate means through experiencing the results of unsuccessful actions and thereby suggest an additional step in the scale.

CHAPTER 13

Scale IIIa, The Development of Vocal Imitation, and Scale IIIb, The Development of Gestural Imitation

Imitation is highly dependent on the motivation of the infant. This means that when an infant fails to imitate, it is exceedingly difficult to tell whether he cannot or will not. It is only when an infant imitates certain acts or vocalizations and attempts to imitate, or at least shows an interest in imitating others, that one may infer with some confidence that he cannot imitate those acts which he does not even attempt. Consequently, it is very important to have the infant's mood, the infant's relationship with the examiner, and the arrangement of the eliciting situation as favorable as possible.

It is important, first of all, especially with younger infants, to catch them in a happy mood and when they are not yet tired of the examination situation. It is important, second, to give the infant time to become acquainted with the examiner. Once an infant begins to direct his behavior toward the examiner (by smiling at the examiner, by giving a toy back to the examiner, etc.) rather than primarily toward toys, one may assume that an atmosphere conducive to imitation has been established. With older infants, particularly, it is important to avoid making them self-conscious. It usually helps to present the models for imitation in a playful atmosphere, possibly when an infant has already found the examiner's acts interesting and may have already attempted to reproduce some aspect of them. It is also usually better to try to obtain imitation at several different times during an examination rather than to progress routinely from one situation to the next, especially in the face of failure to obtain imitation. Either persistence or insistence on the part of the examiner or the person taking care of the infant often destroys rapport and only diminishes the chances of obtaining either pseudo-imitation or imitation.

Scale IIIa: Vocal Imitation

A. DIFFERENTIATION IN VOCAL PRODUCTIONS

1. USE OF VOCALIZATION OTHER THAN CRYING

Location:	Any position comfortable for the infant.
Object:	None.
Directions:	Listen for spontaneous vocalizations of the infant and note whether he vocalizes sounds other than those indicating distress. Observe the infant by himself and also while maintaining face to face contact with him.
Infant Actions:	a. Vocalizes only distress sounds.
	*b. Vocalizes (coos) when not distressed.

2. RESPONSE TO FAMILIAR COOING VOCALIZATIONS

Location:	Same as in situation 1.
Object:	Listen for spontaneous vocalizations of the infant or ask the person caring for the infant what non-distress (cooing) sounds he typically produces.
Directions:	While the infant is not vocalizing spontaneously, face the infant and talk to him in adult fashion. After a few moments of observing the infant's expression and behavior, utter one of the cooing sounds without genuine consonants that the infant typically makes himself (e.g., *ah-i-ya, eh-uh-e, uh-ah-a*—each with rising and falling pitch—*uuh, alia*, etc.). Vocalize the sound a few times, then stop to observe the in-

fant's expression and behavior. Repeat the familiar vocalization. If the infant has been observed to utter several different cooing sounds, shift to a different sound in his repertoire after three or four presentations of the first one.

Repeat: 2–3 different vocalizations.
Infant Actions: a. Shows little interest in either adult or infantlike sounds from the examiner.
                  b. Listens attentively to both adult and infantlike sounds, but does not vocalize.
                  *c. Shows a more positive response to cooing sounds as indicated by brighter expression, smile, and mouth-movements, but does not vocalize.
                  *d. Vocalizes in response to the examiner's presentation of familiar cooing sounds, though the vocalization may or may not be like that of the examiner.
                  e. Vocalizes similar sounds in response to the examiner, but does not shift to match the examiner when the examiner changes the cooing sound presented.
                  f. Vocalizes similar sounds in response to the examiner and changes his vocalization to match that of the examiner.

3. RESPONSE TO FAMILIAR BABBLING SOUNDS

Location: Same as in situation 1.
Object: Listen for spontaneous vocalizations of the infant or ask the person caring for the infant what sound patterns (babbling) the infant has often made.
Directions: While the infant is not vocalizing spontaneously, gain the infant's attention and utter one of the sound patterns the infant typically makes himself (e.g., *ba-ba-ba*, *at-da-da*, *ma-ma-ma*, etc.). Vocalize the sound pattern a few times and then pause to observe the infant's expression and behavior. Repeat the

familiar sound pattern. If the infant has been observed to make several babbling sounds frequently, shift to a different sound pattern in the infant's repertoire after three or four presentations of the first one.

Repeat: 2–3 different sound patterns.

Infant Actions:
  a. Shows little interest in the examiner's vocalizations.
  b. Listens attentively to the examiner, but does not vocalize.
  *c. Shows interest in the babbling sounds as indicated by a smile, mouth-movements, and continued looking at the examiner during pauses, but does not vocalize.
  *d. Vocalizes in response to the examiner's presentation of familiar sound patterns, but the vocalization may not be like that of the examiner.
  e. Vocalizes similar sounds in response to the examiner, but does not shift to match the examiner when the examiner changes the sound pattern presented.
  *f. Vocalizes similar sounds in response to the examiner and changes his vocalization to match that of the examiner.

B. DEVELOPMENT IN IMITATION OF SOUND PATTERNS

4. IMITATION OF FAMILIAR WORDS

Location: Same as in situation 1.

Object: Listen for the spontaneous vocalizations of the infant and ask the person taking care of the infant what words or wordlike sounds the infant has in his repertoire.

Directions: Inasmuch as the first words frequently denote familiar objects, it is often helpful in this situation to present the infant with a toy replica or a picture of an object corresponding to one of the words used by the infant. While the infant is not too engrossed in play with the object, repeat the appropriate word one or two times, wait to observe the infant's behavior, repeat it again, and so forth.

Repeat: 2–3 different words.
Infant Actions: a. Listens attentively to the word uttered by the examiner, but does not vocalize in response.
             *b. Vocalizes in response to the examiner, but with sounds which are unlike the ones modeled by the examiner.
             *c. Imitates several familiar words modeled by the examiner.

5. IMITATION OF UNFAMILIAR SOUND PATTERNS

Location: Same as in situation 1.
Object: Listen for the spontaneous vocalizations of the infant in order to be able to select sound patterns clearly different from those which are familiar to him (e.g., *brr, zzz, ree-ree-ree, faa-faa*, etc.). Check with the person caring for the infant whether the sound patterns chosen are, in fact, novel.
Directions: While the infant is not vocalizing spontaneously, gain his attention and utter one of the unfamiliar sounds. Repeat the sound several times, wait to observe the infant's behavior, repeat again, and so forth. If the infant's behavior is not clear after several presentations, repeat the situation by presenting a different unfamiliar sound pattern.
Repeat: 2–3 different sound patterns.
Infant Actions: a. Shows unhappiness or cries.
             b. Shows no interest in unfamiliar sounds.
             c. Listens to the sounds attentively while they are being uttered by the examiner, but does not vocalize himself.

d. Vocalizes in response to the examiner, but does not make sounds like those presented by the examiner.

e. Vocalizes in response to the examiner with sounds which approximate those modeled more closely with successive repetitions.

f. Vocalizes in response to the examiner with sounds which immediately resemble quite closely those modeled by the examiner.

6. IMITATION OF NEW WORDS

Location: Same as in situation 1.

Object: Listen for the spontaneous vocalizations of the infant and ask the person caring for the infant what words or wordlike utterances the infant has in his repertoire in order to be able to select for presentation words new to the infant. Choose simple new words for presentation.

Directions: To maintain a playful mood, present the infant with a toy for which the mother says the infant does not have a name (e.g., "fish," "flower," "bus" are words often unfamiliar to infants). While the infant is not too engrossed in play with the toy, repeat the name corresponding to the toy one or two times, wait to observe the infant's behavior, repeat it again, and so forth. Alternatively, use adjectives which are not in the infant's vocabulary appropriate to objects highly familiar to the infant. With the object a baby doll, the words "young," "blond," "pretty," etc. may be tried. With a ball for the object, words like "blue," "red," "bouncy," etc. may be appropriate. Say each word distinctly, pause to observe the infant, then repeat once or twice more before trying a different word.

Repeat: 6–7 different words.

Infant Actions: a. Listens to new words, but does not vocalize in response.

b. Vocalizes in response to the examiner, but the infant's vocalizations do not resemble the words modeled.

 c. Vocalizes approximations of the new words which become closer to the model with repetition.

d. Imitates a few (1–2) simple new words directly.

*e. Imitates practically all simple new words (at least 5) directly.

Scale IIIb: Gestural Imitation

A. IMITATION OF FAMILIAR GESTURES

1. SYSTEMATIC IMITATION OF FAMILIAR SIMPLE SCHEMES

Location: Any position comfortable for the infant.
Object: None.
Directions: Observe the infant's play with objects in order to determine which simple schemes are familiar to him (e.g., patting an object, waving the arm, turning the wrist, etc.). When the infant is *not* applying a particular scheme, perform that action several times and wait to observe the infant's behavior. Perform it again a few times and wait. When the infant's behavior seems clear, perform a different familiar action.
Repeat: 2–3 different actions.
Infant Actions: a. Shows interest in the examiner's action, but does not even attempt to reproduce it.

 *b. Performs some action in response to the examiner, consistently, but does not imitate the scheme presented.

 *c. Imitates a scheme presented by the examiner.

2. IMITATION OF COMPLEX ACTIONS COMPOSED OF FAMILIAR SCHEMES

Location: Same as in situation 1.

Object: Use simple objects to demonstrate a more complex action for the infant. For example, blocks and a cup may be used to demonstrate putting a block into the cup and shaking it; several blocks or pieces of foil may be used to demonstrate hitting two objects together; and so on.

Directions: Select a scheme which the infant has spontaneously applied to objects and incorporate it into a more complex action. For instance, if hitting is a scheme which the infant has applied, spread out several blocks in front of the infant, take one in each hand, and hit them together several times. Observe the infant's behavior. If necessary, help the infant to get a block into each hand. Repeat the demonstration or model with pauses for observing the infant's behavior several times. Or, if the infant has been observed to shake objects, model the shaking of a block inside a cup by presenting the infant with several blocks and a cup, putting one block inside the cup, and shaking the cup vigorously several times before placing the cup in front of the infant.

Repeat: 2–3 different actions.

Infant Actions:
    a. Attends to the examiner's demonstration, but does not even attempt to imitate the action.

    b. Performs some action in response to the examiner, consistently, but does not imitate the one demonstrated.

    *c. Attempts to imitate the action, but does not come any closer to success on repeated attempts (e.g., hits a block in the examiner's hand rather than the one he holds, tries to shake the cup, but spills out the block immediately).

d. Imitates the action modeled through gradual approximation.

e. Imitates the action modeled immediately.

B. IMITATION OF UNFAMILIAR GESTURES

Note: A gesture is called visible if the infant is able to see himself performing it. For example, hitting a surface is a visible gesture, since the infant can observe his own hand while he attempts to hit, but wrinkling the nose is not visible, since without a mirror, the infant cannot observe himself performing this action.

3. IMITATION OF UNFAMILIAR GESTURES VISIBLE TO THE INFANT

Location: Same as in situation 1.
Object: None.
Directions: Select several gestures that are thought to be unfamiliar to the infant (e.g., opening and closing the fisted hand, bending and straightening the index finger, drumming on a surface, scratching a surface, clapping hands, and so on). If at all possible, ask the person taking care of the infant whether the selected gestures are actually unfamiliar, since some of them may have been taught or frequently demonstrated to the infant. Demonstrate the unfamiliar gesture several times while the infant is attentive and observe his behavior.
Repeat: 2–3 different gestures.
Infant Actions: a. Shows interest in the examiner's performance, but does not attempt to imitate the gesture.
                 b. Performs some movement in response to the examiner, consistently, but does not imitate the gesture.
                 c. Imitates the gesture modeled through gradual approximation.
                *d. Imitates the gesture modeled immediately.

4. IMITATION OF UNFAMILIAR GESTURES INVISIBLE TO THE INFANT

Location: Same as in situation 1.
Object: None.
Directions: While the infant is attentive, model a gesture which
                  the infant is unable to observe himself perform (e.g.,
                  opening and closing the mouth, blinking the eyes,
                  patting the top of the head, patting the cheek,
                  pulling the ear lobe, wrinkling the nose, etc.). If
                  possible, ascertain whether any of these gestures
                  have been taught or frequently demonstrated to the
                  infant. Repeat the unfamiliar gesture several times
                  and pause to observe the infant's behavior.
Repeat: 3–4 different gestures.
Infant Actions: a. Shows interest in the examiner's performance,
                      but does not attempt to imitate the gesture.
                  *b. Makes some movement in response to the ges-
                      ture modeled, consistently, but does not imitate
                      the gesture.
                   c. Imitates the gesture modeled through gradual
                      approximation.
                  *d. Imitates at least one invisible gesture im-
                      mediately.
                  *e. Imitates several invisible gestures immedi-
                      ately.

CHAPTER 14

Scale IV: The Development of Operational Causality

A. EFFORTS TO PROLONG INTERESTING INPUTS

1. APPEARANCE OF HAND-WATCHING BEHAVIOR

Location: The infant may be supine on any flat surface. There should be no other visually attractive objects within sight.

Object: None.

Directions: Observe whether the infant will engage in hand-watching activities. Pay particular attention to whether the infant seems able to bring his hands into view and to move them while they are being held in view. Allow a few minutes for this observation.

Infant Actions: a. Hand-watching behavior is not observed.
                  *b. Hand-watching is observed.

2. REPETITION OF ACTIONS PRODUCING AN INTERESTING SPECTACLE

Location: Any position suitable for eliciting a "secondary circular reaction" from the infant, usually a sitting position in an infant seat or a high chair.

Object: An object which can be activated by one of the earliest motor schemes, such as hitting, and which provides a change of visual and/or auditory input when so activated has been found to be most effective. For example, a brightly colored musical toy in the shape of a clown, a musical rattle in the shape of a cylinder attached to a handle, and a set of multi-colored discs on a chain have been used.

Directions: The presentation of this situation depends on finding some object on which the infant will act and, through his actions, produce a result which he finds interesting. After selecting an object, hold it within easy reach of the infant's preferred hand, but in a way that discourages grasping (i.e., either the part of the toy closest to the infant should be too large for grasping or the toy should be held securely at a height where it can be touched, but not grasped by the infant). If the infant does not touch or hit the toy within 15 seconds, strike the toy against the infant's hand once, allowing the infant to see that the toy does create a spectacle. Hold the toy in position again for 15–20 seconds.

Repeat: 2–3 times.

Infant Actions:
  a. Shows interest in the object only by looking at it.
  b. Intensifies arm movements in the direction of the object and activates it occasionally, but not regularly.
  *c. Repeats arm movements systematically and keeps the object active consistently.
  d. Only tries to grasp the object.

3. Use of a specific action as "procedure"

Location: Same as in situation 2. It is important that the infant's arms and legs be free to move.

Object: Any object which produces a spectacle interesting to the infant when it is activated by the examiner may be used. Such objects as a musical toy, which can be made to tinkle while swinging back and forth, a colorful pinwheel, which can be twirled, or a jumping jack, which can be activated by pulling a string, have been found to be fairly successful.

Directions: Hold the object in front of the infant and activate it while the infant is focusing on it; stop abruptly. Observe the infant's behavior for a few moments and then activate the object again. Alternate activation and pause 3–4 times. Observe whether some act stands out in the infant's behavior during the pauses. Acts which frequently serve as "procedures" include: a consistent vocalization, the hitting of a surface with the palm of the hand, kicking the legs, waving one arm, a swiping arm movement, etc.

Repeat: 1–2 different spectacles.

Infant Actions: a. Shows interest only while the spectacle is being produced.

  b. Shows excitement and a higher level of activity throughout or only during the pauses, but no single act is dominant during the pauses.

  *c. Performs some act during the pauses consistently, suggesting that it serves as a "procedure" for the infant.

  d. Reaches out to grasp the object, but does not attempt to activate it once he has it.

B. ACTIONS TO REINSTATE INTERESTING SPECTACLES

4. BEHAVIOR IN A FAMILIAR GAME SITUATION

Location: A position suitable for and customarily used in the game to be played must be arranged.

Object: Usually none.

Directions: Find out from the person taking care of the infant what games are frequently played with the infant, such as pulling the infant up to a sitting or standing position repeatedly, jouncing the infant on the knee or foot, raising him up into the air repeatedly, playing a hand game, and so forth. Start one of the games familiar to the infant and stop after a few repetitions, while the infant appears to be enjoying the game. Observe his actions and then start it again. Include 3–4 pauses in the game.

Repeat: 1–2 different games.

Infant Actions:
    a. Shows no interest in playing the game with the examiner.

    b. Appears to enjoy the game, but remains passive during the pauses.

    c. Performs some act which can be considered a "procedure" during the pauses.

    d. Attempts to start the game during the pauses by performing part of the activity (e.g., jumps up on the knee, strains to sit up or stand up, makes a hand movement).[1]

    e. Touches the examiner during the pauses as if to attract attention, but waits for the examiner to start the game.

5. Behavior to a Spectacle Created by an Agent

Location: The infant may be seated in an infant seat, a high chair, or a feeding table. The examiner should be able to face the infant and to have a working surface in front of the infant.

Object: None.

Directions: Attempt to create a spectacle which the infant finds interesting by using your hands and face. Actions such as drumming on a surface with the fingers, snapping the fingers, or making facial grimaces often are successful. Stop abruptly and observe the infant's behavior for a few moments, then resume again. Pause 2–3 times during the spectacle. Leave

---

[1] None of these infant actions carries an asterisk because none of them was included in the scaling analysis. This situation is being retained, nevertheless, because the infant actions listed under (d) as well as those listed below under (b) of situation 7, appear to imply at least minimal appreciation of causality outside the self and thereby suggest the possibility of an additional step in this scale falling between present steps 3 and 4.

your hand or face within the infant's reach during each pause.

Repeat: 1–2 different spectacles.

Infant Actions: a. Shows interest only during the spectacle.
                    b. Shows excitement, but no single act stands out as an attempt to reinstitute the spectacle.
                    *c. Performs some act which can be considered a "procedure" during the pauses.
                    *d. Touches the examiner lightly during the pauses and waits.
                    e. Attempts to imitate the examiner.

6. BEHAVIOR TO A SPECTACLE CREATED BY AN AGENT ACTING ON AN OBJECT

Location: Same as in situation 5.

Object: Any object which can be manipulated to create a spectacle of interest to the infant may be used. For example, a roly-poly toy which can be made to spin around on a surface, a music box that has to be started by pulling a cord, a pendulum toy, or a "Slinky" toy create interesting spectacles.

Directions: Obtain the infant's attention and set off the object. Once the object stops, wait a few moments to observe the infant's behavior, leaving both the object and your hand within the infant's reach. In contrast to situation 3, it is important that the examiner's role in creating the spectacle be quite obvious. However, this situation is most successful when the act setting off the object is not an easy one for the infant to perform. Set off each spectacle 2–3 times.

Repeat: 2–3 different spectacles.

Infant Actions: a. Shows interest during the spectacle, but does not attempt to recreate it.
                 b. Performs some act which can be considered a "procedure" when the object stops.
                 *c. Touches the object or the examiner's hand lightly when the object stops and waits.

d. Picks up the object and gives it to the examiner to activate.

e. Attempts to activate the object himself.

7. BEHAVIOR TO A SPECTACLE CREATED BY A MECHANICAL OBJECT

Location:	Same as in situation 5.
Object:	A mechanically moving toy which executes a definite action when wound is needed. For example, a duck which wobbles in a characteristic way, a bear drumming on a drum, a chicken pecking at a ball, and so on may be used. It is assumed the infant has not been taught to wind mechanical toys.
Directions:	Wind the object without letting the infant see it being done and present him with the object in motion. After the object stops, observe the infant's behavior toward the object. Wind the object up once more, surreptitiously, and present the moving object to the infant. Finally, demonstrate the action of winding up the object to the infant and again observe his behavior after the object stops.
Repeat:	1–2 different objects.
Infant Actions:	a. Plays with the object, seemingly forgetting the spectacle.

                b. Makes the object perform its activity manually (i.e., wobbles the duck, pushes the chicken to peck, etc.).[2]

                c. Touches the object or the examiner's hand lightly when the object stops and waits.

                d. Gives the object back to the examiner and waits.

                e. Attempts to activate the object by manipulating the winding mechanism after demonstration (the infant need not succeed).

                f. Attempts to find a way to activate the object prior to demonstration by the examiner.

[2] See Footnote 1, above.

CHAPTER 15

Scale V: The Construction of Object Relations in Space

A. DEVELOPMENT IN LOCALIZATION
OF OBJECTS IN SPACE

▸ 1. OBSERVING TWO OBJECTS ALTERNATELY

Location:
The infant may be supine on a flat surface, in an infant seat, or sitting up by himself.

Object:
Two differing objects which are both attractive to the infant (e.g., two checkerboards of different colors, a large plastic flower and a colorful rattle) are needed.

Directions:
Hold the two objects in front of the infant, about 10 inches from his eyes and separated by about 6 inches from each other. After about 20 seconds, reverse the positions of the two objects. Observe the movements of the infant's eyes while he looks at the two objects. If the infant focuses on the examiner's face, attempt to move out of the infant's line of sight and hold the two objects at arm's length in front of the infant's face.

Repeat:
2–3 times.

Infant Actions:
a. Looks in the direction of only one object each time.

b. Looks at both objects, but switches the glance slowly from one to the other (once or twice in 20 seconds).

c. Looks at both objects, switching the glance quickly from one to the other in each burst of looking activity (four or five times in 5 seconds).

2. LOCALIZING AN OBJECT BY ITS SOUND

Location: Same as in situation 1.

Object: A sound-making object such as a rattle, a bell, or a squeaking toy may be used.

Directions: Stand behind the infant and produce the sound for a few seconds to the right, the left, and above the infant's head in a random sequence. Make sure the infant cannot see the movements of your hand while producing the sound. After each presentation of the sound, hold the sound-making object in position and allow a few moments of silence before starting another presentation. Observe whether the infant searches for the source of the sound with his eyes and whether he stops upon seeing the sound-making object.

Repeat: 5–7 times.

Infant Actions:
    a. Does not turn head to the source of sound.
    b. Turns head toward the source of sound in one direction only.
    c. Turns head in the direction of sound, but does not localize the source object visually.
   *d. Localizes the source of sound with his eyes.

3. GRASPING A VISUALLY PRESENTED OBJECT

Location: The infant may be supine or seated, as long as both arms are free to reach out.

Object: Any small, attractive object such as a rattle, a plastic animal, or a plastic flower may be used. Make sure a portion of the object is small enough for the infant's hand to close around.

Directions: Hold the object about 12 inches in front of the infant for at least 30 seconds. Observe the infant's attempts to grasp the object.

Repeat: 2–3 times.

Infant Actions: a. Raises arms and moves them in the direction of the object, but does not touch it.
  b. Moves arms in the direction of the object, but clasps hands in front of the object.
  c. Touches the object, but fails to grasp it.
  *d. Grasps the visually presented object.

4. FOLLOWING VISUALLY THE TRAJECTORY OF A RAPIDLY MOVING OBJECT

Location: The infant may be propped in a sitting position on a sofa or seated in a high chair, as long as he is off the floor and free to lean forward and sideways from his seat. A sound-absorbing surface around the infant is helpful.

Object: Any small, light object attractive to the infant is suitable. The object should not make much noise when released to fall to the floor. For example, a small plastic flower, a crumpled piece of aluminum foil, or a ball of cotton may be used.

Directions: Hold the object slightly above the infant's line of sight so that he must raise his eyes to focus on it. Once the infant is looking at the object, release it to have it fall to the left or to the right of the infant, at random, retaining your hand in position above the infant's head. The object should land to the side of the infant, within view. After several presentations, release the object in such a way that it falls all the way to the floor, and thus, lands out of view for the infant. Observe the infant's attempts to locate the object.

Repeat: 3–4 times.
Infant Actions: a. Does not follow the falling object and remains focused on the examiner's hand.

b. Turns eyes to the correct side or follows part of the object's trajectory, but does not locate the object.

*c. Follows the falling object and finds it with his eyes when the object remains in view, but fails to locate it visually when the object falls outside his field of view.

d. Looks around for the object at the point where it was last visible (along the edge of the surface on which the infant is sitting), but does not extrapolate the trajectory of the object to its probable location on the floor and does not lean to find it there.

*e. Leans forward to search for the object in the direction in which it fell, even though the last portion of the trajectory taken by the object was not observed by the infant.

5. RECOGNIZING THE REVERSE SIDE OF OBJECTS

Location: Same as in situation 3.
Object: Any object of interest to the infant which has a definite reverse or nonfunctional side, such as a baby's bottle, a plastic animal designed to float in water, etc., may be used.
Directions: Hold the object in front of the infant within his reach, with its functional or "right" end or side facing him. When the infant begins to reach for the object, quickly reverse it so that the infant is faced with the object's opposite end or side. Observe the infant's behavior after the reversal.
Repeat: 2–3 times.
Infant Actions: a. Continues to reach and grasps the object, showing no indication that the reversal was appreciated.

b. Withdraws hands and appears surprised at seeing the reverse end or side of the object.

*c. Grasps the object, but turns it to the "right"
end or side immediately each time, or, turns
the object over several times and examines both
sides intently.

B. DEVELOPMENT IN APPRECIATION
OF SPATIAL RELATIONSHIPS
BETWEEN OBJECTS

*6. USING THE RELATIONSHIP OF THE CONTAINER AND THE CONTAINED

Location:　　　　The infant may be seated in an infant feeding table,
a high chair, by himself in a crib or on the floor so
long as there is some working space in front of the
infant.

Object:　　　　Several small objects such as blocks or large plastic
beads and a container large enough to hold them
are needed.

Directions:　　　Present the infant with the small objects and the
container. If the infant does not initiate play with
the objects and the container spontaneously, put
some of the objects into the container, without permitting the infant to see the procedure, and present
the filled container to the infant. Observe the infant's behavior in both instances.

Repeat:　　　　2–3 times.

Infant Actions:　　a. Does not put objects into the container and
only touches objects already inside the con-
tainer.

b. Takes objects out of a filled container, but does
not put any into it.

c. Places objects in the container and takes them
out one by one.

*d. Places or drops objects into the container and
turns the container over to remove the objects
inside.

7. PLACING OBJECTS IN EQUILIBRIUM ONE UPON ANOTHER

Location: Same as in situation 6.
Object: Small 1-inch blocks or small stacking-rings may be used.
Directions: Present several objects to the infant and observe his play. If he does not begin placing them one upon another spontaneously, demonstrate by making a tower, 3 or 4 objects high. Scatter the objects in the tower, so that the infant does not start a game of knocking down the examiner's tower, and encourage the infant to build one himself.
Repeat: 2–3 times.
Infant Actions: a. Does not attempt to build a tower.
                 b. Approximates two objects one on top of another, but does not leave the second one in place when removing his hand, or places it so that it falls off immediately.
                 *c. Builds a tower of at least two objects.

8. APPRECIATING GRAVITY IN PLAY WITH OBJECTS

Location: Same as in situation 6.
Object: A small toy of interest to the infant which rolls readily on an incline (e.g., a small toy car, an animal toy on wheels, a spool), a piece of cardboard to make the incline, and a piece of sturdy string are needed.
Directions: Construct an incline by raising one end of a piece of cardboard. Place an object on the top, release it, and let it roll down the incline. Encourage the infant to do the same and observe his behavior. Alternately, tie a piece of string around an object which the infant desires. Lower it to the floor and pull it up by means of the string. Lower the toy again, leaving one end of the string within the infant's reach, and encourage the infant to pull up the toy.

Repeat: 2–3 times.
Infant Actions: a. Does not attempt the action demonstrated by
                      the examiner.
                   b. Acts without taking gravity into account (e.g.,
                      guides the toy along the incline without re-
                      leasing it, pulls the string to bring the object
                      closer and, then, releases it before grasping the
                      object).
                   *c. Acts with appreciation of the force of gravity
                      (e.g., releases the object on the incline, or holds
                      the string while grasping the object).

9. EXPLORING THE FALL OF DROPPED OBJECTS

Location: Same as in situation 4.
Object: Several small objects which can be safely dropped
                   to the floor (e.g., wood or plastic farm animals,
                   large plastic beads, small stuffed animals) are
                   needed.
Directions: Spread the objects in front of the infant. Observe
                   his activities with them.
Repeat: 1–2 times.
Infant Actions: a. Does not drop any of the objects to the floor.
                   b. Drops several objects repeatedly, but does not
                      attempt to see where they land.
                   c. Drops several objects repeatedly and looks to
                      see where each lands.[1]

10. MAKING DETOURS

Location: The infant may be seated on the floor or in a chair
                   from which he can get out on his own.
Object: Any object which is of interest to the infant and
                   which can be propelled along the floor (e.g., a toy
                   car, a ball, a pull-toy on wheels) may be used.

---

[1] None of the infant actions for situation 9 and none for situation 10 is marked with an asterisk, because these infant actions were not included in the scaling analysis. The situations are, nevertheless, retained in order to increase the likelihood of eliciting actions pertinent to the two highest steps of this scale, listed under *c* for both situations.

Directions: While the infant is interested in playing with the object, take it and roll it behind a barrier created by an armchair or a low table. Try to make the object come to rest underneath the more distant side of the barrier from the infant. Observe the infant's attempts to obtain the object.

Repeat: 2–3 times.

Infant Actions: a. Loses interest in the object.
   b. Attempts to reach the object by following the same path as the object took (i.e., attempts to reach underneath the barrier for the object).
   c. Goes directly around the barrier and attempts to retrieve the object from behind.[2]

11. INDICATING ABSENCE OF FAMILIAR PERSONS

Directions: Find out from the person taking care of the infant which member of the family is not present in the home and whose leaving was observed by the infant. Ask the infant where this person is or to be taken to that person. Observe the infant's actions and his reply.

Infant Actions: a. Does not seem to comprehend the question or request.
   b. Goes to look for the person where he may be most often found.
   *c. Indicates knowledge of the absence of that person by pointing to the door or to the outside, saying "gone," or "bye-bye," etc.

[2] See Footnote 1, above.

CHAPTER 16

Scale VI: The Development of Schemes for Relating to Objects

In order to determine the repertoire of sensorimotor schemes which an infant can manifest in acting on objects, a relatively large number of varied objects should be available to be presented. While there is considerable consistency in the schemes which young infants demonstrate with different objects, certain objects definitely tend to elicit particular schemes. All of the objects should not be presented in succession. If too many objects are presented one after another, older infants quickly shift from play with the objects presented to inquiry about what other objects they may yet be shown. When some other activity is interspersed between every two or three objects, infants will usually maintain active interaction with each of the objects presented. If the young infant fails to grasp the object held out to him, or to pick it up off a surface, the object should be placed in the infant's hand.

The form of the directions for this scale is somewhat different from that for the preceeding five scales in that the situations and the infant actions comprising the scale are less closely related. In the examination record form for this scale (see Chapter 17, Scale VI), the various infant actions are listed under the specific objects presented rather than under the three situations arranged for their presentation.

We describe three different situations for presenting objects to determine the infant's repertoire of schemes for relating to them.

There is no particular order in which the various objects should be presented. It is wise, however, to avoid presenting one of relatively little attractiveness right after one in which the infant has shown a great deal of interest, lest frustration result. The infant should ordinarily be allowed to play with each object until he loses interest, until he starts repeating schemes already manifested with this same object, or until about three minutes have elapsed.

Following the directions for arranging the three eliciting situations, we present the specific infant actions commonly shown and their groupings with respect to the steps in this scale; the groupings are indicated by a letter marked with an asterisk and a descriptive phrase.

1. ACTING ON SIMPLE OBJECTS

Location:	Any position comfortable for the infant which leaves the hands free to manipulate the objects is appropriate.
Object:	Simple objects such as a rattle, a plastic doll, a plastic animal, a piece of aluminum foil, a large block, a cup, or a necklace may be used.
Directions:	Present the objects one at a time and observe the infant's actions with each object. Encourage the infant to play with each object, but do not demonstrate any possible activities.
Repeat:	3–5 different objects.

2. ACTING ON SEVERAL OBJECTS AVAILABLE TOGETHER

Location:	The infant may be seated in an infant feeding table, on a sofa, or in a high chair to have him off the floor.
Object:	Objects which can be used jointly and may facilitate elicitation of more complex schemes should be presented (e.g., 6 blocks at once, 3 or 4 blocks and a cup, a doll and a doll's shoe, a ball of cotton and a piece of aluminum foil, a plastic animal, a musical roly-poly toy, a toy car).
Directions:	Present one of the objects and, following some time

to observe the infant's behavior, add a second object which might be used jointly with the first. After
an interval for joint play, remove the first object and
observe the infant's actions with the second.

Repeat: 3–5 different objects.

3. ACTING ON OBJECTS WITH SOCIAL MEANING

Location: The infant may sit on the floor or in a chair from
which he can get out on his own.

Object: Objects which have socially designated ways for
using them should be selected (e.g., a doll, a
stuffed animal, a cup, a necklace, several blocks, a
ball, a doll's shoe, a plastic flower, a toy car).

Directions: Present the objects one at a time and observe the
infant's actions. If the infant requests another object
for joint play, present the second object after an
interval for play with the first object.

Repeat: 3–5 different objects.

Infant Actions: a. Holding an object for at least 30 seconds.

*b. Mouthing of objects: Brings the object to the
mouth immediately or after other actions with
it. In very young infants, the intent to mouth an
object may be seen from anticipatory opening
of the mouth.

*c. Visual inspection of objects: Brings the object
before the eyes or holds it and looks at it for a
few moments in the course of other actions with
it.

*d. Simple motor schemes: The infant appears to be
exercising his schemes for acting on objects and
pays very little attention to the kind of object
that is presented to him. He may (1) hit or pat
the object with his hand, (2) hit a surface with
the object, (3) hit two objects together, (4)
shake the object, (5) wave the object in the air,
and so forth.

*e. Examining of objects: When the infant begins

to focus his attention on the objects themselves, he begins to show examining activity. This is distinguished from mere visual inspection by a combination of both visual attention to the object and manipulation of the object in an exploratory manner such as turning it around, feeling its surface, touching various protuberances on the object, and so on.

*f. Complex motor schemes: The infant begins to accommodate his schemes to the characteristics of particular objects and, thus, begins to show a number of more varied actions adapted to specific objects rather than applied indiscriminately. These actions include (1) sliding objects on a surface, (2) crumpling objects which are flexible, (3) swinging objects, (4) tearing objects which may be torn or stretching objects out, (5) rubbing one object against another or putting one object into another, and so on.

*g. "Letting go" activities: The infant may (1) drop objects repeatedly and intentionally or (2) throw them considerable distances when playing with them. These actions may be differentiated from an infant's attempt merely to get rid of an uninteresting object by his willingness, even eagerness, to pick up the object dropped or thrown as soon as it is retrieved and offered to him.

*h. Socially instigated activities: The particular schemes shown depend on the objects presented to the infant, but they all indicate some appreciation of the activities deemed appropriate for the object in the culture. For example, (1) pretending to drink from the cup, (2) wearing the necklace, (3) driving the toy car, (4) building a structure with the blocks, (5) hugging a doll or a soft animal, (6) dressing a doll or putting the shoe on the doll, (7) sniffing a plastic flower, (8) making the doll or animal "walk," and so on, are considered socially instigated behaviors.

*i. Showing of objects: When another person is present while the infant plays with objects, he may show some of these objects to the other person in a way suggesting social interaction or a beginning in sharing of experiences. The infant extends the hand holding the object in the direction of the other person and waits a moment, or, he brings the object over to the other person to look at. This action may be differentiated from an attempt to get rid of the object by the infant's unwillingness to give up the object for more than a moment. The infant may also bring an object of his own like the one presented or in some way associated with the one presented, and show that object to the other person.

*j. Naming of objects in recognition: The infant spontaneously names an object or a part of an object either immediately upon being presented with it or after a period of examining the object. The name used may be a childish name and it may be accompanied by showing of the object to another person. Naming in recognition may be differentiated from the use of the name to express desire for an object by its occurrence in the presence of the object.

CHAPTER 17

Record Forms

The kind of record of infant performances to be kept depends upon the purpose of the examination. We provide in this chapter two kinds of forms: examination record forms and summary record forms.

The *examination record forms* are designed for use in the course of the examination. They retain a near-maximal amount of information and are useful in investigations aimed at extending information about the actions elicited by each of the situations and at refining the scales by uncovering steps intermediate between those we have identified in our scaling analysis. These forms list the situations described in the directions for arranging them, with the number and heading corresponding to those in the directions. Under each situation, the infant actions which the situation has elicited according to our observations, are listed with condensed descriptions. These actions are lettered as they were lettered in the directions: the letters for those actions which are considered critical are in italics and, if they were included in the scaling analysis, an asterisk appears before the letter. For Scales I through V, where it is appropriate, space is provided for indicating the action elicited by each presentation of each situation. For Scale VI, the schemes commonly elicited are listed in relation to the various objects which may be presented instead of to the eliciting situations.

The *summary record forms* are designed to be completed following the examination. They retain less information, but they are useful where interest is focused chiefly on levels of development. We shall describe them below immediately before presenting them.

SAMPLE EXAMINATION RECORD FORMS

SCALE I: THE DEVELOPMENT OF VISUAL PURSUIT AND THE PERMANENCE OF OBJECTS

Name:

Birthdate:

Date of Examination:

SITUATION	PRESENTATION *(Suggested number of presentations for each situation is indicated in parentheses)*						
	1	2	3	4	5	6	7
1. *Following a Slowly Moving Object through a 180° Arc* (3–4)							
a. Does not follow object	___	___	___	___	___	___	___
b. Follows jerkily through part of arc	___	___	___	___	___	___	___
c. Follows smoothly through part of arc	___	___	___	___	___	___	___
*d. Follows object smoothly through complete arc	___	___	___	___	___	___	___
Other:	___	___	___	___	___	___	___
2. *Noticing the Disappearance of a Slowly Moving Object* (3–4)							
a. Does not follow to point of disappearance	___	___	___	___	___	___	___
b. Loses interest as soon as object disappears	___	___	___	___	___	___	___
*c. Lingers with glance on point of disappearance	___	___	___	___	___	___	___
*d. Returns glance to starting point after several presentations	___	___	___	___	___	___	___
e. Searches around point of disappearance	___	___	___	___	___	___	___
Other:	___	___	___	___	___	___	___
3. *Finding an Object Which Is Partially Covered* (3)							
a. Loses interest	___	___	___	___	___	___	___
b. Reacts to the loss, but does not obtain object	___	___	___	___	___	___	___
*c. Obtains the object	___	___	___	___	___	___	___
Other:	___	___	___	___	___	___	___
4. *Finding an Object Which Is Completely Covered* (3)							
a. Loses interest	___	___	___	___	___	___	___

SCALE I (*continued*)

SITUATION	PRESENTATION (*Suggested number of presentations for each situation is indicated in parentheses*)						
	1	2	3	4	5	6	7
b. Reacts to loss, but does not obtain object	—	—	—	—	—	—	—
c. Pulls screen, but not enough to obtain object	—	—	—	—	—	—	—
*d. Pulls screen off and obtains object	—	—	—	—	—	—	—
Other:	—	—	—	—	—	—	—
5. *Finding an Object Completely Covered in Two Places* (2)							
a. Loses interest	—	—	—	—	—	—	—
b. Searches for object where it was previously found	—	—	—	—	—	—	—
c. Searches for object where it is last hidden	—	—	—	—	—	—	—
Other:	—	—	—	—	—	—	—
6. *Finding an Object Completely Covered in Two Places Alternately* (3–5)							
a. Becomes perplexed and loses interest	—	—	—	—	—	—	—
b. Searches haphazardly under one or both screens	—	—	—	—	—	—	—
*c. Searches correctly under each of the screens	—	—	—	—	—	—	—
Other:	—	—	—	—	—	—	—
7. *Finding an Object Completely Covered in Three Places* (5–7)							
a. Loses interest	—	—	—	—	—	—	—
b. Searches haphazardly under some or all screens	—	—	—	—	—	—	—
*c. Searches directly under correct screen	—	—	—	—	—	—	—
Other:	—	—	—	—	—	—	—
8. *Finding an Object after Successive Visible Displacements* (3–5)							
a. Does not follow successive hidings	—	—	—	—	—	—	—
b. Searches only under the first screen	—	—	—	—	—	—	—
c. Searches under screen where object was previously found	—	—	—	—	—	—	—
d. Searches haphazardly under all screens	—	—	—	—	—	—	—
e. Searches in order of hiding	—	—	—	—	—	—	—

SCALE I (continued)

SITUATION	PRESENTATION (Suggested number of presentations for each situation is indicated in parentheses)						
	1	2	3	4	5	6	7
f. Searches directly under the last screen in path	—	—	—	—	—	—	—
Other:	—	—	—	—	—	—	—
9. *Finding an Object under Three Superimposed Screens* (2–3)							
a. Loses interest	—	—	—	—	—	—	—
b. Lifts one or two screens, but fails to find object	—	—	—	—	—	—	—
*c. Removes all screens and obtains object	—	—	—	—	—	—	—
Other:	—	—	—	—	—	—	—
10. *Finding an Object Following One Invisible Displacement* (3)							
a. Loses interest	—	—	—	—	—	—	—
b. Reacts to loss, does not search	—	—	—	—	—	—	—
c. Searches only in the box	—	—	—	—	—	—	—
*d. Checks the box and searches under the screen	—	—	—	—	—	—	—
*e. Searches under screen directly	—	—	—	—	—	—	—
Other:	—	—	—	—	—	—	—
11. *Finding an Object Following One Invisible Displacement with Two Screens* (2)							
a. Searches only in box	—	—	—	—	—	—	—
b. Searches under screen where object was previously found	—	—	—	—	—	—	—
*c. Searches directly under correct screen							
Other:	—	—	—	—	—	—	—
12. *Finding an Object Following One Invisible Displacement with Two Screens Alternated* (3)							
a. Loses interest	—	—	—	—	—	—	—
b. Searches haphazardly under screens	—	—	—	—	—	—	—
*c. Searches directly under correct screen	—	—	—	—	—	—	—
Other:	—	—	—	—	—	—	—
13. *Finding an Object Following One Invisible Displacement with Three Screens* (5–7)							
a. Loses interest	—	—	—	—	—	—	—
b. Searches haphazardly under all screens	—	—	—	—	—	—	—

SCALE I (*continued*)

SITUATION	PRESENTATION (*Suggested number of presentations for each situation is indicated in parentheses*)						
	1	2	3	4	5	6	7
*c. Searches directly under correct screen	___	___	___	___	___	___	___
Other:	___	___	___	___	___	___	___
14. *Finding an Object Following a Series of Invisible Displacements* (4–6)							
a. Searches only in E's hand	___	___	___	___	___	___	___
b. Searches only under first one or two screens in the path	___	___	___	___	___	___	___
*c. Searches under all screens in the path in the order of hiding	___	___	___	___	___	___	___
*d. Searches directly under the last screen in the path	___	___	___	___	___	___	___
15. *Finding Object Following a Series of Invisible Displacements by Searching in Reverse of the Order of Hiding* (2)							
a. Searches only under last screen	___	___	___	___	___	___	___
b. Searches haphazardly under all screens	___	___	___	___	___	___	___
*c. Searches systematically from the last screen back to the first	___	___	___	___	___	___	___
Other:	___	___	___	___	___	___	___

SCALE II: THE DEVELOPMENT OF MEANS FOR OBTAINING DESIRED ENVIRONMENTAL EVENTS

Name:

Birthdate:

Date of Examination:

	PRESENTATION *(Suggested number of presentations for each situation are indicated in parentheses)*			
SITUATION	1	2	3	4

1. *Appearance of Hand-Watching Behavior* (1); also Scale IV-1
    a. Hand-watching is not observed   ___ ___ ___ ___
    *b. Hand-watching is observed   ___ ___ ___ ___
        Comments: ___ ___ ___ ___
2. *Achievement of Visually Directed Grasping* (3); also Scale V–3
    a. Reaches for, but does not grasp object   ___ ___ ___ ___
    *b. Grasps object when both hand *and* object in view ___ ___ ___ ___
    *c. Grasps object by bringing hand up to object   ___ ___ ___ ___
    d. Grasps object by shaping hand in anticipation of
        contact with object   ___ ___ ___ ___
        Other: ___ ___ ___ ___
3. *Repetition of Actions Producing an Interesting Spectacle* (2); also
    Scale IV–2
    a. Shows interest   ___ ___ ___ ___
    b. Intensifies arm movements and activates occasion-
        ally   ___ ___ ___ ___
    *c. Repeats arm movements systematically and keeps
        toy active consistently   ___ ___ ___ ___
    d. Only tries to grasp object   ___ ___ ___ ___
        Other: ___ ___ ___ ___
4. *Letting Go of an Object in Order to Reach for Another* (3)
    a. Reaches for third object while holding the others ___ ___ ___ ___
    b. Reaches for third object with filled hands and drops
        one in the process of reaching   ___ ___ ___ ___
    *c. Drops one of the objects prior to reaching for third ___ ___ ___ ___
        Other: ___ ___ ___ ___
5. *Use of Locomotion As Means* (2)
    a. No attempt to retrieve object, continues play   ___ ___ ___ ___
    b. Indicates desire for object, but does not try to re-
        trieve it   ___ ___ ___ ___
    *c. Moves to regain the object and resumes play using
        it   ___ ___ ___ ___
        Other: ___ ___ ___ ___

SCALE II (*continued*)

		PRESENTATION (*Suggested number of presentations for each situation are indicated in parentheses*)			
SITUATION		I	2	3	4

6. *Use of the Relationship of Suppport* (2)
   a. Reaches for object on the support ⎯ ⎯ ⎯ ⎯
   b. Tries to get object by climbing ⎯ ⎯ ⎯ ⎯
   c. Appeals to another person to get the object ⎯ ⎯ ⎯ ⎯
   *d. Pulls the support after demonstration ⎯ ⎯ ⎯ ⎯
   *e. Pulls support without demonstration ⎯ ⎯ ⎯ ⎯
   Other: ⎯ ⎯ ⎯ ⎯

7. *Understanding of the Relationship of Support* (1–2)
   a. Pulls support expecting to obtain object ⎯ ⎯ ⎯ ⎯
   b. Pulls support, but reaches for object at same time ⎯ ⎯ ⎯ ⎯
   *c. Does not pull the support without the object on it ⎯ ⎯ ⎯ ⎯
   Other: ⎯ ⎯ ⎯ ⎯

8. *Use of String Horizontally* (2)
   a. Reaches for the object, ignoring string ⎯ ⎯ ⎯ ⎯
   b. Manipulates the string, but does not pull it enough to get object ⎯ ⎯ ⎯ ⎯
   *c. Pulls string and gets object after demonstration ⎯ ⎯ ⎯ ⎯
   *d. Pulls string and gets object without demonstration ⎯ ⎯ ⎯ ⎯
   Other: ⎯ ⎯ ⎯ ⎯

9. *Use of String Vertically* (2–3)
   a. Indicates desire for object, ignoring the string ⎯ ⎯ ⎯ ⎯
   b. Drops string to floor and becomes unhappy ⎯ ⎯ ⎯ ⎯
   c. Plays with the string itself ⎯ ⎯ ⎯ ⎯
   d. Pulls the string, but not sufficiently to get the object ⎯ ⎯ ⎯ ⎯
   *e. Pulls string and obtains object after demonstration ⎯ ⎯ ⎯ ⎯
   *f. Pulls string and obtains object without demonstration ⎯ ⎯ ⎯ ⎯
   Other: ⎯ ⎯ ⎯ ⎯

10. *Use of Stick as Means* (2)
    a. Plays only with stick ⎯ ⎯ ⎯ ⎯
    b. Reaches for object, disregarding stick ⎯ ⎯ ⎯ ⎯
    c. Plays with stick and object, does not get object closer ⎯ ⎯ ⎯ ⎯
    *d. Uses stick to get object after demonstration ⎯ ⎯ ⎯ ⎯
    *e. Uses stick to get object without demonstration ⎯ ⎯ ⎯ ⎯
    Other: ⎯ ⎯ ⎯ ⎯

11. *Foresight in the Problem of the Necklace and the Container* (2–3)
    a. Does not try to put necklace into container ⎯ ⎯ ⎯ ⎯
    b. Attempts to put necklace in, but fails repeatedly ⎯ ⎯ ⎯ ⎯
    c. Succeeds in putting necklace in after several unsuccessful attempts ⎯ ⎯ ⎯ ⎯

SCALE II (*continued*)

	PRESENTATION (*Suggested number of presentations for each situation are indicated in parentheses*)			
SITUATION	1	2	3	4
d. Invents a method which is successful after a failure	___	___	___	___
*e. Adopts a method which is successful from the first	___	___	___	___
Other:	___	___	___	___
12. *Foresight in the Problem of the Solid Ring* (2–3)				
a. Does not stack rings	___	___	___	___
b. Uses force in trying to stack solid ring repeatedly	___	___	___	___
c. Attempts to stack solid ring once and avoids it subsequently	___	___	___	___
*d. Sets aside the solid ring without attempting to stack it	___	___	___	___
Other:	___	___	___	___

SCALE III: THE DEVELOPMENT OF IMITATION: VOCAL AND GESTURAL

Name:

Birthdate:

Date of Examination:

IIIa. VOCAL IMITATION

	PRESENTATION (*Suggested number of presentations for each situation is indicated in parentheses*)						
SITUATION	1	2	3	4	5	6	7
1. *Use of Vocalization Other than Crying* (1)							
a. Only vocalizes distress sounds	___	___	___	___	___	___	___
*b. Vocalizes (coos) when not distressed	___	___	___	___	___	___	___
Comments:	___	___	___	___	___	___	___
2. *Response to Familiar Vocalizations* (2–3)	List vocalizations presented:						
a. Shows no interest	___	___	___	___	___	___	___
b. Listens, does not vocalize himself	___	___	___	___	___	___	___
*c. Positive response to infantlike sounds	___	___	___	___	___	___	___

SCALE III (*continued*)

SITUATION	PRESENTATION (*Suggested number of presentations for each situation is indicated in parentheses*)						
	1	2	3	4	5	6	7
d. Vocalizes in response to E's infantlike sounds	—	—	—	—	—	—	—
e. Vocalizes similar sounds, but does not shift to match E	—	—	—	—	—	—	—
f. Vocalizes similar sounds and shifts to match E	—	—	—	—	—	—	—
Other:	—	—	—	—	—	—	—

3. *Response to Familiar Sound Patterns* (2–3)   List vocalizations presented:

	1	2	3	4	5	6	7
a. Shows no interest	—	—	—	—	—	—	—
b. Listens, does not vocalize himself	—	—	—	—	—	—	—
c. Positive response to familiar sound patterns	—	—	—	—	—	—	—
d. Vocalizes in response	—	—	—	—	—	—	—
e. Vocalizes similar sounds in response, but does not shift to match E	—	—	—	—	—	—	—
f. Vocalizes similar sound patterns and shifts to match E	—	—	—	—	—	—	—

4. *Imitation of Familiar Words* (2–3)   List words presented:

	1	2	3	4	5	6	7
a. Listens, does not vocalize	—	—	—	—	—	—	—
b. Vocalizes, but sounds fail to match model's	—	—	—	—	—	—	—
c. Imitates familiar words	—	—	—	—	—	—	—
Other:	—	—	—	—	—	—	—

5. *Imitation of Unfamiliar Sound Patterns* (2–3)   List vocalizations presented:

	1	2	3	4	5	6	7
a. Shows unhappiness or cries	—	—	—	—	—	—	—
b. Shows no interest	—	—	—	—	—	—	—
c. Listens, does not vocalize himself	—	—	—	—	—	—	—
d. Vocalizes, but not similar sounds	—	—	—	—	—	—	—
e. Vocalizes with sounds becoming gradually closer approximations of model's	—	—	—	—	—	—	—
f. Vocalizes with sounds similar to model's immediately	—	—	—	—	—	—	—
Other:	—	—	—	—	—	—	—

6. *Imitation of New Words* (6–7)   List words presented:

— — — — — — —

SCALE III (*continued*)

		PRESENTATION (*Suggested number of presentations for each situation is indicated in parentheses*)						
SITUATION		1	2	3	4	5	6	7
a. Listens, does not vocalize		—	—	—	—	—	—	—
b. Vocalizes, but not similar sounds		—	—	—	—	—	—	—
c. Imitates by gradual approximation								
d. Imitates a few words immediately		—	—	—	—	—	—	—
*e. Imitates most simple words immediately		—	—	—	—	—	—	—
Other:		—	—	—	—	—	—	—

IIIb. GESTURAL IMITATION

	PRESENTATION			
SITUATION	1	2	3	4
1. *Systematic Imitation of Familiar Simple Schemes* (2–3)	List actions presented:			
a. Shows interest, but no attempt to imitate	—	—	—	—
*b. Performs some action consistently, does not imitate	—	—	—	—
*c. Imitates	—	—	—	—
Other:	—	—	—	—
2. *Imitation of Complex Actions Composed of Familiar Schemes* (2–3)	List actions presented:			
a. Attends, but makes no attempt to imitate	—	—	—	—
b. Performs some action consistently, does not imitate	—	—	—	—
*c. Attempts to imitate, but does not approximate on successive attempts	—	—	—	—
*d. Imitates by gradual approximation	—	—	—	—
*e. Imitates model immediately	—	—	—	—
Other:	—	—	—	—
3. *Imitation of Unfamiliar Gestures Visible to the Infant* (2–3)	List gestures presented:			
a. Shows interest, but no attempt to imitate	—	—	—	—
b. Performs some action consistently, but does not imitate	—	—	—	—
c. Imitates by gradual approximation	—	—	—	—

SCALE III (*continued*)

SITUATION	PRESENTATION			
	1	2	3	4
*d. Imitates immediately	___	___	___	___
Other:	___	___	___	___
4. *Imitation of Unfamiliar Gestures Invisible to the Infant* (3–4)	List gestures presented:			
a. Shows interest, but no attempt to imitate	___	___	___	___
*b. Performs some action consistently, does not imitate	___	___	___	___
c. Imitates by gradual approximation	___	___	___	___
*d. Imitates at least one invisible gesture immediately	___	___	___	___
*e. Imitates most invisible gestures immediately	___	___	___	___
Other:	___	___	___	___

SCALE IV: THE DEVELOPMENT OF OPERATIONAL CAUSALITY

Name:

Birthdate:

Date of Examination:

SITUATION	PRESENTATION (*Suggested number of presentations for each situation is indicated in parentheses*)		
	1	2	3
1. *Appearance of Hand-Watching Behavior* (1); also Scale II–1			
a. Hand-watching is not observed	___	___	___
*b. Hand-watching is observed	___	___	___
Comment:	___	___	___
2. *Repetition of Actions Producing an Interesting Spectacle* (2–3); also Scale II–3			
a. Shows interest in object	___	___	___
b. Intensifies arm movements and activates occasionally	___	___	___
*c. Repeats arm movements systematically and keeps object active consistently	___	___	___
d. Only tries to grasp object	___	___	___
Other:	___	___	___

SCALE IV (*continued*)

	PRESENTATION (*Suggested number of presentations for each situation is indicated in parentheses*)		
SITUATION	1	2	3
3. *Use of Specific Action as "Procedure"* (1–2)			
a. Shows interest only during spectacle	___	___	___
b. Shows excitement, but no dominant act during pauses	___	___	___
*c. A dominant act during pauses suggests a "procedure"	___	___	___
d. Reaches for object only	___	___	___
Other:	___	___	___
4. *Behavior in a Familiar Game Situation* (2–3)			
a. Shows no interest	___	___	___
b. Remains passive during pauses	___	___	___
c. A dominant act during pauses suggests a "procedure"	___	___	___
d. Performs part of the act during pauses	___	___	___
e. Touches E and waits during pauses	___	___	___
Other:	___	___	___
5. *Behavior to a Spectacle Created by an Agent* (1–2)			
a. Shows interest only during spectacle	___	___	___
b. Shows excitement, but no dominant act during pauses	___	___	___
*c. A dominant act during pauses suggests a "procedure"	___	___	___
*d. Touches E and waits during pauses	___	___	___
e. Attempts to imitate E	___	___	___
Other:	___	___	___
6. *Behavior to a Spectacle Created by an Agent Acting on an Object* (2–3)			
a. Shows interest only during spectacle	___	___	___
b. A dominant act during pauses suggests a "procedure"	___	___	___
*c. Touches E or the object and waits	___	___	___
*d. Gives object back to E	___	___	___
e. Attempts to activate object	___	___	___
Other:	___	___	___
7. *Behavior to a Spectacle Created by a Mechanical Agent* (1–2)			
a. Plays with object only	___	___	___
b. Makes object perform its activity manually	___	___	___
c. Touches E or object and waits	___	___	___
*d. Gives object back to E	___	___	___
*e. Attempts to activate object mechanically after demonstration	___	___	___
*f. Attempts to discover a way to activate object mechanically before demonstration	___	___	___
Other:	___	___	___

SCALE V: THE CONSTRUCTION OF OBJECT
RELATIONS IN SPACE

Name:

Birthdate:

Date of Examination:

	PRESENTATION *(Suggested number of presentations for each situation is indicated in parentheses)*						
SITUATION	1	2	3	4	5	6	7
1. *Observing Two Objects Alternately* (2–3)							
a. Looks at one object only							
*b. Alternates glance slowly between objects							
*c. Alternates glance rapidly between objects							
Other:							
2. *Localizing an Object by Its Sound* (5–7)							
a. Does not turn to sound							
b. Turns to sound in one direction only							
c. Turns to sound, does not locate its source							
*d. Localizes the source of sound visually							
Other:							
3. *Grasping a Visually Presented Object* (2–3); also Scale II–2							
a. Moves arms in the direction of object, does not touch it							
b. Clasps arms in front of the object							
c. Touches object, but fails to grasp it							
*d. Grasps object							
Other:							
4. *Following the Trajectory of a Rapidly Moving Object* (3–4)							
a. Does not follow object, continues to look at E's hand							
b. Follows some, but does not locate object							
*c. Follows object and locates it visually only when it lands in view							
d. Searches with the eyes for object when it lands out of view, but does not lean							

SCALE V (*continued*)

	PRESENTATION *(Suggested number of presentations for each situation is indicated in parentheses)*						
SITUATION	I	2	3	4	5	6	7
*e. Leans to search for object in the direction where it must have landed	—	—	—	—	—	—	—
Other:	—	—	—	—	—	—	—
5. *Recognizing the Reverse Side of Objects* (2–3)							
a. Grasps object with no sign of appreciation of reversal	—	—	—	—	—	—	—
b. Withdraws hands and appears surprised at reversal	—	—	—	—	—	—	—
*c. Grasps object, but turns it around immediately or by comparing both sides indicates appreciation of reversal	—	—	—	—	—	—	—
Other:	—	—	—	—	—	—	—
6. *Using the Relationship of the Container and the Contained* (2–3)							
a. Does not put objects in; only touches those inside	—	—	—	—	—	—	—
b. Takes objects out, does not put any in	—	—	—	—	—	—	—
c. Puts objects in and takes them out one by one	—	—	—	—	—	—	—
*d. Puts or drops objects in, reverses container to get them out	—	—	—	—	—	—	—
Other:	—	—	—	—	—	—	—
7. *Placing Objects in Equilibrium One upon Another* (2–3)							
a. Does not try to build tower	—	—	—	—	—	—	—
b. Approximates two objects, but does not leave the second on the first	—	—	—	—	—	—	—
*c. Builds a tower of at least two objects	—	—	—	—	—	—	—
Other:	—	—	—	—	—	—	—
8. *Appreciating Gravity in Play with Objects* (2–3)							
a. Does not attempt action	—	—	—	—	—	—	—
b. Acts without showing appreciation of gravity	—	—	—	—	—	—	—

SCALE V (*continued*)

SITUATION	PRESENTATION (*Suggested number of presentations for each situation is indicated in parentheses*)						
	1	2	3	4	5	6	7
*c. Acts with appreciation of the force of gravity	—	—	—	—	—	—	—
Other:	—	—	—	—	—	—	—
9. *Exploring Fall of Dropped Objects* (1–2)							
a. Does not systematically drop objects	—	—	—	—	—	—	—
b. Drops several objects repeatedly, does not look at where they land	—	—	—	—	—	—	—
c. Drops several objects repeatedly and looks to see where they land	—	—	—	—	—	—	—
Other:	—	—	—	—	—	—	—
10. *Making Detours* (2–3)							
a. Loses interest in objects	—	—	—	—	—	—	—
b. Attempts to reach for the object using the same path as object	—	—	—	—	—	—	—
c. Goes directly around the barrier, thus making a detour	—	—	—	—	—	—	—
Other:	—	—	—	—	—	—	—
11. *Indicating Absence of Familiar Persons* (1)							
a. Does not comprehend question	—	—	—	—	—	—	—
b. Goes to the usual location of the person	—	—	—	—	—	—	—
*c. Indicates knowledge of absence by gesture or word	—	—	—	—	—	—	—
Other:	—	—	—	—	—	—	—

SCALE VI: THE DEVELOPMENT OF SCHEMES
FOR RELATING TO OBJECTS

Name:

Birthdate:

Date of Examination:

		OBJECTS PRESENTED TO INFANT					
		1	2	3	4	...	15
				Plastic			
SCHEMES SHOWN	For Example:	Rattle	Doll	Fish	Foil		
a. Holding		——	——	——	——	...	——
*b. Mouthing		——	——	——	——	...	——
*c. Visual inspection		——	——	——	——	...	——
*d. Simple motor schemes:							
1. Hits or pats with hand		——	——	——	——	...	——
2. Hits surface with object		——	——	——	——	...	——
3. Hits two together		——	——	——	——	...	——
4. Shakes		——	——	——	——	...	——
5. Waves		——	——	——	——	...	——
Other:		——	——	——	——	...	——
*e. Examining		——	——	——	——	...	——
*f. Complex motor schemes:							
1. Slides		——	——	——	——	..	——
2. Crumples		——	——	——	——	..	——
3. Swings		——	——	——	——	..	——
4. Tears or stretches		——	——	——	——	..	——
5. Rubs or pats		——	——	——	——	..	——
Other:		——	——	——	——	...	——
*g. "Letting go" actions:							
1. Drops		——	——	——	——	...	——
2. Throws		——	——	——	——	...	——
Other:		——	——	——	——	...	——
*h. Socially instigated actions:							
1. Drinks		——	——	——	——	...	——
2. Wears		——	——	——	——	...	——
3. Drives		——	——	——	——	...	——
4. Builds		——	——	——	——	...	——
5. Hugs		——	——	——	——	...	——
6. Dresses		——	——	——	——	...	——
7. Sniffs		——	——	——	——	...	——
8. Making "walk"		——	——	——	——	...	——
Other:		——	——	——	——	...	——
*i. Showing		——	——	——	——	...	——
*j. Naming		——	——	——	——	...	——
(List name used by infant)							

SAMPLE SUMMARY RECORD FORMS

These summary record forms list first, on the left, the scale steps by number (see Chapter 8 for description). They list next the situation relevant to each step on the scale by the number associated with it in the directions for arranging the situations as well as in the examination record forms. Third, they list the infant action critical for each numbered step by the letter associated with that action under the eliciting situation indicated by number for each scale step. Finally, there is a place to list the infant actions observed in each of the eliciting situations. These can be listed by means of the letters for the infant actions given under each eliciting situation. Once the infant actions observed in each of the eliciting situations are filled in, it is possible to determine at a glance the highest step in the scale achieved by the infant. Such a record form is quite adequate where the purpose of the investigation is to identify the level of each infant on each scale.

Scale VI is an exception to the description above, for the critical actions for the several steps are related to the objects presented rather than to the three eliciting situations. The critical actions for each scale are indicated by letter, except in the case of steps 3 and 4, where they are further specified by the number of the particular action listed under the grouping in the examination record forms, which are given in parentheses.

SCALE I: THE DEVELOPMENT OF VISUAL
PURSUIT AND THE PERMANENCE OF OBJECTS

Infant Code Number:

Age:

Scale Step	Relevant Situation Number	Critical Infant Action	Infant Actions Observed (List situation by no. and response by letter)
1	1	d	_____
2	2	c	_____
3	3	c	_____
4	2	d	_____
5	4	d	_____
6	6 (and 5)	6c (and 5c)[a]	_____
7	7	c	_____
8	9	c	_____
9	10	d or e	_____
10	11	c	_____
11	12	c	_____
12	13	c	_____
13	14	c	_____
14	14 and 15	14d plus 15c	_____

[a] Infant actions in situations 5 and 8 were not included in the scaling analysis. The scale step for which actions in situation 5 may be relevant is indicated in parentheses.

SCALE II: THE DEVELOPMENT OF MEANS FOR OBTAINING DESIRED ENVIRONMENTAL EVENTS

Infant Code Number:

Age:

Scale Step	Relevant Situation Number	Critical Infant Action	Infant Actions Observed (List situation by no. and response by letter)
1	1	b	_____
2	3	c	_____
3	2	b	_____
4	2	2c (or 2d)	_____
5	4	c	_____
6	6	d or e	_____
7	5	c	_____
8	7	c	_____
9	8	c or d	_____
10	9	e or f	_____
11	10	d or e	_____
12	11	e	_____
13	12	d	_____

SCALE III: THE DEVELOPMENT OF IMITATION: VOCAL AND GESTURAL

Infant Code Number:

Age:

IIIa. Vocal Imitation

Scale Step	Relevant Situation Number	Critical Infant Action	Infant Actions Observed (List situation by no. and response by letter)
1	1	b	_____
2	2, 3	2c or 3c	_____
3	2	2d (or 2e)	_____
4	3, 4	3d or 4b (or 3e)	_____
5	3, 4	3f or 4c	_____
6	5	d	_____
7	5 (and 6)	5e (and 6c)[a]	_____
8	5	f	_____
9	6	e	_____

IIIb. Gestural Imitation

Scale Step	Relevant Situation Number	Critical Infant Action	Infant Actions Observed (List situation by no. and response by letter)
1	1 (and 2)	1b (and 2b)[a]	_____
2	1	c	_____
3	2	c	_____
4	2 (and 3, 4)	2d (and 3c, 4c)	_____
5	2	e	_____
6	3	d	_____
7	4	b	_____
8	4	d	_____
9	4	e	_____

[a] The infant actions to situations listed in parentheses were not included in the scaling analysis; however, the scale steps for which they may be appropriate are indicated to facilitate further investigation.

SCALE IV: THE DEVELOPMENT OF OPERATIONAL CAUSALITY

Infant Code Number:

Age:

Scale Step	Relevant Situation Number	Critical Infant Action	Infant Actions Observed (List situation by no. and response by letter)
1	1	b	_____
2	2	c	_____
3	3, 5, 6 (and 4)	3c or 5c (and 6b, 4c)[a]	_____
4	5, 6, 7	5d or 6c (and 7c)	_____
5	6, 7	6d or 7d	_____
6	7	e	_____
7	7	f	_____

[a] Situation 4 was not included in the scaling analysis; the infant action which may be appropriate for one of the scale steps is indicated in parentheses.

SCALE V: THE CONSTRUCTION OF OBJECT RELATIONS IN SPACE

Infant Code Number:

Age:

Scale Step	Relevant Situation Number	Critical Infant Action	Infant Actions Observed (List situation by no. and response by letter)
1	1	b	_____
2	1	c	_____
3	2	d	_____
4	3	d	_____
5	4	c	_____
6	4	e	_____
7	5	c	_____
8	6	d	_____
9	7	c	_____
10	8 (and 9)	8c (and 9c)[a]	_____
11	11 (and 10)	11c (and 10c)	_____

[a] Situations 9 and 10 were not included in the scaling analysis; the infant actions in these situations which may be appropriate for particular scale steps are indicated in parentheses.

SCALE VI: THE DEVELOPMENT OF SCHEMES
FOR RELATING TO OBJECTS

Infant Code Number:

Age:

Scale Step	Critical Infant Action	Objects with Which Actions Were Demonstrated (List)
1	b	_____
2	c	_____
3	d (1–3)ᵃ	_____
4	d (4–5)	_____
5	e	_____
6	f	_____
7	g	_____
8	h	_____
9	i	_____
10	j	_____

ᵃ These numbers in parentheses refer to the particular infant actions listed by number in the directions under *d* and also in the Examination Record Forms under *d*.

APPENDIX A

Mean Inter-observer Agreement for Actions in the Eliciting Situations: Percentages of Agreement Averaged for the Two Observation Sessions

ELICITING SITUATIONS AND INFANT ACTIONS	AGE GROUP OF SUBJECTS IN MONTHS					Total Sample	Total N
	0–3	*4–7*	*8–11*	*12–17*	*18–24*		
1. Following a Slowly Moving Object.							
Follows through part of arc with jerky accommodations	100	—	—	—	—	100	15
Follows through part of arc with smooth accommodations	100	—	—	—	—	100	15
Follows through complete arc with smooth accommodations	100	—	—	—	—	100	15
2. Disappearance of a Slowly Moving Object.							
Follows, but loses interest as soon as ring disappears	96.6	100	—	—	—	98.5	30
Lingers with glance on point of disappearance	80.0	96.6	—	—	—	91.0	30
Lingers, then returns eyes to starting point	93.3	83.3	—	—	—	87.7	30
Returns glance to starting point, then searches around point of disappearance	96.6	83.3	—	—	—	89.2	30
Searches with eyes around point of disappearance	96.6	93.3	—	—	—	94.7	30
3. Partial Hiding.							
Obtains toy.	96.1	96.8	100	100	100	98.6	82
5. Hiding Under One or More Single Screens.							
Fingers screen	—	91.8	100	100	100	97.7	67
Obtains toy with one screen	—	94.4	100	100	100	98.5	67
Searches only under first screen with two screens	—	97.2	100	100	100	99.2	67
Searches haphazardly with two screens	—	94.4	100	100	100	98.5	67
Searches directly under the correct screen with two screens	—	97.2	100	100	100	99.2	67
Searches haphazardly with three screens	—	97.2	100	100	100	99.2	67

NOTE: Situations 4, 6, 23, 24, 27, 31, and 38 were not presented to enough infants to warrant presentation of percentages of inter-observer agreement and inter-session stability.

APPENDIX A (continued)

ELICITING SITUATIONS AND INFANT ACTIONS	AGE GROUP OF SUBJECTS IN MONTHS					Total Sample	Total N
	0–3	4–7	8–11	12–17	18–24		
Searches directly under the correct screen with three screens	—	97.2	100	100	100	99.2	67
7. Superimposed Screens.							
Reacts to loss, but does not touch screens	—	—	95.0	100	100	97.9	48
Lifts one or two screens and gives up	—	—	92.5	100	100	96.8	48
Lifts all screens and obtains toy	—	—	95.0	100	100	97.9	48
8. Hiding with Invisible Displacements under One or More Single Screens.							
Reacts to loss of object with one screen	—	—	100	100	100	100	45
Searches only in box top with one screen	—	—	100	100	100	100	45
Searches in box top and then under the screen with one screen	—	—	94.4	95.8	100	96.5	45
Searches directly under the screen with one screen	—	—	97.2	100	92.8	96.7	45
Searches only in box top with two screens	—	—	97.2	100	100	98.8	44
Searches only under the first screen with two screens	—	—	97.2	100	100	98.8	44
Searches directly under the second screen with two screens	—	—	100	100	100	100	44
Searches haphazardly with two screens alternated	—	—	100	100	100	100	44
Searches directly under the correct screen with two screens alternated	—	—	100	100	100	100	44
Searches haphazardly under all screens with three screens	—	—	100	100	100	100	44
Searches directly under the correct screen with three screens	—	—	100	95.8	88.7	95.4	44
9. Hiding with Successive Invisible Displacements.							
Searches under the first screen or haphazardly	—	—	100	91.6	96.4	96.5	44
Searches successively under all screens in the path of hiding	—	—	100	91.3	92.9	95.4	44

							N
Starts search with the last screen and then retraces the path of hiding	—	—	100	95.8	85.7	94.5	44
10. Hand-Eye Coordination.							
Hand-watching behavior is observed	86.7	—	—	—	—	86.7	15
11. Hand-Mouth Coordination.							
Mouthing of fingers at will is observed	86.5	—	—	—	—	86.5	15
12. Smiling.							
Smiling at mother or E is observed	86.5	—	—	—	—	86.5	15
Smiling at familiar objects is reported	93.3	—	—	—	—	93.3	14
13. Maintaining an Interesting Spectacle, Secondary Circular Reaction.							
Watches spectacle	90.9	100	—	—	—	96.0	30
Shows positive excitation to spectacle	95.4	100	—	—	—	98.0	30
Intensifies hand or leg movements	90.9	94.7	—	—	—	93.0	30
Attempts to keep toy in motion	90.9	94.7	—	—	—	93.0	30
Attempts to obtain toy directly	100	92.1	—	—	—	95.6	30
14. Eye-Hand Coordination, Visually Directed Grasping.							
Reaches for toy when both hand and toy are in view	90.0	100	—	—	—	95.6	34
Reaches when just toy is in view	90.0	100	—	—	—	95.6	34
Grasps toy when both hand and toy are in view	100	100	—	—	—	100	34
Grasps toy when just toy is in view	96.6	97.3	—	—	—	97.0	34
15. Means and Ends, Dropping One Object to Pick Up Another.							
Reaches for third object while holding on to those already in hands	—	—	100	—	—	100	14
Reaches for third object and drops one already held in the process	—	—	100	—	—	100	14
Quickly drops one or both objects already held and then reaches for third	—	96.4	96.4	—	—	96.4	14
16. Means and Ends, Support.							
Reaches for toy	—	—	100	100	100	100	41

APPENDIX A (continued)

ELICITING SITUATIONS AND INFANT ACTIONS	AGE GROUP OF SUBJECTS IN MONTHS					Total Sample	Total N
	0-3	4-7	8-11	12-17	18-24		
Tries to climb onto table to obtain toy or appeals for help	—	—	95.8	96.4	100	97.2	41
Pulls the support and obtains toy after demonstration	—	—	100	100	100	100	41
Pulls the support and obtains toy without demonstration	—	—	100	100	96.6	98.9	41
Does *not* pull the support when toy is held above it	—	—	100	96.4	90.0	96.0	40
7. Means and Ends, Locomotion as Means.							
Reacts to loss of toy, but does not move to retrieve it	—	—	89.5	92.3	—	90.6	32
Moves to retrieve toy	—	—	94.7	92.3	—	93.7	32
18. Means and Ends, String.							
Reaches for toy or tries to climb onto table to obtain it	—	—	—	100	100	100	27
Pulls string horizontally to obtain toy after demonstration	—	—	—	91.6	100	95.9	27
Pulls string horizontally to obtain toy without demonstration	—	—	—	95.8	100	98.0	27
Reacts to loss of toy, does not use string vertically	—	—	—	100	100	100	27
Plays with string only when toy is lowered	—	—	—	100	100	100	27
Pulls string vertically, but not enough to get toy	—	—	—	96.1	100	98.1	27
Pulls string vertically to obtain toy after demonstration	—	—	—	100	100	100	27
Pulls string vertically to obtain toy without demonstration	—	—	—	96.4	100	98.3	27
19. Means and Ends, Stick.							
Reaches for toy or attempts to climb onto table to obtain it	—	—	—	89.0	96.6	92.9	28
Plays with stick only	—	—	—	100	96.6	98.2	28
Plays with stick and toy, but does not get toy within reach	—	—	—	89.0	96.6	92.9	28
Uses stick to obtain toy after demonstration	—	—	—	100	93.1	96.4	28
Uses stick to obtain toy without demonstration	—	—	—	100	96.6	98.2	28
20. Foresight in Manipulation, Necklace and Container.							
Attempts to put in piece by piece and fails	—	—	—	100	95.0	97.4	23

	A	B	C	N
Puts in piece by piece after some failures	100	95.0	97.4	23
Adopts a successful method after a failure	95.0	90.0	92.4	23
Foresees the falling of the container and adopts a successful method from the start	100	95.0	97.4	23
21. Foresight Indicated by Recognition of Solidity.				
Tries to stack the solid ring by force	100	100	100	21
Tries the solid ring but does not persist in attempts to stack it	95.0	95.4	95.2	21
Does not attempt to stack the solid ring	100	95.4	97.6	21
22. Foresight in Manipulation, Nested Boxes.				
Tries to put larger boxes into smaller ones by force	67.8	100	84.4	24
Tries to put larger boxes into smaller ones but readily realizes when they do not fit	57.1	93.3	75.8	24
Gets the boxes together after groping	64.3	96.6	81.0	24
Gets the boxes together without overt groping	67.8	100	84.4	24
25. Differentiation of Vocalizations.				
Vocalization other than crying is observed			86.6	15
26. Recognition by Infant of Own Vocalizations.				
Stops ongoing activity to "adult" sounds			90.0	15
Smiles and/or makes mouth movements to "adult" sounds			86.7	15
Vocalizes in response to "adult" sounds			86.6	15
Shows interest or smiles in response to "own" sounds			96.4	15
Makes mouth movements in response to "own" sounds			96.4	15
Vocalizes in response to "own" sounds			89.5	15
Vocalizes sounds similar to ones made by E			96.6	14
28. Vocal Imitation of Familiar Syllables.				
Shows interest	94.7	97.6	96.2	39
Vocalizes, but not same sounds	86.4	90.4	88.5	39
Vocalizes similar sounds	71.0	76.2	73.7	39
29. Vocal Imitation of Unfamiliar Sounds.				
Shows interest	90.0	92.1	93.4	50
Vocalizes, but not same sounds	90.0	87.3	91.5	50

234

APPENDIX A (continued)

ELICITING SITUATIONS AND INFANT ACTIONS	AGE GROUP OF SUBJECTS IN MONTHS					Total Sample	Total N
	0-3	4-7	8-11	12-17	18-24		
Vocalizes sounds similar to E's by gradual approximation	—	100	89.9	100	—	96.1	50
Vocalizes sounds similar to E's directly	—	100	97.3	92.3	—	96.9	50
30. Vocabulary.							
Has a few words	—	—	—	96.4	100	98.3	29
Has over five words	—	—	—	100	100	100	29
Repeats most new words	—	—	—	100	100	100	29
32. Representation Indicated by Verbal Memory.							
Verbal reference to a past event is observed	—	—	—	—	93.3	93.3	15
33. Imitation of Familiar Gestures.							
Makes a movement other than E's	—	88.7	—	—	—	88.7	13
Makes same movement as E	—	95.8	—	—	—	95.8	13
34. Maintaining an Interesting Spectacle, Hitting.							
Shows interest in spectacle	—	91.6	92.8	100	100	95.4	67
Touches E's hand or a block	—	80.5	95.2	96.4	100	92.4	67
Hits a block in E's hand or one on the floor	—	97.2	95.2	96.4	100	97.0	67
Hits two blocks together after groping	—	100	92.8	96.4	100	97.1	67
Hits two blocks together immediately	—	100	92.8	92.9	100	96.4	67
35. Imitation of Unfamiliar Gestures.							
Makes a movement other than E's	—	92.8	92.8	100	—	94.7	50
Makes same movement as E with or without groping	—	96.4	97.6	96.4	—	96.9	44
36. Imitation of Unfamiliar Gestures, Facial Gestures.							
Makes a movement other than E's	—	—	95.0	100	96.6	96.8	47
Makes same movement directly at least once	—	—	92.0	100	100	96.6	47
37. Maintaining an Interesting Spectacle, "Procedure."							
Reacts with a definite "procedure"	93.3	82.1	—	—	—	87.0	31
Tries to obtain the toy involved	93.6	97.0	—	—	—	96.8	31

235

Item								N
39. Maintaining an Interesting Spectacle, Shaking.								
Touches E's hand or container	—	100	97.6	92.9	100	97.8		64
Makes some movement in response, but not shaking	—	81.3	97.6	92.9	100	92.7		64
Spills blocks in attempt to shake	—	100	100	100	96.6	99.7		64
Shakes container after groping	—	100	100	100	100	100		64
Shakes container directly	—	100	95.2	96.4	100	97.8		64
40. Maintaining an Interesting Spectacle, Spinning Musical Toy.								
Resumes previous play with toy	—	88.7	90.5	96.1	100	93.2		57
Touches toy or E's hand	—	85.7	85.7	100	90.9	89.7		57
Gives toy back to E for repetition of spectacle	—	100	97.6	100	95.4	98.2		57
Tries to spin toy himself	—	100	100	100	90.9	98.0		57
41. Maintaining an Interesting Spectacle, Mechanical Toy.								
Touches toy and waits	—	—	—	100	100	100		24
Imitates toy's movements himself	—	—	—	82.5	100	91.5		24
Gives toy to E or mother to activate	—	—	—	87.5	100	94.0		24
Explores for a way to activate toy himself and concentrates on key after demonstration	—	—	—	—	—	100		24
Attempts to activate toy appropriately with or without demonstration	—	—	—	100	96.6	98.2		24
42. Alternate Glancing.								
Alternates glance slowly	93.3	—	—	—	—	93.3		15
Alternates glance rapidly	93.3	—	—	—	—	93.3		15
43. Eye-Ear Coordination, Localization of Sound.								
Turns head in direction of sound to one side only	93.3	100	—	—	—	97.0		29
Turns head in direction of sound to both sides	100	100	—	—	100	100		29
Localizes source of sound	96.6	96.6	—	—	—	96.6		29
44. Following a Rapidly Moving Object.								
Turns to correct side or follows a short way	90.9	86.5	100	—	—	92.8		49
Follows toy to about where it falls	100	94.7	100	—	—	98.2		50
Follows and searches with eyes around point of disappearance, when object goes out of sight	100	94.7	100	—	—	98.2		50

Appendix A (continued)

ELICITING SITUATIONS AND INFANT ACTIONS	AGE GROUP OF SUBJECTS IN MONTHS					Total Sample	Total N
	0–3	4–7	8–11	12–17	18–24		
Leans forward to search for the object in the direction in which it fell	100						
45. Construction of the Object, Reverse Side.		100	97.5	—	—	99.0	50
Indicates appreciation of reversal by withdrawal or repeated turning of toy		97.3	95.2	—	—	96.2	40
46. Construction of the Object, Container and Contained.		—	97.0	100	90.9	96.0	38
Places or drops objects into the container		—	100	100	100	100	49
47. Construction of the Object, Building a Tower.							
Scatters tower, does not build		—	100	—	—		
Approximates two blocks, does not leave one on top of the other		—	97.6	100	100	99.0	49
Builds a tower of at least two blocks		—	100	100	100	100	49
48. Phenomenon of the Fall.							
Deliberately watches the fall of an object		—	100	89.3	—	95.7	35
49. Orientation in Space, Absence of a Familiar Person.							
Indicates knowledge of absence		—	—	—	96.4	96.4	14
62. Representation Indicated by Action.							
An instance is observed		—	—	75.0	93.3	84.5	26
63. Recognition of Objects Indicated by Naming.							
Names one object spontaneously		—	—	96.4	93.3	94.8	29
Names more than one object spontaneously		—	—	96.4	93.3	94.8	29

SCHEMES FOR RELATING TO OBJECTS	AGE GROUP OF SUBJECTS IN MONTHS					Total Sample	Total N
	0–3	4–7	8–11	12–17	18–24		
Eliciting Situations Used[a]	50–52	50–57	51–61	51–61	51–61		
Mean Percentages of Agreement on Actions across Infants and Objects							
Mouthing	92.1	93.3	93.6	95.3	94.7	93.7	84
Visual Inspection	91.5	85.3	81.1	84.2	80.6	84.3	84
Hitting	100	94.1	92.4	92.6	91.1	93.9	84
Shaking	87.2	89.8	91.5	91.5	90.8	90.2	84
Examining	100	90.4	89.3	90.4	81.5	90.2	84
Differentiated schemes	98.5	89.4	90.3	92.3	94.4	92.6	84
Dropping	100	97.2	94.0	94.1	89.9	95.1	84
Throwing	100	98.6	94.0	89.3	84.6	93.6	84
Socially instigated behaviors	100	99.5	95.9	96.3	91.2	96.7	84
Showing	100	100	99.3	95.9	89.2	97.2	84
Naming	100	100	97.0	95.5	90.3	96.7	84
Mean for all actions:	94.5	93.1	96.2	95.8	96.9	96.1	84

[a] Numbers refer to the eliciting situations described in Chapter 6. Since the schemes for relating to objects have been elicited by presenting infants with various objects, each of these numbers refers to an object: 50, the rattle; 51, doll; 52, foil; 53, musical toy; 54, necklace; 55, toy animal; 56, toy car; 57, six blocks; 58, familiar toy; 59, cup; 60, ball of cotton; 61, doll's shoe.

APPENDIX B

Mean Inter-session Stability of Actions in the Eliciting Situations: Percentages of Agreement Averaged for the Two Observers

ELICITING SITUATIONS AND INFANT ACTIONS	AGE GROUP OF SUBJECTS IN MONTHS					Total Sample	Total N
	0–3	4–7	8–11	12–17	18–24		
1. Following a Slowly Moving Object							
Follows through part of arc with jerky accommodations	100	—	—	—	—	100	15
Follows through part of arc with smooth accommodations	100	—	—	—	—	100	15
Follows through complete arc with smooth accommodations	93.3	—	—	—	—	93.3	15
2. Disappearance of a Slowly Moving Object.							
Follows, but loses interest as soon as ring disappears	83.3	100	—	—	—	92.6	30
Lingers with glance at point of disappearance	73.3	96.6	—	—	—	86.3	30
Lingers, then returns eyes to starting point	86.6	63.3	—	—	—	73.6	30
Returns glance to starting point, then searches around point of disappearance	90.0	70.0	—	—	—	78.8	30
Searches with eyes around point of disappearance	90.0	73.3	—	—	—	80.7	30
3. Partial Hiding.							
Obtains toy.	89.0	81.5	100	100	100	93.8	82
5. Hiding under One or More Single Screens.							
Handles the one screen	—	55.2	95.2	100	100	86.2	67
Obtains toy with one screen	—	78.9	95.2	100	100	92.7	67
Searches only under first screen with two screens	—	81.5	95.2	100	100	93.4	67
Searches haphazardly with two screens	—	73.7	90.5	100	100	89.9	67
Searches directly under the correct screen with two screens	—	76.3	85.7	92.3	100	87.6	67
Searches haphazardly with three screens	—	81.5	95.2	100	100	93.4	67
Searches directly under correct screen with three screens	—	92.1	81.0	100	100	92.0	67

						N
7. Superimposed Screens.						
Reacts to loss, but does not touch screens	—	81.0	100	100	92.0	48
Lifts one or two screens and gives up	—	78.6	100	100	91.0	48
Lifts all screens and obtains toy	—	61.9	100	100	84.0	48
8. Hiding with Invisible Displacements under One or More Single Screens.						
Reacts to loss of object with one screen	—	85.0	100	93.3	91.7	45
Searches only in box top with one screen	—	85.0	100	93.3	91.7	45
Searches in box top and then lifts the one screen	—	67.5	79.1	93.3	78.5	45
Searches directly under the one screen	—	70.8	83.3	73.3	75.0	45
Searches only in box top with two screens	—	82.5	100	80.0	86.6	44
Searches only under the first screen with two screens	—	72.5	83.3	80.0	77.8	44
Searches directly under the second screen	—	85.0	75.0	73.3	78.7	44
Searches haphazardly with two screens alternated	—	85.0	83.3	80.0	83.0	44
Searches directly under the correct screen with two screens alternated	—	85.0	83.3	73.3	81.0	44
Searches haphazardly under all screens with three screens	—	85.0	83.3	80.0	83.0	44
Searches directly under the correct screen with three screens	—	85.0	87.5	66.7	80.2	44
9. Hiding with Successive Invisible Displacements.						
Searches under the first screen or haphazardly	—	80.0	70.8	76.6	76.4	44
Searches successively under all screens in the path	—	80.0	83.3	60.0	74.9	44
Starts search with the last screen and then retraces the path of E's hand	—	85.0	87.5	53.3	76.2	44
10. Hand-Eye Coordination.						
Hand-watching behavior is observed	73.3	—	—	—	73.3	15
11. Hand-Mouth Coordination.						
Mouthing of fingers is observed	53.3	—	—	—	53.3	15
12. Smiling.						
Smiling at mother or E is observed	53.3	—	—	—	53.3	15
Smiling at familiar objects is reported	86.7	—	—	—	86.7	14

APPENDIX B (continued)

ELICITING SITUATIONS AND INFANT ACTIONS	AGE GROUP OF SUBJECTS IN MONTHS					Total Sample	Total N
	0-3	4-7	8-11	12-17	18-24		
13. Maintaining an Interesting Spectacle, Secondary Circular Reaction.							
Watches spectacle	63.6	100	—	—	—	83.9	30
Shows positive excitation to spectacle	59.0	100	—	—	—	81.9	30
Intensifies movements of hand or leg	54.9	94.7	—	—	—	77.0	30
Attempts to keep toy in motion	63.6	89.5	—	—	—	78.1	30
Attempts to obtain toy directly	100	71.0	—	—	—	83.8	30
14. Eye-Hand Coordination, Visually Directed Grasping.							
Reaches for toy when both hand and toy are in view	76.6	94.7	—	—	—	86.7	34
Reaches when just toy is in view	83.3	94.7	—	—	—	89.7	34
Grasps toy when both hand and toy are in view	100	100	—	—	—	100	34
Grasps when just toy is in view	90.0	97.3	—	—	—	94.1	34
15. Means and Ends, Dropping One Object to Pick Up Another.							
Reaches for third object while holding onto those already in hands	—	—	81.2	—	—	81.2	14
Reaches for third object and drops one already held in the process	—	—	68.7	—	—	68.7	14
Quickly drops one or both objects already held and then reaches for third	—	—	46.8	—	—	46.8	14
16. Means and Ends, Support.							
Reaches for toy	—	—	91.7	100	100	96.5	41
Tries to climb onto table to obtain toy or appeals for help	—	—	87.5	96.4	100	94.6	41
Pulls the support and obtains toy after demonstration	—	—	83.3	85.7	100	89.0	41
Pulls the support and obtains toy without demonstration	—	—	75.0	64.3	90.0	76.5	41

							N
Does not pull the support when the toy is held above it	—	—	58.3	75.0	43.3	58.5	40
17. Means and Ends, Locomotion as Means.							
Reacts to loss of toy, but does not move to retrieve it	—	—	71.4	60.7	—	67.1	32
Moves to retrieve toy	—	—	71.4	70.3	—	71.0	32
18. Means and Ends, String.							
Reaches for toy or tries to climb onto table to obtain toy	—	—	—	85.7	93.3	89.6	27
Pulls string horizontally to obtain toy after demonstration	—	—	—	57.1	93.3	75.8	27
Pulls string horizontally to obtain toy without demonstration	—	—	—	60.7	93.3	77.6	27
Reacts to loss of toy, does not use string vertically	—	—	—	92.9	100	96.6	27
Plays with string only when toy is lowered	—	—	—	92.9	100	96.6	27
Pulls string vertically, but not enough to get toy	—	—	—	67.8	100	84.4	27
Pulls string vertically to obtain toy after demonstration	—	—	—	57.1	85.7	71.9	27
Pulls string vertically to obtain toy without demonstration	—	—	—	82.1	71.4	76.6	27
19. Means and Ends, Stick.							
Reaches for toy or attempts to climb onto table to obtain toy	—	—	—	85.7	96.6	91.3	28
Plays with stick only	—	—	—	92.9	96.6	94.8	28
Plays with stick and toy, but does not get toy within reach	—	—	—	78.5	89.8	84.3	28
Uses stick to obtain toy after demonstration	—	—	—	92.9	65.7	78.8	28
Uses stick to obtain toy without demonstration	—	—	—	85.7	96.6	91.3	28
20. Foresight in Manipulation, Necklace and Container.							
Attempts to put in piece by piece and fails	—	—	—	57.1	50.0	53.4	23
Puts in piece by piece after some failures	—	—	—	42.9	50.0	46.6	23
Adopts a successful method after a failure	—	—	—	53.3	46.6	49.9	23
Foresees the falling of the container and adopts a successful method from the start	—	—	—	64.3	50.0	56.9	23
21. Foresight Indicated by Recognition of Solidity.							
Tries to stack the solid ring by force	—	—	—	80.0	100	90.3	21
Tries the solid ring but does not persist in attempts to stack it	—	—	—	95.0	86.3	90.5	21
Does not attempt to stack the solid ring	—	—	—	100	77.2	88.2	21

APPENDIX B (continued)

ELICITING SITUATIONS AND INFANT ACTIONS	AGE GROUP OF SUBJECTS IN MONTHS					Total Sample	Total N
	0-3	4-7	8-11	12-17	18-24		
22. Foresight in Manipulation, Nested Boxes.							
Tries to put larger boxes into smaller ones by force	—	—	—	50.0	100	75.9	24
Tries to put larger boxes into smaller ones but readily realizes when they do not fit	—	—	—	32.1	80.0	56.9	24
Gets the boxes together after trial and error	—	—	—	60.7	76.6	68.9	24
Gets the boxes together without overt groping	—	—	—	64.3	93.3	79.3	24
25. Differentiation of Vocalizations.							
Vocalization other than crying is observed	60.0	—	—	—	—	60.0	15
26. Recognition by Infant of Own Vocalizations.							
Stops ongoing activity in response to "adult" sounds	70.0	—	—	—	—	70.0	15
Smiles and/or makes mouth movements to "adult" sounds	73.3	—	—	—	—	73.3	15
Vocalizes in response to "adult" sounds	80.0	—	—	—	—	80.0	15
Shows interest or smiles in response to "own" sounds	76.6	—	—	—	—	76.6	15
Makes mouth movements in response to "own" sounds	43.3	—	—	—	—	43.3	15
Vocalizes in response to "own" sounds	43.3	—	—	—	—	43.3	15
Vocalizes sounds similar to the ones made by E	76.6	—	—	—	—	76.6	14
28. Vocal Imitation of Familiar Syllables.							
Shows interest	—	89.4	97.6	—	—	93.7	39
Vocalizes, but not same sounds	—	55.2	76.2	—	—	66.2	39
Vocalizes similar sounds	—	71.0	76.2	—	—	73.7	39
29. Vocal Imitation of Unfamiliar Sounds.							
Shows interest	—	47.0	87.2	85.7	—	72.6	50
Vocalizes, but not same sounds	—	47.0	71.7	78.6	—	64.8	50
Vocalizes sounds similar to E's by gradual approximation	—	83.3	79.6	57.1	—	75.1	50
Vocalizes sounds similar to E's directly	—	83.3	87.2	57.1	—	78.0	50

							N
30. Vocabulary.							
Has a few words	—	—	—	96.4	100	93.3	29
Has over five words	—	—	—	100	93.3	96.5	29
Repeats most new words	—	—	—	100	86.7	93.1	29
32. Representation Indicated by Verbal Memory.							
Verbal expression of some memory is observed	—	—	—	—	86.7	86.7	15
33. Imitation of Familiar Gestures.							
Makes a movement other than E's	—	43.3	—	—	—	43.3	13
Makes same movement as E	—	63.3	—	—	—	63.3	13
34. Maintaining an Interesting Spectacle, Hitting.							
Shows interest in spectacle	—	75.2	88.1	92.9	80.0	83.7	67
Touches E's hand or a block	—	63.9	66.6	75.0	86.7	71.9	67
Hits a block in E's hand or one on the floor	—	86.1	71.4	82.1	86.7	80.9	67
Hits two blocks together after groping	—	100	69.0	82.1	86.7	84.0	67
Hits two blocks together immediately	—	100	54.7	85.7	80.0	79.0	67
35. Imitation of Unfamiliar Gestures.							
Makes a movement other than E's	—	62.4	64.2	100	—	72.8	50
Makes same movement as E with or without groping	—	78.1	64.3	96.4	—	77.5	44
36. Imitation of Unfamiliar Gestures, Facial Gestures.							
Makes a movement other than E's	—	—	57.1	78.6	56.6	63.0	47
Makes same movement directly at least once	—	—	69.0	78.6	60.0	69.0	47
37. Maintaining an Interesting Spectacle, "Procedure."							
Reacts with a definite "procedure"	70.0	65.7	—	—	—	67.6	31
Tries to obtain the toy involved	96.6	85.7	—	—	—	90.5	31
39. Maintaining an Interesting Spectacle, Shaking.							
Touches E's hand or container	—	100	83.3	78.5	80.0	86.2	64
Makes some movement in response, but not shaking	—	53.5	83.3	78.5	80.0	73.4	64
Spills blocks in the attempt to shake	—	64.3	66.7	71.4	83.3	70.6	64
Shakes container after groping	—	64.3	66.7	71.4	66.7	67.0	64
Shakes container directly	—	85.7	66.7	53.5	73.3	70.7	64

APPENDIX B (continued)

ELICITING SITUATIONS AND INFANT ACTIONS	AGE GROUP OF SUBJECTS IN MONTHS					Total Sample	Total N
	0–3	4–7	8–11	12–17	18–24		
40. Maintaining an Interesting Spectacle, Spinning Musical Toy.							
Resumes previous play with toy	—	45.8	76.2	67.8	90.9	69.3	57
Touches toy or E's hand	—	41.7	47.6	57.1	81.8	55.3	57
Gives toy back to E for repetition of spectacle	—	58.3	83.3	64.3	68.1	69.2	57
Tries to spin toy himself	—	58.3	90.5	92.9	54.5	74.3	57
41. Maintaining an Interesting Spectacle, Mechanical Toy.							
Touches toy and waits	—	—	—	80.0	93.3	86.9	24
Imitates toy's movements himself	—	—	—	45.0	86.7	66.6	24
Gives toy to E or mother to activate	—	—	—	50.0	86.7	69.0	24
Explores for a way to activate toy himself	—	—	—	60.0	73.3	66.9	24
Attempts to activate toy appropriately with or without demonstration	—	—	—	80.0	70.0	74.8	24
42. Alternate Glancing.							
Alternates glance slowly	80.0	—	—	—	—	80.0	15
Alternates glance rapidly	86.7	—	—	—	—	86.7	15
43. Eye-Ear Coordination, Localization of Sound.							
Turns head in direction of sound to one side only	80.0	93.3	—	—	—	87.4	29
Turns head in direction of sound to both sides	86.7	93.3	—	—	—	90.4	29
Localizes source of sound	90.0	90.0	—	—	—	90.0	29
44. Following a Rapidly Moving Object.							
Turns to correct side or follows a short way	81.8	81.5	95.2	—	—	86.8	49
Follows toy to about where it falls	100	89.5	90.5	—	—	92.7	50
Follows and searches with eyes around point of disappearance, when object goes out of sight	100	86.8	90.5	—	—	91.2	50
Leans forward to search for the object in the direction in which it fell	100	84.2	78.6	—	—	86.4	50

45. Construction of the Object, Reverse Side.						
Indicates appreciation of reversal by withdrawal or turning of toy	81.5	90.5	—	—	86.2	40
46. Construction of the Object, Container and Contained.						
Places or drops objects into the container	—	73.5	80.0	77.2	76.4	38
47. Construction of the Object, Building a Tower.						
Scatters tower, does not build	—	95.2	100	93.3	95.9	49
Approximates two blocks, does not leave one on top of the other	—	88.1	78.6	66.7	75.5	49
Builds a tower of at least two blocks	—	100	92.9	73.3	90.0	49
48. Phenomenon of the Fall.						
Watches the fall of an object	—	90.5	67.8	—	81.4	35
49. Orientation in Space, Absence of a Familiar Person.						
Indicates knowledge of absence	—	—	—	76.6	76.6	14
62. Representation Indicated by Action.						
An instance is observed	—	—	71.4	53.3	62.0	26
63. Recognition of Objects Indicated by Naming.						
Names one object spontaneously	—	—	96.4	82.1	89.0	29
Names more than one object spontaneously	—	—	80.0	72.3	76.5	29

APPENDIX B (continued)

SCHEMES FOR RELATING TO OBJECTS	AGE GROUP OF SUBJECTS IN MONTHS					Total Sample	Total N
	0–3	4–7	8–11	12–17	18–24		
Eliciting Situations Used[a]	50–52	50–57	51–61	51–61	51–61	51–61	
Mean Percentages of Inter-session Stability of Actions across Infants and Objects							
Mouthing	66.0	69.2	69.9	70.8	87.6	73.3	84
Visual Inspection	67.5	70.0	63.0	57.1	55.2	63.0	84
Hitting	96.9	78.0	75.6	77.8	82.4	81.5	84
Shaking	78.5	78.7	75.6	67.1	77.8	75.8	84
Examining	95.4	75.7	69.2	68.9	64.4	74.4	84
Differentiated Schemes	86.3	84.2	78.1	55.0	78.2	77.1	84
Dropping	95.4	95.5	78.8	70.2	78.8	84.1	84
Throwing	90.9	93.4	70.2	71.4	69.1	79.1	84
Socially Instigated Behaviors	95.4	93.4	87.8	70.5	69.2	84.2	84
Showing	95.4	98.0	97.3	78.6	63.6	88.0	84
Naming	100	100	97.0	85.2	72.1	91.8	84
Mean for all actions:	81.2	79.0	79.3	79.0	81.9	79.9	84

[a] Numbers refer to the eliciting situations described in Chapter 6. Since the schemes for relating to objects have been elicited by presenting infants with various objects, each of these numbers refers to an object: 50, the rattle; 51, doll; 52, foil; 53, musical toy; 54, necklace; 55, toy animal; 56, toy car; 57, six blocks; 58, familiar toy; 59, cup; 60, ball of cotton; 61, doll's shoe.

References

Altman, J., and Das, G. D. 1964. Autoradiographic examination of enriched environment on the rate of glial multiplication in the adult rat brain. *Nature* 204: 1161–65.

Anderson, L. D. 1939. The predictive value of infancy tests in relation to intelligence at five years. *Child Development* 10:203–12.

Bartoshuk, A. K. 1962. Response decrement with repeated elicitation of human neonatal cardiac acceleration to sound. *Journal of Comparative and Physiological Psychology* 55:9–13.

Bayley, N. 1933. Mental growth during the first three years. A developmental study of 61 children by repeated tests. *Genetic Psychology Monographs* 14:1–92.

———. 1940. Mental growth in young children. *Yearbook, National Society for Studies in Education* 39(2):11–47.

———. 1969. *Bayley scales of infant development.* New York: Psychological Corporation.

Bennett, E. L.; Diamond, M. C.; Krech, D.; and Rosenzweig, M. R. 1964. Chemical and anatomical plasticity of the brain. *Science* 146:610–19.

Berlyne, D. E. 1960. *Conflict, arousal, and curiosity.* New York: McGraw-Hill.

Boole, G. 1854. *An investigation of the laws of thought.* New York: Dover (1953).

Brattgård, S. O. 1952. The importance of adequate stimulation for the chemical composition of retinal ganglion cells during early post-natal development. *Acta Radiologica* (Stockholm) Suppl. 96: 1–80.

Bridger, W. H. 1961. Sensory habituation and discrimination in the human neonate. *American Journal of Psychiatry* 117:991–96.

Bühler, C., and Hetzer, H. 1927. Inventar der Verhaltungsweisen des ersten Lebensjahres. *Quellen und Studien zur Jugenkunde* 5:125–250.

Cattell, P. 1947. *The measurement of intelligence of infants and young children.* New York: Psychological Corporation.

Coghill, G. E. 1929. *Anatomy and the problem of behavior.* Cambridge: Cambridge University Press (New York: Macmillan).

Cohen, L. B. 1969. Observing responses, visual preferences and habituation to visual stimuli in infants. *Journal of Experimental Child Psychology* 7:419–33.

Cohen, L. B.; Gelber, E. R.; and Lazar, M. A. 1971. Infant habituation and generalization to differing degrees of stimulus novelty. *Journal of Experimental Child Psychology* 11:379–89.

Coleman, P. D., and Riesen, A. H. 1968. Environmental effects on cortical dendritic fields. I, Rearing in the dark. *Journal of Anatomy* (London) 102:363–74.

Coombs, C. H. 1964. *Theory of data*. New York: Wiley.

Corman, H. H., and Escalona, S. K. 1969. Stages of sensorimotor development: A replication study. *Merrill-Palmer Quarterly* 15:351–61.

Curcio, F. 1969. The role of age and experience in infants' selective attention to novelty and incongruity. Ph.D. dissertation, Clark University.

Décarie, T. G. 1965. *Intelligence and affectivity in early childhood*. New York: International University Press.

Dennis, W. 1941. Infant development under conditions of restricted practice and of minimum social stimulation. *Genetic Psychology Monographs* 23:143–89.

———. 1960. Causes of retardation among institutional children: Iran. *Journal of Genetic Psychology* 96:47–59.

Disher, D. R. 1934. The reactions of newborn infants to chemical stimuli administered nasally. *Ohio State University Studies of Infant Behavior*, No. 12: 1–52. Columbus: Ohio State University Press.

Dodge, R. 1923. Habituation to rotation. *Journal of Experimental Psychology* 6:1–35.

Engen, T., and Lipsitt, L. P. 1965. Decrement and recovery of responses to olfactory stimulation in the human neonate. *Journal of Comparative and Physiological Psychology* 59:312–16.

Engen, T.; Lipsitt, L. P.; and Kaye, H. 1963. Olfactory responses and adaptation in the human neonate. *Journal of Comparative and Physiological Psychology* 56:73–77.

Fantz, R. L. 1961. The origin of form perception. *Scientific American* 204(5):66–72.

———. 1963. Pattern vision in newborn infants. *Science* 140:296–97.

———. 1964. Visual experience in infants: Decreased attention to familiar patterns relative to novel ones. *Science* 146:668–70.

Ferguson, G. A. 1954. On learning and human ability. *Canadian Journal of Psychology* 8:95–112.

Flavell, J. H. 1972. An analysis of cognitive-developmental sequences. *Genetic Psychology Monographs* 86:279–350.

Flavell, J. H., and Wohlwill, J. F. 1969. Formal and functional aspects of cognitive development. In D. Elkind and J. H. Flavell, eds., *Studies in cognitive development*. New York: Oxford University Press, pp. 67–120.

Forbes, H. S., and Forbes, H. B. 1927. Fetal sense reaction: hearing. *Journal of Comparative Psychology* 7:353–55.

Friedlander, B. Z. 1970. Receptive language development in infancy: Issues and problems. *Merrill-Palmer Quarterly* 16:7–51.

Friedman, S.; Nagy, A. N.; and Carpenter, G. C. 1970. Newborn attention: Differential response decrement to visual stimuli. *Journal of Experimental Child Psychology* 10:44–51.

Furfey, P. H., and Muehlenbein, J. 1932. The validity of infant intelligence tests. *Journal of Genetic Psychology* 40:219–23.

Furth, H. G. 1969. *Piaget and knowledge: Theoretical foundations*. Englewood Cliffs, N.J.: Prentice-Hall.

Gagné, R. M. 1965. *The conditions of learning*. New York: Holt, Rinehart and Winston.

Gagné, R. M., and Paradise, N. E. 1961. Abilities and learning sets in knowledge acquisition. *Psychological Monographs* 75, No. 14 (Whole No. 518).

Gesell, A. 1954. The ontogenesis of infant behavior. In L. Carmichael, ed., *Manual of child psychology*. New York: Wiley, Ch. 6.

Gesell, A., and Armatruda, C. S. 1941. *Developmental diagnosis: Normal and abnormal child development, clinical methods and practical applications*. New York: Hoeber.

Gesell, A.; Halverson, H. M.; Thompson, H.; Ilg, F. L.; Castner, B. M.; and Bates, L. 1940. *The first five years of life*. New York: Harper.

Goodenough, F. L. 1939. A critique of experiments on raising the IQ. *Educational Method* 19:73–79.

Goodenough, F. L., and Maurer, K. M. 1942. *The mental growth of children from two to fourteen years: A study of the predictive value of the Minnesota Preschool Scales*. Minneapolis: University of Minnesota Press.

Green, B. F. 1956. A method of scalogram analysis using summary statistics. *Psychometrika* 21:79–88.

Greenberg, D. J.; Užgiris, I. Č.; and Hunt, J. McV. 1968. Hastening the development of the blink-response with looking. *Journal of Genetic Psychology* 113:167–76.

———. 1970. Attentional preference and experience: III, Visual familiarity and looking time. *Journal of Genetic Psychology* 117:123–35.

Gunther, M. 1961. Infant behavior at the breast. In B. M. Foss, ed., *Determinants of infant behaviour*. London: Methuen, pp. 37–44.

Gyllesten, L. 1959. Postnatal development of the visual cortex in darkness (mice). *Acta Morphologica* (Neerlando-Scandinavica) 2:331–45.

Harlow, H. F. 1949. The formation of learning sets. *Psychological Review* 56:51–65.

Harris, J. D. 1943. Habituation response decrement in the intact organism. *Psychological Bulletin* 40:385–422.

Haynes, H.; White, B. L.; and Held, R. 1965. Visual accommodation in human infants. *Science* 148:528–30.

Hebb, D. O. 1949. *The organization of behavior*. New York: Wiley.

Honzik, M. P.; Macfarlane, J. W.; and Allen, L. 1948. The stability of mental test performance between two and 18 years. *Journal of Experimental Education* 17:309–24.

Hunt, J. McV. 1961. *Intelligence and experience*. New York: Ronald Press.

———. 1963a. Motivation inherent in information processing and action. In O. J. Harvey, ed., *Motivation and social interaction: The cognitive determinants*. New York: Ronald Press, pp. 35–94.

———. 1963b. Piaget's observations as a source of hypotheses concerning motivation. *Merrill-Palmer Quarterly* 9:263–75.

———. 1965. Intrinsic motivation and its role in psychological development. In D. Levine, ed., *Nebraska Symposium on Motivation* 13:189–282. Lincoln: University of Nebraska Press.

———. 1966. Toward a theory of guided learning in development. In R. H. Ojemann and K. Pritchett, eds., *Giving emphasis to guided learning*. Cleveland: Educational Research Council, pp. 99–160.

———. 1970. Attentional preference and experience: I, Introduction. *Journal of Genetic Psychology* 117:99–107.

———. 1971a. Early childhood learning. In L. C. Deighton, ed., *The encyclopedia of education*, Vol. 3. New York: Macmillan Co. and The Free Press, pp. 173–86.

———. 1971b. Intrinsic motivation and psychological development. In H. M. Schroder and P. Suedfeld, eds., *Personality theory and information processing*. New York: Ronald Press, Ch. 5.

Hunt, J. McV.; Paraskevopoulos, J.; Schickedanz, D.; and Užgiris, I. Č. 1975.

Variations in mean ages of achieving object permanence under diverse conditions of rearing. In B. Z. Friedlander, G. Sterritt, and G. E. Kirk, eds., *The exceptional infant*, Vol. 3: *Assessment and intervention*. New York: Bruner/Mazel (in press).

Hydén, H. 1943. Protein metabolism in the nerve cell during growth and function. *Acta Physiologica Scandinavica*, Suppl. 17: 1–70.

———. 1950. Spectroscopic studies on nerve cells in development, growth and function. In P. Weiss, ed., *Genetic neurology; International conference on the development, growth, and regeneration of the nervous system*. Chicago: University of Chicago Press.

———. 1960. The neuron. In H. Brachet and A. E. Mirsky, eds., *The cell: Biochemistry, physiology, morphology*. Vol. 4, *Specialized cells*. New York: Academic Press, Ch. 5.

Inhelder, B. 1956. Comments in discussion on the criteria of stages of mental development. In J. M. Tanner and B. Inhelder, eds., *Discussions on child development*, Vol. I. London: Tavistock Publication, pp. 75–107.

Inhelder, B., and Piaget, J. 1955. *The growth of logical thinking from childhood to adolescence: An essay on the construction of formal operational structures*, trans. by A. Parsons and S. Milgram. New York: Basic Books, 1958.

Jeffrey, W. E., and Cohen, L. B. 1971. Habituation in the human infant. In H. W. Reese, ed., *Advances in child development and behavior*, Vol. 6. New York: Academic Press, pp. 63–97.

Jones, H. E. 1954. The environment and mental development. In L. Carmichael, ed., *Handbook of child psychology*. New York: Wiley.

Kaplan, B. 1966. The comparative developmental approach and its application to symbolization and language in psychopathology. In S. Arieti, ed., *American handbook of psychiatry*, Vol. III. New York: Basic Books, pp. 659–88.

———. 1967a. Meditations on genesis. *Human Development* 10:65–87.

———. 1967b. Strife of systems: The tension between organismic and developmental points of view. Unpublished manuscript, submitted on invitation for a volume of essays in honor of L. von Bertalanffy.

Kaye, H. 1965. The conditioned Babkin reflex in human newborns. *Psychonomic Science* 2:287–89.

Kessen, W. 1966. Questions for a theory of cognitive development. *Monographs of the Society for Research in Child Development* 31, No. 5 (Whole No. 107): 55–70.

King, W. L., and Seegmiller, B. 1973. Performance of 14- to 22-month-old black, firstborn male infants on two tests of cognitive development: The Bayley Scales and the Infant Psychological Development Scale. *Developmental Psychology* 8:317–26.

Kohen-Raz, R. 1967. Scalogram analysis of some developmental sequences of infant behavior as measured by the Bayley Infant Scales of Mental Development. *Genetic Psychology Monographs* 76:3–21.

Langer, J. 1969. *Theories of development*. New York: Holt, Rinehart and Winston.

Levine, S., and Lewis, G. W. 1963. Developmental pattern of adrenal ascorbic acid in the rat. *Science* 139:118–19.

Liberman, R. 1962. Retinal cholinesterase and glycolysis in rats raised in darkness. *Science* 135:372–73.

Lipsitt, L. P. 1967. Learning in the human infant. In H. W. Stevenson, R. Hess, and H. L. Rheingold, eds., *Early Behavior: Comparative and developmental approaches*. New York: Wiley, pp. 225–47.

———. 1969. Learning capacities of the human infant. In R. J. Robinson, ed., *Brain and early behavior*. New York: Academic Press, pp. 227–45.

Lipsitt, L. P., and Kaye, H. 1964. Conditioned sucking in the human newborn. *Psychonomic Science* 1:29–30.

———. 1965. Change in neonatal response to optimizing and nonoptimizing sucking stimulation. *Psychonomic Science* 2:221–22.

Lipsitt, L. P.; Kaye, H.; and Bosack, T. 1966. Enhancement of neonatal sucking through reinforcement. *Journal of Experimental Child Psychology* 4:163–68.

Marquis, D. P. 1931. Can conditioned responses be established in the newborn infant? *Journal of Genetic Psychology* 39:479–92.

McGraw, M. B. 1943. *The neuromuscular maturation of the human infant*. New York: Columbia University Press.

McKee, J. P., and Honzik, M. P. 1962. The sucking behavior of mammals: An illustration of the nature-nurture question. In L. Postman, ed., *Psychology in the making*. New York: Knopf, pp. 585–661.

Meier, G. W. 1961. Infantile handling and development in Siamese kittens. *Journal of Comparative and Physiological Psychology* 54:284–86.

Millar, W. S. 1972. A study of operant conditioning under delayed reinforcement in early infancy. *Monographs of the Society for Research in Child Development* 37, No. 2 (Whole No. 147).

Miller, D. J.; Cohen, L. B.; and Hill, K. T. 1970. A methodological investigation of Piaget's theory of object concept development in the sensory-motor period. *Journal of Experimental Child Psychology* 9:59–85.

Moreau, T.; Birch, H. G.; and Turkewitz, G. 1970. Ease of habituation to repeated auditory and somesthetic stimulation in the human newborn. *Journal of Experimental Child Psychology* 9:193–207.

Murphy, L. B. 1944. Childhood experience in relation to personality. In J. McV. Hunt, ed., *Personality and the behavior disorders*, Vol. 2. New York: Ronald Press, Ch. 21.

Papoušek, H. 1969. Individual variability in learned responses in human infants. In R. J. Robinson, ed., *Brain and early behavior*. New York: Academic Press, pp. 251–63.

Paraskevopoulos, J., and Hunt, J. McV. 1971. Object construction and imitation under differing conditions of rearing. *Journal of Genetic Psychology* 119:301–21.

Piaget, J. 1936. *The origins of intelligence in children*, trans. by M. Cook. New York: International Universities Press (1952).

———. 1937. *The Construction of reality in the child*, trans. by M. Cook. New York: Basic Books (1954).

———. 1945. *Play, dreams, and imitation in childhood*, trans. by C. Gattegno and F. M. Hodgson. New York: Norton (1951).

———. 1947. *The psychology of intelligence*, trans. by M. Piercy and D. E. Berlyne. Paterson, N.J.: Littlefield, Adams and Co. (1960).

———. 1960. The general problems of psychobiological development of the child. In J. M. Tanner and B. Inhelder, eds., *Discussions on child development*, Vol. IV. London: Tavistock Publications, pp. 3–27.

———. 1968. *Structuralism*, trans. by C. Maschler. New York: Basic Books (1970).

Pinard, A., and Laurendeau, M. 1969. "Stage" in Piaget's cognitive developmental theory: Exegesis of a concept. In D. Elkind and J. H. Flavell, eds., *Studies in cognitive development*. New York: Oxford University Press, pp. 121–70.

Provence, S., and Lipton, R. C. 1962. *Infants in institutions*. New York: International University Press.

Ramey, C. T., and Ourth, L. L. 1971. Delayed reinforcement and vocalization rates of infants. *Child Development* 42:291–97.

Rasch, E. R.; Swift, H.; Riesen, A. H.; and Chow, K. L. 1961. Altered structure and composition of retinal cells in dark-reared mammals. *Experimental Cellular Research* 25:348–63.

Razran, G. 1961. The observable unconscious and the inferable conscious in current Soviet psychophysiology: Interoceptive conditioning, semantic conditioning, and the orienting reflex. *Psychological Review* 68:81–147.

Reese, H. W., and Overton, W. F. 1970. Models of development and theories of development. In L. R. Goulet and P. B. Baltes, eds., *Life-span developmental psychology*. New York: Academic Press, pp. 115–45.

Ribble, M. A. 1944. Infantile experience in relation to personality development. In J. McV. Hunt, ed., *Personality and the behavior disorders*, Vol. 2. New York: Ronald Press, Ch. 20.

Riesen, A. H. 1958. Plasticity of behavior: Psychological aspects. In H. F. Harlow and C. N. Woolsey, eds., *Biological and biochemical bases of behavior*. Madison: University of Wisconsin Press, pp. 425–50.

Ruiz-Marcos, A., and Valverde, F. 1969. The temporal evolution of the distribution of dendritic spines in the visual cortex of normal and dark raised mice. *Experimental Brain Research* 8:284–94.

Saayman, G.; Ames, E. W.; and Moffett, A. 1964. Response to novelty as an indicator of visual discrimination in the human infant. *Journal of Experimental Child Psychology* 1:189–98.

Salama, A. A., and Hunt, J. McV. 1964. "Fixation" in the rat as a function of infantile shocking, handling, and gentling. *Journal of Genetic Psychology* 105:131–62.

Sameroff, A. J. 1968. The components of sucking in the human newborn. *Journal of Experimental Child Psychology* 6:607–23.

———. 1971. Can conditioned responses be established in the newborn infant? *Developmental Psychology* 5:1–12.

Scott, J. P. 1962. Critical periods in behavioral development. *Science* 138:949–58.

Sharpless, S., and Jasper, H. H. 1956. Habituation of the arousal reaction. *Brain* 79:655–80.

Shirley, M. M. 1931. A motor sequence favors the maturation theory. *Psychological Bulletin* 28:204–5.

———. 1933. *The first two years.* 3 vols. Minneapolis: University of Minnesota Press.

Siqueland, E., and Lipsitt, L. P. 1966. Conditioned head-turning behavior in newborns. *Journal of Experimental Child Psychology* 3:356–76.

Skeels, H. M. 1966. Adult status of children with contrasting early life experiences. *Monographs of the Society for Research in Child Development* 31, No. 3 (Whole No. 105).

Skeels, H. M., and Dye, H. B. 1939. A study of the effects of differential stimulation of mentally retarded children. *Proceedings of the American Association on Mental Deficiency* 44:114–36.

Skeels, H. M.; Updegraff, R.; Wellman, B. L.; and Williams, H. M. 1938. A study of environmental stimulation: An orphanage preschool project. *University of Iowa Studies of Child Welfare* 15, No. 4.

Skinner, B. F. 1953. *Science and human behavior.* New York: Macmillan.

Sokolov, E. N. 1960. Neuronal models and the orienting reflex. In M. A. B. Brazier, ed., *The central nervous system and behavior*. New York: Josiah Macy, Jr., Foundation, pp. 187–276.

Sontag, L. W.; Baker, C. T.; and Nelson, V. L. 1958. Mental growth and personality development: A longitudinal study. *Monographs of the Society for Research in Child Development* 23, No. 2 (Whole No. 68).

Spearman, C. 1904. "General intelligence" objectively determined and measured. *American Journal of Psychology* 15:201–93.

Spitz, R. A. 1945. Hospitalism: An inquiry into the genesis of psychiatric conditions in early childhood. *The Psychoanalytic Study of the Child* 1:53–74.

———. 1946a. Hospitalism: A follow-up report. *The Psychoanalytic Study of the Child* 2:113–17.

———. 1946b. Anaclitic depression. *The Psychoanalytic Study of the Child* 2:313–42.

Stern, W. 1914. *The psychology of early childhood*, trans. from 3d ed. by A. Burwell. New York: Holt (1924).

Thompson, R. F., and Spencer, W. A. 1966. Habituation: A model phenomenon for the study of neuronal substrates of behavior. *Psychological Review* 73:16–43.

Užgiris, I. Č. 1967. Ordinality in the development of schemas for relating to objects. In J. Hellmuth, ed., *The exceptional infant*, Vol. I. Seattle: Special Child Publications, pp. 315–34.

———. 1972. Patterns of vocal and gestural imitation in infants. In F. J. Mönks, W. H. Hartup, and J. de Wit, eds., *Determinants of behavioral development*. New York: Academic Press, pp. 467–71.

———. 1973. Patterns of cognitive development in infancy. *Merrill-Palmer Quarterly* 19:181–204.

Užgiris, I. Č., and Hunt, J. McV. 1965. A longitudinal study of recognition learning. Paper read at Society for Research in Child Development, Minneapolis, March 27.

———. 1970. Attentional preference and experience: II, An exploratory longitudinal study of the effects of visual familiarity and responsiveness. *Journal of Genetic Psychology* 117:109–21.

Valverde, F. 1967. Apical dendritic spines of the visual cortex and light deprivation in the mouse. *Experimental Brain Research* 3:337–52.

———. 1968. Structural changes in the area striata of the mouse after enucleation. *Experimental Brain Research* 5:274–92.

Volkmar, F. R., and Greenough, W. T. 1972. Rearing complexity affects branching of dendrites in the visual cortex of the rat. *Science* 176:1445–47.

Watson, J. S. 1967. Memory and "contingency analysis" in infant learning. *Merrill-Palmer Quarterly* 13:55–76.

Watson, J. S., and Ramey, C. T. 1969. Reactions to response-contingent stimulation in early infancy. Paper presented at biennial meeting of the Society for Research in Child Development, Santa Monica, Calif., March 26–29.

Weiskrantz, L. 1958. Sensory deprivation and the cat's optic nervous system. *Nature* 181:1047–50.

Werner, E. E., and Bayley, N. 1966. The reliability of Bayley's Revised Scale of Mental and Motor Development during the first year of life. *Child Development* 37:39–50.

White, B. L. 1967. An experimental approach to the effects of experience on early human development. In J. P. Hill, ed., *Minnesota Symposia on Child Development*. Minneapolis: University of Minnesota Press, pp. 201–26.

White, B. L.; Castle, P.; and Held, R. 1964. Observations on the development of visually-directed reaching. *Child Development* 35:349–64.

White, B. L., and Held, R. 1966. Plasticity of sensorimotor development in the human infant. In J. F. Rosenblith and W. Allinsmith, eds., *The causes of behavior: Readings in child development and educational psychology* (2d ed.). Boston: Allyn and Bacon.

White, R. W. 1959. Motivation reconsidered: The concept of competence. *Psychological Review* 66:297–333.

————. 1960. Competence and the psychosexual stages of development. In M. R. Jones, ed., *Nebraska Symposium on Motivation* 8:97–141. Lincoln: University of Nebraska Press.

Wiesel, T. N., and Hubel, D. H. 1963. Effects of visual deprivation on morphology and physiology of cells in the cat's lateral geniculate body. *Journal of Neurophysiology* 26:978–93.

Wohlwill, J. F. 1973. *The study of behavioral development*. New York: Academic Press.

Woodworth, R. S. 1947. Reinforcement of perception. *American Journal of Psychology* 60:119–24.

Author Index

255

Subject Index

Accommodation: visual, 31
Action: knowledge implied by, 15
Age: stages and, 22; separating developmental sequence from, 22–28; rearing conditions, achievement, and, 132
Assessment: implications of ordinality for, 18; foresight in, 23–24; spontaneous actions in, 50; arranging eliciting situations in, 50–51; criteria of accuracy in, 54; levels vs. stages in, 54; reliability by sensorimotor stage, 56–59; abandonment of Piaget's stages in, 59; coordinations in, 64–66; means-end differentiation in, 66–69; problems demanding foresight in, 69–70; learning new tasks in, 70, 71; imitation in, 71–75; maintaining interesting spectacles in, 75; alternate glancing in, 77; visual following in, 78; repertoire of schemes in, 79–85; inter-observer agreement in, 90–93; between-session stability in, 93–98; operational causality in, 116–18; object relations in space in, 119–22, 192–99; uses of ordinal scales for, 140. See also Infant tests; Instrument; Psychological development
—Theoretical approach: reflected in second version, 53; and repetition of presentations, 53; standardization in, 53; and eliciting situations, 53, 59–60; and additivity of achievements, 54; development and experience in, 54;

numerical scores in, 54; to levels of achievement, 59–60

Blink response, 27, 31

Causality. *See* operational causality
Child rearing: differences in, 19
Chronological age: separation of developmental sequences from, 22–28
Circulatory reactions, 21
Cognition: emotional aspect of, 40–41
Cognitive structures: age of achieving, 15, 16; actions implying, 16
Competence motivation, 40
Complexity, 41
Concrete operations: behavioral characteristics of, 22
Consistency: Green's index of, 129
Construction of reality, 17–18
Container and contained, 196
Coordination: eye-hand, 64, 66, 165–66; hand-mouth, 65; eye-ear, 77

Dendrites, 25–26
Detours, 198
Developmental age (DA): compensatory theory of data in, 13; mental age (MA) and, 14, 15
Developmental change: accretion in, 4; nature of transformations in, 5; bases for ordering states in, 6–7; environ-

259